RcJ

SURVEY
OF
WORLD
CULTURES

SURVEY OF WORLD CULTURES

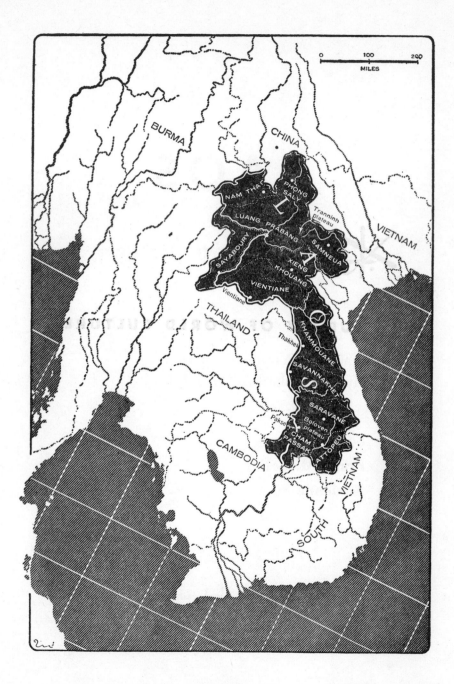

BURMA

CHINA

VIETNAM

NAM THA

PHONG SALY

Tranninh plateau

LUANG PRABANG

SAMNEUA

SAYABOURY

XIENG KHOUANG

THAILAND

VIENTIANE

Vientiane

Thakhek

KHAMMOUANE

SAVANNAKHET

SARAVANE

Pakse

Boloven plateau

CAMBODIA

CHAM PASSAK

ATTOPEU

SOUTH VIETNAM

0   100   200
MILES

LAOS

its people   its society   its culture

by the
Staff and Associates of the
Human Relations Area Files

Editors
Frank M. LeBar
Adrienne Suddard

HRAF PRESS *New Haven*

Already Published in this Series

1 **Poland**
2 **Jordan**
3 **Iraq**
4 **Saudi Arabia**
5 **Cambodia**
6 **China**
7 **USSR**

LIBRARY OF CONGRESS CATALOG CARD NUMBER: 60-7381

© COPYRIGHT 1960
HUMAN RELATIONS AREA FILES, INC.
NEW HAVEN, CONN.
MANUFACTURED IN THE UNITED STATES OF AMERICA BY
UNITED PRINTING SERVICES, INC.

PROBABLY AT NO TIME IN HISTORY have thoughtful men everywhere been so conscious of the need to know about the different peoples of the world. Such knowledge is not in itself a formula for human understanding but it is an indispensable first step. The Survey of World Cultures, of which Laos is the eighth in the series, is one of several means by which the Human Relations Area Files seeks to promote and facilitate the comparative study of human behavior and a greater understanding of cultures other than our own.

These surveys, though augmented by original research, are primarily a collation and synthesis of the best and most authoritative materials, published and unpublished, on the societies selected. For many of these societies excellent specialized studies exist, but the materials are often so widely scattered as to be virtually unavailable to all except the most determined scholar. It was to meet the need for a comprehensive readable volume, bringing together all those aspects of a country and culture usually studied separately, that these books were undertaken.

The present series is based in part on background studies prepared for limited distribution. Under the direction of the Human Relations Area Files an interdisciplinary team with area competence was assembled for each study. The enterprise involved, in all, contributions from several hundred scholars resident at some twenty universities.

The original studies have been extensively revised: materials have been added and the body of the work rewritten, edited, and adapted to a new format. Owing to special requirements imposed on the program, footnotes and citations customary in works of this nature were omitted. Both lack of funds and dispersal of the original teams of scholars have unfortunately made it impossible to supply this critical apparatus. However there are cited in the bibliography at the end of each volume the most important materials on which each study is based.

One result of the process of collecting and selecting information from many, often widely scattered, sources has been to reveal new relationships, making explicit in these surveys much which had remained implicit in previous separate studies. Gaps in existing knowledge have become apparent. The series should, then, raise a number of general questions, at the same time offering certain factual answers and providing guidance for further research. That there will also result increased understanding of the seemingly endless and diverse ways in which men approach the experience of living with one another is the wish of all who have participated in producing this series.

ACKNOWLEDGMENTS

THE HISTORY OF THE PREPARATION of this study is the history of a research project engaging many persons for longer or shorter periods over the last five years. To thank individually each person who contributed, directly or indirectly, to the realization of the final manuscript would be a formidable task. The acknowledgments here are necessarily limited.

Much of the background material came from a monograph on Laos prepared under contract to HRAF in 1955 at the University of Chicago under the general direction of Professors Norton Ginsburg and Fred Eggan. We gratefully acknowledge our indebtedness to the authors of this monograph: Gerald C. Hickey, who also acted as editor, Albert Androsky, Ann Larimore, Naomi Noble, Hong-phuc Vo, and Mitchell Zadrozny.

The preparation of a second manuscript, differing in scope and form and incorporating additional material, was completed in 1958 at a former Washington branch of HRAF by a team headed by Wendell Blanchard and including Chester A. Bain, Lloyd Burlingham, Russell G. Duff, Bernard B. Fall, Joel M. Halpern, and David J. Steinberg.

Original material for certain chapters in the sociological and political sections of this book was contributed by George L. Trager, Department of Anthropology and Linguistics, University of Buffalo; William Davenport, Department of Anthropology, Yale University; and Sebastian de Grazia, Department of Politics, Princeton University, now with the Twentieth Century Fund.

A preliminary revision and updating of this manuscript for general publication was begun in 1959 by Herbert H. Vreeland III, and Thomas Fitzsimmons, editor of previous volumes in this series. Their suggestions proved helpful in many ways.

Robert B. Textor, Research Fellow in Anthropology and Southeast Asia Studies in Yale University carefully read the chapter on religion in the present volume and in addition offered comments on other chapters in the book. John Musgrave, Head of the Oriental Division in the Yale University Library, contributed expert advice on a number of ethnic and linguistic problems, as did Li Fang-Kuei, Professor of Anthropology in the University of Washington, and William Gedney, Professor of Comparative Literature in State University Teachers College, New Paltz, New York. Wu-chi Liu, Associate Research Director in HRAF, read portions of the manuscript and did an extensive revision of the chapter on art and literature. Arthur N. Young, economist and monetary expert, checked the chapter on the Laotian financial system and made substantive additions to it. John D. Montgomery, currently Research Fellow in the Council on Foreign Relations, Elden Johnson, Assistant Professor of Anthropology in the University of Minnesota, and Raymond Fink of Berkeley, California, all read parts of the manuscript and offered helpful comments and criticisms. Finally, Thephathay Vilaihongs, Permanent Delegate of the Royal Kingdom of Laos to the United Nations very kindly checked several of the chapters and offered his expert advice and criticism. Acknowledgment is hereby made to all these individuals for their very generous assistance.

Special thanks go to Joel M. Halpern, Assistant Professor of Anthropology at the University of California, Los Angeles, who read and commented on many chapters, helped in locating current statistical information, and made contributions to the chapter on public health and welfare. Dr. Halpern freely offered the use of prepublication manuscript materials from his own book, *People of Laos,* to be published by the University of California Press.

Bernard B. Fall, who is Associate Professor of Government in Howard University, very kindly checked the chapters on government and politics and in addition contributed the chapter on foreign relations. This chapter is largely based on Dr. Fall's article, "International Relations of Laos" which appeared in *Kingdom of Laos,* published in Saigon by *France-Asie* in 1959, with additions and corrections by the author made especially for the present volume.

Standard French transliterations of Lao words have been retained in most instances. The symbol *x* indicates a pronunciation somewhat like English *ch.*

Although credit for any contribution this volume may make to an understanding of Laos belongs to many scholars, responsibility for the final form and any shortcomings rests solely with the staff and associates of the Human Relations Area Files and more particularly with the editors, who divided the task, problems of factual content being the special province of Frank LeBar and those of an editorial nature that of Adrienne Suddard.

THE EDITORS

New Haven, Connecticut
July 1960

THE HUMAN RELATIONS AREA FILES

THE HUMAN RELATIONS AREA FILES is a nonprofit research corporation affiliated with Yale University and sponsored and supported by its twenty member organizations. HRAF was established in 1949 "to collect, organize, and distribute information of significance to the natural and social sciences and the humanities." It has concentrated upon furthering a fresh approach to the study of societies, culture, and social behavior.

The Files themselves contain carefully selected sources analyzed according to G. P. Murdock's *Outline of Cultural Materials*. Located at each of the member institutions, they are a new kind of reference library in which basic information about nearly two hundred peoples can be consulted with ease and speed. Preparation of the present study was facilitated by the use of the following Files: Indochina, the Cambodians, the Laotians, the Vietnamese, and Thailand.

MEMBERS

University of Chicago
University of Colorado
Cornell University
École Pratique des Hautes
    Études, Paris
Harvard University
University of Hawaii
University of Illinois
Indiana University
State University of Iowa

University of Michigan
University of North Carolina
University of Oklahoma
University of Pennsylvania
Princeton University
Smithsonian Institution
University of Southern California
Southern Illinois University
University of Utah
University of Washington

Yale University

CONTENTS

Contents *(continued)*

LIST OF PLATES

LIST OF TABLES

List of Tables (*continued*)

LAOS

THE CULTURE AND THE SOCIETY

IN THE CONTINUING COLD WAR between East and West one of the more critical battlegrounds — militarily, economically, and psychologically — is Laos, a small Southeast Asian country strategically located on the periphery of the Communist Chinese colossus. But although millions of dollars in economic assistance from France, the United States, and other countries of the free world are spent annually to strengthen this tropical outpost, few Westerners have any clear picture of the Lao and their culture — fewer still understand the capabilities and probable future of this new and important potential ally.

The independent Kingdom of Laos is less than twenty years old, dating from the signing of an agreement in 1949 with France, which for over half a century had administered Laos as a protectorate. The history of modern Laos may be said to begin with the arrival of the French in 1893, but the Lao people — the dominant ethnic group politically as well as culturally — trace their history back to their flight south from China before the advancing forces of Kublai Khan in the thirteenth century A.D. and the founding of the Lao kingdom of Lan Xang in 1353. By the seventeenth century Lan Xang (Land of a Million Elephants) had reached a political apex and controlled sections of Yunnan, of the southern Shan States, of the Vietnamese and Cambodian mountain plateaus, and large stretches of present-day northeastern Thailand. For the next two centuries Lan Xang went through a slow but continuing decline dominated by wars, periodic invasions and conquests of Lao territory by the Annamese, Siamese, and Burmese, and division of the kingdom into separate princedoms — Luang Prabang, Vientiane, Xieng Khouang, and Champassak.

The country the French found was, as it is today, almost completely agricultural. Following centuries-old patterns, the overwhelming majority of the people of Laos — as many as 95 percent — are subsistence wet-rice farmers living in tiny villages along the Mekong river and its tributaries or, in the case of the minority hill tribes, dry-rice farmers leading a seminomadic life based on slash-and-burn cultivation in the highlands.

To the villagers, most of whom are illiterate, life is an annual routine of planting, cultivation, and harvest — dictated by the monsoon cycle and punctuated by exuberant village celebration of the numerous religious festivals. In many ways the Buddhist temple in every village is the very center of a villager's life and his concept of the world or even the rest of his own country is often ill-formed.

Sharing basic values and attitudes with the villagers but strongly influenced by their contact with the French and other foreigners are the Laotians living in the towns, particularly the five largest — Luang Prabang, Vientiane, Thakhek, Savannakhet, and Pakse. Here amid surroundings still reminiscent of the village are the evidences of Western influence — air-conditioned movies, bars, night clubs, postal and telephone service, newspapers. In Vientiane, the administrative capital, are the central government offices, the foreign embassies, police headquarters, an airport, the most advanced schools, and the country's only broadcasting station, Radio Vientiane. Luang Prabang, more provincial in atmosphere, is the royal residence, center of Buddhist activities, and social capital.

The wealthier townspeople, mostly merchants and government officials, have been moving rapidly toward a Western standard of living, but the social gap between the urban and rural populations remains much less pronounced than might be expected, one reason being the low level of industrial development.

The most important distinction is between the ruling elite, who usually live in the towns, and the politically apathetic villagers. It was this political elite, comprising a few hundred people from less than twenty historically important families, upon whom the French relied during the protectorate for implementation of colonial policy. Though reserving all real control to a *résident supérieur* appointed by France and using Vietnamese as interpreters and minor functionaries, the French ruled through the king and the local elite wherever possible. The appositeness of this at least nominal recognition of the Lao nobility to the gentle but proud Lao had the effect of encouraging loyalty and cooperation but provided little opportunity for the kind of political experience the Lao would have to have to handle the complex problems of sovereignty in the modern world.

Perhaps the most urgent problem facing the newly independent nation has been the creation of a viable economy. To the French Laos was only part of the larger entity, Indochina, and primarily useful as a buffer against the eastern expansion of the Thai and against the British in Burma. A rudimentary communications network to facilitate military and political administration and a limited amount of private investment in tin and coffee production was the practical sum of French economic development. But whereas perennial Laotian deficits in the colonial period could be made up from Cambodian and Vietnamese surpluses, postindependence deficits have had to be covered by foreign aid.

To put Laos on a sound economic basis will require, it is agreed, fundamental changes in the structure of the economy and in traditional attitudes. But economic development is a complex process in a country where farmers still tend to show interest in improved agricultural methods primarily as a means to maintain their subsistence standard of living with less work, where except for very recently trained airplane mechanics and truck drivers skilled labor is almost nonexistent, or where the primitive condition of much of the road network leaves large areas of the country without land transportation during the rainy season.

Lao leaders have exhibited a fairly realistic grasp of their problems and with foreign technical and economic assistance have begun such basic projects as the expansion of communications, the development with Cambodia and Thailand of the power and transport potentialities of the Mekong river, and the technical training abroad of a growing number of Laotians. To create a basis for future changes in attitudes the dual problem of illiteracy and a low level of participation in the national life is being attacked by a conscientious effort to improve the education system.

Superimposed on the traditional religious and vocational schooling a young Lao receives from the bonzes (every male Buddhist should spend some time, however brief, as a novice in the pagoda) is the compulsory public education in schools closely modeled on the secular schools introduced by the French colonial administration. The Laotian public school system has had a spectacular growth and although still seriously handicapped by insufficient funds and a shortage of qualified teachers is providing educational advantages only possible for the wealthy up to a generation ago. Higher education, which must be obtained abroad, is also being offered to deserving students in the form of generous scholarships from the Lao government as well as France and the United States.

A predictable result of the greater educational opportunities will be the creation of a middle class — engineers, doctors, lawyers, career government and army officers — a development perhaps heralded by the growing influence of a group of young civilian and army leaders with a vigorous program of social and economic reform. The first decade of independence had been dominated politically by a handful of influential personalities, often related to the royal families, whose bland pronouncements on domestic policy were almost indistinguishable and whose major differences were confined to their attitudes toward the Pathet Lao threat and to foreign policy.

The Pathet Lao, or Lao Country, movement nominally headed by Lao Prince Souphanouvong has by practical control for four years of two northern provinces (1953–57) and by intermittent guerrilla warfare kept the new nation in a state of continual crisis. A patient and personal attitude toward the disaffection of Prince Souphanouvong led the royal government through a long series of negotiations with the Pathet Lao culminating in an integration agreement in 1957. The uneasy truce, during which the Pathet Lao gained a legal political status — still valid — and during which Prince Souphanouvong held an important cabinet post, ended a year later with a new outbreak of guerrilla activity.

The Pathet Lao rebellion presents a dilemma to the royal government as Communist China and North Vietnam have been psychologically and reportedly militarily supporting the movement, making effective action against the Pathet Lao subject to interpretation as an unfriendly act against these powerful states on the Laotian border.

In this dilemma Laos, having realized the hesitancy of the SEATO powers to enter a dispute which could erupt into full-scale war, turned to the United Nations. A lull in the fighting was the immediate result but even more significant was the subsequent acceptance by the Lao government of a continuing United Nations "presence" for the arrangement of technical and economic assistance. It may well be that this most recent series of events foreshadows an increasingly important United Nations role in the troubled affairs of Laos wherein the country's economic development and political education can take place gradually and peacefully with the help of a force uncommitted to either of the major power blocs.

1. *The Culture and the Society*

Whatever the future, one may suppose that the Lao will react with characteristic resourcefulness to preserve their cultural and national identity. Located, along with Thailand, in almost the exact geographical center of Southeast Asia, the Lao have for centuries absorbed the impact of foreign cultural influences and immigrations into the country of foreign nationals. Lao culture today shows a mixture of Hindu, Buddhist, Thai, Vietnamese, Khmer, French, and more recently American influences. In their lowland valley villages the Lao, themselves immigrants from southwest China, have witnessed the continuous movement of peoples southward into Laos from Yunnan and northern Vietnam and are today faced with a vastly greater potential thrust from the north in the form of Red China's expansionist tendencies.

Despite these diverse historical influences the Lao today possess a viable culture — marked by a characteristic Buddhist tolerance and gentleness, a lack of interest in personal aggrandizement, and a fondness for the simple pleasures of life. Balancing these traits, however, is a hardheaded practicality in the face of threats to individual or national identity which the Westerner sometimes finds difficult to reconcile with his image of the "happy and carefree" Laotian.

The peasant's way of life is a "given" — something he rarely philosophizes about and which he characteristically refrains from forcing on others. But there is much in the traditional Lao solutions to the problems of life on which the Westerner might reflect with profit.

HISTORICAL SETTING

THE KINGDOM OF LAOS DESCENDS from Lan Xang (Land of a Million Elephants), a unified Lao nation that emerged in the fourteenth century and included an area considerably larger than that of the present state. Lan Xang endured until about the end of the seventeenth century when it separated into three kingdoms—Luang Prabang, Vientiane, and Champassak — each headed by a member of the old royal house. When the present constitutional monarchy was established in 1946 the king of Luang Prabang, a direct descendant of the Lan Xang royal line, became king of modern Laos.

To the elite — virtually all Lao — the history of Laos is the story of the Lao. Modern writings on history stress the continuity of the Lao tradition as the sole unifying human factor of the Laotian state. Lan Xang is to the Lao the Golden Age and to this period belong all the national heroes — the legendary ancestors Khoun Borom and his son Khoun Lo, the founder Fa Ngoun, the consolidator Sam Sene Thai, the pious Photisarath, the defender Setthathirath, and the stern but just Souligna Vongsa. It is with pride that the Lao list their kings (see Table 1), all of the same family, for six hundred years of recorded history and for two hundred years before that according to legend.

For the vast majority of the population, however, of whatever ethnic group, understanding of history derives much more from legend than from fact. The history taught in the pagoda schools, before the French came, was history by word of mouth. Following their pattern in Cambodia and Vietnam, the French during their protectorate combined the teaching of French history, to promote understanding of their rule, with stimulation of research into Laotian history. But knowledge of ancient historical records or of recent research is limited to a few, and until the school

system — still poor — can be expanded and improved most Lao
will continue to learn their history from the tales of priests and
the songs of balladiers. Even more dependent on legend are the
ethnic minorities, who are, as far as is known, without written
histories of any kind.

Origins and Legends

It is not possible to fix upon any one definite ethnic strain as constituting the aborigines of Laos. Various Negroid peoples apparently were established there in prehistoric times when land bridges
connected Southeast Asia with Indonesia, Borneo, and the Philippines, in each of which common Negrito characteristics are noted
in the most primitive and oldest known inhabitants. Later came
peoples of so-called Indonesian or proto-Malay stock, from whom
developed the Cham, Mon, and Khmer peoples, and who interbred
with the earlier inhabitants.

The Lao are one of the Thai peoples who, long before they
began to record their history, occupied a vast area in southern
China — the present Yunnan and southern Sikang provinces. They
appear in Chinese records from the sixth century B.C. on as the "bar-
barians" beyond the Yangtze. At times subject to Chinese suzerainty, often independent, they were always moving very slowly
southward. By the eighth century A.D. they had established in
western Yunnan a strong military kingdom, Nan Chao, that survived until attacked by the Mongols of Kublai Khan in the
thirteenth century (see the map, Historical References).

To the Thai nation, Nan Chao, belonged among others the
peoples now known as the Lao, the Shan, the Siamese Thai, the
Lu, and, more distantly connected, the Man and Miao (Meo).
All of them, at different times and by different routes, moved
down the valleys of the Irrawaddy, the Salween, the Menam (Chao
Phraya), and the Mekong, infiltrating into the kingdoms of the
Burmese, the Mon (of present-day eastern Burma and western
Thailand), and the Khmer (of central and eastern Thailand, middle and southern Laos, and Cambodia). Only as the migrants
achieved local dominance by reason of numbers and superior
organization did they begin to set up tiny, village-based, petty
principalities.

The Lao entered history later than the Shan, the Lu, and the
Siamese Thai but the pattern of infiltration and settlement was
the same as that of the other Nan Chao peoples. Entering a

remote, rugged, and sparsely populated part of the still powerful Khmer empire, perhaps almost unnoticed, they found a people less advanced than themselves living under Khmer overlords who referred to them collectively, regardless of differences, as Kha (slaves), a name their descendants retain to this day. These the Lao gradually displaced, forcing them from the more desirable sites into the hills and forests.

Lao tradition assigns a dozen successive non-Lao rulers to Muong Swa (later to become Luang Prabang), some of them Cambodian, some Kha, before the first Lao chieftain. It appears therefore that early infiltration was very gradual and probably peaceful and that the Lao were either content to live under Khmer overlordship or too weak to do otherwise.

The slow southward migration from Yunnan was accelerated in the middle of the thirteenth century by the conquests of Kublai Khan, whose forces captured Ta-li, capital of Nan Chao, in 1253. It is believed that this had the effect of reinforcing the earlier Lao migrants in the Indochinese peninsula to the point where their leaders could seize power.

Despite their proximity to the literate Chinese, the Lao apparently developed the art of writing only after leaving Nan Chao and through later association with the Indianized Khmer. Consequently, there are only legends and half-remembered dynastic lists (cited in the earliest annals) to account for the period of the migration.

The legend of origin takes a number of forms. Reduced to its essentials it provides a semidivine ancestor, the sage Khoun Borom, sent to rule on earth by the King of Heaven (a possible allusion to China, the Celestial Kingdom). Mounted on a white elephant and furnished with all the appurtenances of royalty, including two divine wives, Khoun Borom arrived at Muong Theng, in the vicinity of Dien Bien Phu, where he found a vine bearing two enormous gourds. These when pierced gave forth men, women, seed, domestic animals, and all types of useful materials, thus populating the world. (The darker Kha are said to have emerged, sooty, from a hole burned with a poker.) Having seven sons, Khoun Borom divided the land among them, the divisions corresponding to the various lands to which the Thai peoples migrated — Siam, Burma, Laos, and other contiguous regions. Two of these areas never achieved more than loose tribal confederation, but their names still distinguish regions to which it will be necessary to refer from time to time: the Sip Song Pan Na (Twelve Thousand Rice Fields) on the upper Mekong, which overlaps the present boundaries of

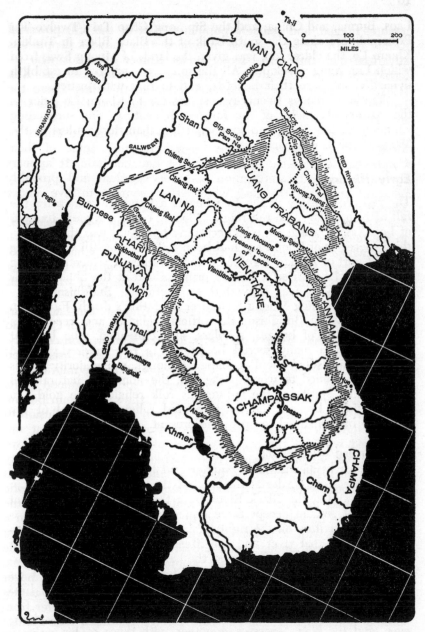

HISTORICAL REFERENCES

Laos, Burma, and China; and the Sip Song Chao Tai (Twelve Tai Principalities) along the south bank of the Black River in Tonkin. Khoun Lo, the eldest son, was given the lands of Muong Swa, from which Lan Xang developed. All the sons were adjured to establish dynasties, to share their benefits, and to rule with justice.

Tradition names twenty-two successors to Khoun Lo prior to the written chronicles of the fourteenth century. The succeeding Kingdom of Lan Xang had somewhat less than thirty rulers in the 350 years of its existence.

Early History

The recorded history of the Lao begins a hundred years after the fall of Nan Chao, with the reign (1353–73) of Fa Ngoun, founder of Lan Xang. Fa Ngoun, who according to legend was the twenty-third successor of Khoun Lo, had been exiled while still very young to the Court of Angkor together with his father, a prince of Muong Swa. There he married a Khmer princess and at the behest of his new father-in-law was converted to Theravada Buddhism.

Upon regaining Muong Swa after his father's death, Fa Ngoun made Theravada Buddhism the official religion and received a Khmer mission of bonzes, scholars, and craftsmen, who brought to Muong Swa many sacred books and a five-hundred-year-old gold Buddha called the Pra Bang. Although the majority of his subjects continued to worship the *phi,* the numerous natural and supernatural spirits of the indigenous folk religion, the gold Pra Bang quickly became the most revered religious symbol of the Lao and has remained so up to the present.

The Founding of Lan Xang

Fa Ngoun was an insatiable warrior and had soon forcibly established his eastern border at the crest of the Annam Cordillera from the south and at the Black River from the north, demanding that the king of Annam accept these boundaries. To the west, he extended his territory on the right bank of the Mekong to the watershed between that river and the Menam and forced the king of Ayutthaya to promise tribute and the hand of his daughter in marriage. Fa Ngoun's territory now included all of present-day Laos and much of what is today northern and eastern Thailand. In 1353 he united his conquests as the Lao state, Lan Xang.

Continual wars had been a heavy burden on the people, however, and the king's excesses, together with those of his military lieutenants, who oppressed the Lao and the conquered alike, led to his deposition twenty years later in 1373.

He was succeeded by his son, Sam Sene Thai (1373–1416) – organizer, consolidator, and man of peace. Besides showing exemplary devoutness and building many pagodas, Sam Sene Thai developed an administrative structure that lasted for centuries. Based on the principle of absolute monarchy the system employed princes of the royal blood as the king's ministers or principal advisers, supported by a hierarchy of officials, judges, taxgatherers, and minor functionaries. Officials were graded and titled but these titles existed at the pleasure of the king. Only titles in the royal family were hereditary.

An institution peculiar to this state was the office of *maha oupahat*, or "second king," who was not necessarily of royal blood. Local governors of *muong* (districts) might be royal appointees, or princes, but as often were selected by a local council of notables, usually from among the family of the previous incumbent. In theory, and frequently in practice, any qualified person regardless of birth could rise to high office.

In 1376 the king ordered a census taken. The results showed 300,000 adult males of "Thai race" and 400,000 adult males of non-Thai origin. Since monks, children, and women were excluded the total population probably exceeded two million. On the basis of this census the king chose for his dynastic name Phya Sam Sene Thai, or Lord of Three Hundred Thousand Thai. A standing army of 150,000 – infantry, cavalry, and elephant corps – supported by a supply corps of 20,000 coolies, was divided into an internal garrison or police force, a mobile defense force, and a reserve.

The bonze began to assume the place of honor and prestige traditional in Buddhist countries. He enjoyed status as the practitioner of the state religion; the populace, although continuing its worship of the *phi*, also showed him deference. The pagoda became the center of community life, as place of worship, school (in both letters and crafts), and social gathering place.

The reigns of Fa Ngoun and Sam Sene Thai, totaling sixty-three years, established Lan Xang among its neighbors when they were too weak militarily for effective resistance. The surrounding states to the east, south, and west – Annam, Champa, Angkor, Sukhothai, Ayutthaya, Chieng Mai, and those of the Shans and the Burmese – were all in some way embroiled one with another, or, as in the case of Annam, with China. Although the Khmer state of Angkor had in effect sponsored Lan Xang, it is doubtful if its kings expected such a burgeoning of strength and acquisitiveness. By the time the neighboring states were aware of what was happening, Lan Xang, though sparse in population, controlled more territory than any of them and had become an empire carved mostly from the loosely held border regions of the declining Khmer empire. From this time until after the arrival of the French, the history of Laos is dominated by the struggle to retain the lands conquered and settled by the Lao.

The Decline of Lan Xang

The first enemy was Annam, which Lan Xang offended in 1421 by an act of seeming treachery during one of Annam's long series of defensive wars with the Chinese. Some fifty years later, Annam, free of encumbrances, launched an invasion that succeeded in taking Muong Swa, the Lao capital, before being beaten off.

There followed a considerable period of peace during which Lan Xang tried to consolidate its position by royal intermarriages and by furthering its trade relations (mostly in forest products) with Ayutthaya. During this period the land was ruled by King Photisarath (1520–47), a devout Buddhist noted for his temple building and attempts to suppress the cult of the *phi* by royal edict. These acts doubtless strengthened the position of the established religion in official circles, but they had little effect on the persistent animism of the common people.

Photisarath also placed Lan Xang squarely in a conflict of power that was to disturb all Southeast Asia for the rest of the sixteenth century. Basing his claim on the fact that his mother was a princess of Chieng Mai, Photisarath took advantage of an interregnum in Chieng Mai to obtain its throne for his son, Setthathirath.

An abortive attempt to force Setthathirath from the throne was made by a Siamese army, but a second and more powerful threat loomed in Burma, where the dynamic expansionist King Bayinnaung had just consolidated his power and, looking east for new lands to conquer, saw Chieng Mai as a base for operations against Ayutthaya. Setthathirath had meanwhile returned to Lan Xang, following Photisarath's death in 1547, carrying with him the Emerald Buddha, the Pra Keo, a green jasper carving which was the most cherished religious object of Chieng Mai and an important symbol of sovereignty.

A three-way power conflict developed, leading to more than forty years of warfare involving Burma, Siam, and Lan Xang. The

Burmese king twice invaded Lan Xang, but Setthathirath was able to force his withdrawal and maintain Lan Xang's independence. Perhaps to increase contact with the Siamese, his allies against Burma, certainly to establish a better center for his increasingly important trade with them, Setthathirath moved his capital to Vientiane, which he both fortified and beautified. He built the Wat Keo to enshrine the Pra Keo, or Emerald Buddha, and the That Luang, an even more imposing shrine to house purported Buddhist relics. The That Luang, restored by the French, is still venerated by Laotians today. It was at this time (about 1563) that the old capital, Muong Swa, received its present name of Luang Prabang in honor of the revered gold Buddha, the Pra Bang, which remained there.

The as yet unexplained disappearance of Setthathirath while on a punitive expedition against the Kha tribes of Attopeu in 1571 removed the major obstacle to Burmese conquest. Lan Xang was subjugated for the next twenty years, until the resurgent Siamese finally pushed back the Burmese, incidentally bringing Chieng Mai under Siamese control.

Setthathirath's last surviving son, himself without issue, was on the throne when the Burmese tide receded. After a period of nondynastic rulers the Lan Xang throne passed to a collateral line of the original royal family. A little over sixty years later, in 1637, Souligna Vongsa won a struggle among brothers and cousins and ruled for fifty-seven years until his death in 1694.

It was during Souligna Vongsa's reign that European visitors first arrived. A Dutch visitor, van Wuysthoff, came on a mission of diplomacy and trade, staying but a short time; trade evidently was not established on any permanent basis. Another visitor was a Jesuit who stayed, it is said, five years before he finally despaired of success in his missionary work. Both men recorded their impressions of the beauty of Vientiane and the splendor and ritual of the court.

The long reign of Souligna Vongsa gave the country strength and security, enabling him to establish boundaries peacefully by treaty. (The boundary with Annam was by formal agreement settled on ethnic grounds: lands settled by people who lived in "houses on piles and with verandas" should belong to Lan Xang, those occupied by people in houses "without piles or verandas" went to Annam; ethnically, the distinction remains valid today.)

Other actions of Souligna Vongsa were less helpful to his country. His seizure by force of a Xieng Khouang princess permanently alienated that small but strategically located tributary kingdom, which later drifted into the arms of Annam. And by allowing a sentence of death against his only son (for adultery) he laid the ground for a struggle over the succession. Both actions contributed to the downfall of Lan Xang.

The Period of Division

When Souligna Vongsa died, his grandsons were under age and a nephew, Sai Ong Hué, emerged from exile in Annam to win the throne with Annamese aid — for which, however, he accepted vassalage to Annam and promised heavy tribute.

The victory of Sai Ong Hué ended the unity of Lan Xang. His rival, young King Kitsarath, a grandson of Souligna Vongsa, fled to Luang Prabang, where he established a separate kingdom in 1707. Another prince of the royal house established a third kingdom, Champassak, in the southernmost provinces on both sides of the Mekong in 1713. In the Sip Song Pan Na, to the north, the tribes pursued an almost independent course, though sometimes recognizing the king of Luang Prabang. Left to Vientiane was a considerable area on both sides of the middle Mekong.

Through the eighteenth and nineteenth centuries the Lao states quarreled among themselves and struggled to maintain their independence against outside invaders: Annamese from the east, Chinese and other non-Thai bandits and raiders from the north, Burmese from the west, and Siamese from the south. In 1778, Vientiane was for a time in Siamese hands; independence was regained only by accepting vassalage to Siam as well as to Annam.

Chao (Prince) Anou (1805–28), a former *maha oupahat*, became king with Siamese support. Some years later he involved Vientiane in wars with Siam; expected aid failed to come and in 1828 the city of Vientiane was sacked by the Siamese general, Bodin. The archives of the kingdom were burned and according to tradition a large part of the Vientiane population of ten thousand families was forcibly resettled in Siam. Later campaigns similarly depopulated Khammouane and central Laos. Finally the Siamese invaded Annam through central Laos and on being driven out carried off still more Laotians. Later, Vientiane was directly annexed as a province by Siam, then by Annam, and finally again by Siam.

The centuries-old custom of war in Southeast Asia was to depopulate systematically any conquered territory in order to make good the losses of other wars, to preclude rebellion after the vic-

2. The French Period

torious troops had departed, and to leave a devastated area incapable of supporting the troops of another invader. So thoroughly was the custom applied to the principality of Vientiane that it was practically obliterated and at the middle of the nineteenth century its population was only one quarter of what it had been fifty years earlier.

Luang Prabang fared only a little better, suffering from wars with Vientiane, Burma, and Siam. Later a wave of Meo tribesmen migrated into north Luang Prabang and Tran Ninh (Xieng Khouang); though they generally settled down as seminomadic farmers, they were often rebellious. In the latter half of the nineteenth century the backwash of the T'ai-p'ing and Moslem rebellions to the north hit Laos and upper Tonkin: armies of fleeing rebels and bandits ravaged the area. At the same time France began its expansion into Annam and Cambodia, and Siam, to forestall French encroachments into Laos, strengthened its own control over the area. On one occasion a king of Luang Prabang sought aid from Siam against Chinese bandits; a Siamese army arrived but came to terms with the Chinese and withdrew, again carrying off numbers of Lao.

After the French had established their protectorate over Annam, the Siamese in 1885 reduced King Oun Kham of Luang Prabang to the status of a governor who took orders from Siamese commissioners at his court. In the south other commissioners directed the affairs of the king of Champassak.

The French Period

Beginning their penetration of Indochina in 1858 the French had by 1864 annexed Cochin China and established a protectorate over Cambodia, and by 1884 had also successfully concluded treaties making protectorates of Tonkin and Annam. French interest turned next to the Laos states, where Siam and Annam had long been rivals for suzerainty. In a move to forestall French assertion of prior Annamese claims, the pattern followed by the French in Cambodia, the Siamese in 1885 marched into Xieng Khouang and Houa Phans under the pretext of acting to suppress Chinese bandits in regions predominantly Thai in race and language. Their real purpose became clear, however, when the viceroy of Luang Prabang was seized and taken to Bangkok as a hostage.

The ensuing negotiations resulted in an agreement which, while implicitly recognizing the Siamese claims, secured for the

French the right to maintain a vice-consul in Luang Prabang. The man named to this post, Auguste Pavie, is generally credited by the French with winning Laos for France by a "conquest of hearts." With apparently genuine sympathy for the appealing qualities of his "gentle and carefree Laotians," Pavie convinced the royal court of Luang Prabang that its best interests lay in accepting French protection.

Pavie's innovation in colonization methods, dramatized by his personal role in saving the lives of the aged King Oun Kham and his family during a Chinese bandit raid after the Siamese garrison had fled, ensured a peaceful transition for the Laotians but did not preclude further trouble with the Siamese. It took a blockading of Bangkok by French naval and military forces to get the formal accession to France in 1893 of all Siamese claims in Laos.

This brought France face to face with British territory in the Shan States of Burma. British claims extended into territory sought by France but the dispute was settled by a treaty in 1896 making the Mekong the border between Burma and Laos.

The first Franco-Siamese treaty also set the Mekong as the boundary between Laos and Siam, thereby cutting both Luang Prabang and Champassak into two sections. Subsequently, by new treaties in 1904 and 1905, Siam ceded the west bank sections of Luang Prabang and of the province of Bassac. All of Luang Prabang and Xieng Khouang and about half of the former kingdoms of Champassak and Vientiane were now under French control. Vientiane, Xieng Khouang, and central Laos became French provinces; no effort was made to revive their former royal families. When the cession of the west bank territory of Bassac was completed in 1905 all but one of the sons of the late King Kham Souk of Champassak left for Siam; the exception, Nhouy, took an oath of loyalty to France and was made governor of Bassac province but was accorded no royal status. The king of Luang Prabang retained his royal title and prerogatives under French protection; his realm, however, was in all important respects administered indirectly by French officials.

Vientiane, the seat of the *résident supérieur* since 1899, became the administrative capital of French Laos. From here the *résident* exercised indirect rule of Luang Prabang and a much more direct administration, through French commissioners, of the eight provinces outside that kingdom. One area, now the northernmost province of Phongsaly, was made a military territory under French army administration.

2. The French Period

On the whole French rule rested lightly on Laos. The French accepted the advice and used the services of the local elite, especially the chiefs of the tribal groups. Patterns of local rule were not greatly changed and local custom and tradition went unmolested, insofar as they were not incompatible with the larger French objectives. The French did, however, abolish slavery, and they took firmly into their own hands the administration of all fiscal matters. More gradual French influence was felt on the judicial and educational systems. A later, complete innovation was the establishment of government health and sanitation services.

At one time the French considered the annexation of Laos to Annam, principally for economic convenience because they had finally realized that the Mekong was not the interstate route of communication they had earlier imagined. This idea was, however, abandoned as the force of Laotian resentment became evident. Although Laos had seldom fought Annam and had at times even sought it as an ally, the Lao always mistrusted the people "from the other side of the mountains." Mistrust was intensified into dislike when the French brought in Annamese, already at least partially French-trained, as minor bureaucrats and laborers. The Lao liked neither their tutelage nor their example of greater energy and personal aggressiveness.

Generally the French found Laos easy to govern. Only three incidents required suppression by military force, and none of these involved the Lao. The cause of the first incident was obscure, but probably related to the prohibition of the trade in slaves. The Kha of the Boloven plateau and Attopeu areas were in the habit of kidnapping tribal people from across the border in Annam to sell illicitly to the Lao and the Siamese. In any case, Kha chiefs and sorcerers in 1901 whipped their people into a rebellion that was not entirely subdued until 1907. During World War I the Phongsaly military territory was invaded by Yunnanese bandits, egged on, it is said, by a disgruntled Lu chieftain who had exiled himself to China. This dissidence did not deeply infect the local population, but it kept French colonial troops busy for two years. The last trouble was with the Meo, who had lived isolated on their mountaintops since their immigration in the mid-nineteenth century. In 1919 the Meo started raiding and looting the Lao, Kha, and other non-Meo peoples. It took two years to restore order.

The Lao themselves caused no trouble. King Oun Kham of Luang Prabang turned over his powers to his son Zakarine in 1894, a year before he died; Zakarine continued to accept the French overlordship. He died in 1904, whereupon his son, Sisavang Vong, who had been studying in Paris, returned to Laos and ascended the throne. All in all, Laos left little imprint on history from 1893 to 1940.

World War II and Transition

Laos was wakened from its apathy during World War II. By the time of the fall of France in June 1940, Japan in its southward march had reached almost to the Indochina border and had signed a treaty of friendship with Thailand (formerly Siam). The next Japanese move was to get from the Vichy regime the right to move troops into Indochina. In the meantime Japan permitted Thailand to seize those parts of Luang Prabang and Champassak that had been ceded to France in 1904. In July 1941 all of Indochina was occupied. The Lao did not seem too resentful of either the Thai or the Japanese, and, although a few Lao joined with the Thai in underground resistance to the Japanese, life in general went on much as usual. But the inability of France to protect Laos from Japan, or even from Thailand, was a severe blow to French prestige.

During most of the war the Japanese chose to act through the Vichy authorities in imposing their control on Laos and the rest of Indochina. This, too, lowered French prestige, since it was all too evident to the Laotians that their former colonial masters were simply obeying the orders of an Asiatic power. In August 1941 a treaty with the Vichy regime increased the domain of Luang Prabang by incorporating with it the provinces of Vientiane, Xieng Khouang, and Nam Tha. The king was allowed to form a cabinet composed of a prime minister and four other ministers, all appointed with Vichy concurrence. The *maha oupahat,* Prince Petsarath, became prime minister in addition to his traditional duties.

In March 1945 the Japanese decided to oust the Vichy French, now completely discredited by the total liberation of France by the Allied armies, and declare the colonial regime at an end. Tonkin and Annam united to form the Republic of Vietnam; Cambodia at once declared itself an independent kingdom. The king, Sisavang Vong, and his son, Crown Prince Savang Vatthana, both unalterably pro-French, delayed for a month the assumption of independent status and even then left the southern provinces free to decide for themselves. The Japanese, angered by this delay, caused the Crown Prince to be sent to Saigon, leaving Petsarath a relatively free hand in running the country; they interned the Vichy French officials, replacing them with their own military representatives.

With the surrender of Japan on August 14, 1945 a vacuum was created that invited disturbance and agitation; the worst of these occurred in Khammouane and Savannakhet. The surrender terms required the Japanese to maintain order but they had few troops in Laos and were not averse to seeing anti-European movements develop. By decision of the Potsdam Conference Chinese troops were to receive the surrender of the Japanese as far south as the 16th parallel (the level of Saravane), but the Chinese moved slowly and did not enter Laos until September. The French assumed control in Champassak and prepared to take over the whole country.

Prince Petsarath, in Vientiane, announced on August 18, 1945 that independence from France, proclaimed earlier at the instigation of the Japanese, was not to be compromised and that it applied to all of Laos unified under the King of Luang Prabang. Under Petsarath a committee of Lao Issara (Free Laos) was formed; it comprised members of his family, others of the elite, and a few Vietnamese who held official positions in Laos. Some of the committee were former members of the anti-Japanese resistance; some were unqualifiedly anti-French; but others believed that independence could be attained through French good will.

Late in August a small French force was parachuted in near Vientiane to release the French officials still under Japanese internment. The actions and attitudes of French officers indicated to the Lao Issara that France sought a return to prewar status. Prince Petsarath tried to keep French troops out of the capital by telling the French commander that the safety of his troops could not be guaranteed there. The French successfully employed a ruse to gain peaceful entry to the city and proceeded to alienate the Lao Issara by ignoring them. They then parachuted another group into Luang Prabang and a few days later King Sisavang Vong announced that he had accepted resumption of the French protectorate. Accounts differ as to whether he acted solely under the influence of the French; one report has it that the Chinese, who arrived at that time, presented him with a choice between the French and themselves as protectors.

These events stiffened the reaction of the Lao Issara in Vientiane. On October 10 word arrived from Luang Prabang that Prince Petsarath had been dismissed not only as prime minister but also as *maha oupahat;* in reaction a so-called "committee of the people" was formed and two days later it proclaimed a provisional constitution establishing a free Laotian government.

When the new constitution was offered to King Sisavang Vong for his consideration he refused to approve it. The Assembly thereupon, on October 20, voted to depose him on the grounds that he was no longer a free agent. (In Luang Prabang, he was in fact almost entirely isolated from events in Vientiane.) But no one in a responsible position, including Petsarath, was ready to accept this as a final solution. A delegation was sent to apprise the King of the situation and the attitudes of the factions represented at Vientiane and elsewhere; noting that the vote against him had caused no appreciable popular reaction in his favor and realizing the strength of the constitutional movement, he hastened to accept the constitution. He affirmed his acceptance in writing on November 10 and denied any binding agreement with the French; the Assembly then unanimously voted his reinstatement as a constitutional monarch. On April 23, 1946 he was enthroned king of all Laos, with traditional ceremony.

To reinforce the slender forces previously parachuted in a larger, ground-based French force moved up the Mekong, putting down Lao Issara resistance as it advanced. Vientiane fell on March 25, 1946. The small forces of the Issara, supported by Vietminh troops sent by Ho Chi Minh, broke up into small guerrilla bands and many escaped across the Mekong into Thailand. The whole Free Laos government, which included the majority of the most capable of the Western-educated elite, also took refuge in Thailand, and a government-in-exile under Prince Petsarath (who called himself Regent of Laos) was set up in Bangkok.

After the reoccupation of Vientiane and Luang Prabang the French made conciliatory moves which led, in June, to the formation of a Franco-Lao commission to draft a provisional agreement on future relations between the two countries and the form of the Laotian government. The joint commission produced a document signed in Vientiane on August 27, 1946: it confirmed a unified Laos under the sovereignty of Luang Prabang and established it as a constitutional monarchy. In a protocol to the agreement Prince Boun Oum of Champassak renounced his sovereign rights to that principality; in return his title as Prince (*chao*) was confirmed and made hereditary and he was made Inspector General of the Kingdom for life.

A constituent assembly provided for in the agreement was elected in December 1946. Disturbed conditions practically restricted voting to the larger towns but forty-four delegates were elected and over the next few months produced a constitution that was promulgated by the King on May 11, 1947.

All these events took place during the absence in Thailand of most of the more politically sophisticated of the elite. The government-in-exile was not without its own dissensions. Prince Petsarath, at its head, was obviously ambitious for the crown and remained resolutely anti-French; his next younger half brother, Prince Souvanna Phouma, led a group desiring complete independence but inclined to work with the French to get it; another half brother, Prince Souphanouvong, drawn toward the ideas and methods of the Vietminh, favored armed resistance in concert with them. All shades of sentiment were represented.

A new convention with France in 1949 confirmed the autonomy of Laos within the French Union and gave the country greater liberty in the conduct of foreign relations, including the right to apply for membership in the United Nations. This left the exile government with so little in the way of issues that it dissolved itself in October 1949. Most of the leaders, with the notable exceptions of Prince Petsarath and Prince Souphanouvong, returned to Laos to re-enter government affairs.

Spurred by the open rebellion of the Vietminh in Indochina in 1950, the French hastened toward granting Laos full independence. In October 1953 a new treaty was signed recognizing Laos as a fully sovereign state within the French Union. Laos was empowered to establish its own diplomatic representation abroad without the formerly required French approval; the French courts in Laos, as well as effective French control of government departments concerned with foreign and military affairs and with justice, disappeared. The only remaining apparent concession of sovereignty to France was adherence to the article in the French constitution, in reference to the French Union, whereby France "assumes the co-ordination of . . . means and the direction of policy proper to the preparation and the assurance of . . . defense."

Independence

The government of independent Laos was immediately plunged into trouble — economic, military, and political. Under the French, the perennial Laotian deficit had been made up from the favorable balance of the other states, but the newly independent neighboring governments, having troubles of their own, declined to support a virtually indigent Laos. American aid, first given through France and later directly, has been an essential factor in keeping the country on its feet.

Withdrawal of the bulk of French troops from Laos had begun in 1950. The new government had therefore to meet the expenses of building its own army, which was possible only with complete financial and logistic support furnished by the French from funds and stocks supplied by American aid.

An additional and overriding complication was the constant threat of subversion instigated by the Communist Vietminh regime, itself supported by Communist China. Prince Souphanouvong, who had, as mentioned, split earlier with the Lao Issara, had rallied to the Vietminh cause and in March 1951 appeared as head of the Laotian dissidents in North Vietnam. The formation of this new body, which became known as the Pathet Lao (Lao Country), was announced — with all the propaganda trimmings — as the free government of all Laos and as the center of all true resistance against French colonialism and American imperialism. Operationally, it seems to have done little during the next two years, during which time the Lao, with French help, were able to cope with the scattered guerrilla bands within Laos itself.

By 1953 the Vietminh, encouraged by their increasing success in consolidating their position in North Vietnam, moved in some strength into northern Laos and forced the evacuation of the small French and Laotian forces from the area. With them came the Pathet Lao to set up a "government" in Samneua, the capital of Samneua province. Supported by Vietminh forces, Pathet Lao troops made several incursions into central Laos and civil war ensued.

The Geneva cease-fire of July 1954 left Laos a divided country. Despite Laotian and French protestations, the "regrouping zone" principle adopted by the Geneva conference brought about the award of most of Phongsaly and Samneua provinces to the Pathet Lao pending elections in 1955 which were supposed to reintegrate the two provinces. The Geneva agreements provided that the royal government would administer the provinces, but the Pathet Lao not only resisted by force of arms all attempts of the government to assume control but also attacked government army posts on the borders of the area. In further violation of the agreements they continued to increase the strength and armament of their forces.

2. Independence

On the recommendation of the International Commission for Supervision and Control (referred to as the International Control Commission, or ICC) set up by the Geneva conference, negotiations started in January 1955 concerning problems of administration of the disputed provinces, the elections, and, at the insistence of the Pathet Lao, the integration of Pathet Lao forces into the Laotian army. Laos held elections (after several postponements) in 1955, as required, but the elections were boycotted by the Pathet Lao. Accords in principle were reached twice by the negotiators at the top level (in August and December 1956) but both times working committees at a lower level were unable to settle details in a manner satisfactory to both sides. A final agreement was reached, however, in November 1957 and a month later the two provinces were formally returned to royal government control.

By mid-1958 all of the royal government's commitments under the Geneva agreements had been fulfilled, and on July 20 the ICC in Laos formally adjourned itself. Prince Souphanouvong and one of his aides were included in a coalition cabinet and former Pathet Lao members were elected deputies to the National Assembly and entered the civil service. The country appeared to have been reunified politically and its energies could now be directed to economic and social development.

Almost immediately, however, problems which had been held beneath the surface for several months emerged to plague the government. There were charges in the press of graft and corruption among government officials, neglect of the rural population, and mismanagement of foreign aid. As a result of these and similar charges the government of Prince Souvanna Phouma fell in July 1958.

The new government was headed by Phoui Sananikone and included a group of young pro-Western politicians who called themselves the Committee for the Defense of the National Interest. Sananikone ended the coalition with the Pathet Lao by excluding all former Pathet Lao members from his cabinet, bringing a prompt charge by Prince Souphanouvong that the government was violating the 1957 agreements, using terroristic methods against former Pathet Lao leaders, and permitting United States intervention in Laotian affairs that was both detrimental to the economy and a threat to regional peace. His charges were echoed in Red China, where Laos was accused of allowing itself to be converted into a United States military base, and in North Vietnam, where the government joined Prince Souphanouvong in calling for a revival of the International Control Commission to investigate alleged abrogations of the Geneva agreements.

The spring of 1959 brought renewed fighting in the northern provinces, Samneua and Phongsaly, where Pathet Lao rebels backed and supplied by the North Vietnamese had launched a campaign to regain control. Anticipating a serious struggle to keep the two provinces, Phoui Sananikone on February 11, 1959 declared that Laos had fulfilled the Geneva agreements, in effect dismissing the relatively powerless ICC, and would henceforth rely directly on the United Nations to arbitrate and prevent disputes with other Indochinese states.

As the fighting grew in intensity during the summer, Phoui Sananikone turned more and more to neutralism, over the objections of both his own cabinet and Crown Prince Savang Vatthana, whose aging father had in August turned over his duties to him in the crisis.

A lull in the fighting followed the arrival in mid-September of a United Nations inspection committee requested by Laos. The death of King Sisavang Vong in November brought Crown Prince Savang Vatthana to the throne and pressure against Phoui Sananikone's neutralist policies mounted rapidly. In an effort to strengthen his political defenses, Phoui in December reshuffled his government, eliminating those associated with the Committee for the Defense of the National Interest and his other critics. The ousted politicians hurriedly rallied the army command and a month later, in January 1960, successfully carried out a bloodless military coup.

Two weeks later King Savang Vatthana had replaced the military junta by the appointment of an old royal adviser, Kou Abhay, to serve as prime minister until new elections could be held. These elections, in April 1960, proved a decisive victory for the young CDIN faction, who quickly formed a new government pledged to social and economic reforms for the people, a vigorous campaign against corruption and nepotism in government, and firm action should the Pathet Lao begin a new offensive, which seemed likely.

But the newly formed government was shaken by a coup d'état on August 9, 1960. Although it was impossible to assess the success or failure of the coup as this book went to press, there were strong indications that Laos would return to a policy of neutrality.

3

GEOGRAPHY AND POPULATION

LAOS IS A LANDLOCKED, MOUNTAIN-SEGMENTED, monsoon country of some 91,000 square miles populated by about two million people of various ethnic backgrounds. Mountain barriers, even those pierced by rivers, hinder communication both inside the country and with its neighbors. The Mekong, with its left-bank tributaries, is the grand artery of communication in Laos, but frequent rapids prevent large-scale, long-distance shipments, and the falls at the southern boundary of Laos minimize its international use. The river and its lowlands provide easy access to Thailand, however, and with French influence receding Bangkok is becoming more important to Laos than Saigon.

Agriculture — the basis of life in Laos — is governed by the country's distinct two-season cycle of monsoon winds and resultant precipitation. The northeast monsoon of winter produces a dry season from November to April; the southwest monsoon of summer, a wet season from May to October. Thunderstorms in late April precede the onset of the gentler and steadier rains of the next few months. By July and August, the months of maximum precipitation, rain may fall steadily for several days at a time. As the season nears its end, rains may fall only in the morning and evening; by mid-November rain is a rarity.

During the relatively short colonial regime, the French took only preliminary steps toward exploiting or even surveying the resources that may exist in Laos. Deposits of coal, iron, copper, lead, gold, tungsten, and precious stones are known and have been exploited by primitive means at one time or another. Salt beds have been worked locally from time immemorial, but only tin has been extracted on a commercial scale, by a French company.

Geography

With minor exceptions the eastern frontier of Laos is the main divide in Indochina, the Annam Cordillera, a length of land that runs from Tibet to Vietnam, dividing the watersheds of the east-flowing rivers leading to the China Sea and the south-trending rivers of all of South Asia. Within Laos the divide lies northwest-southeast, branching near the northern tip of Laos into a series of generally parallel northeast-southwest ridges, sharp and steep, between which the rivers run in deep gorges (see the map, Relief and Drainage).

This hilly or mountainous terrain characterizes the whole of northern Laos. The only considerable area of low local relief is the Tranninh plateau 3,600 to 4,500 feet above sea level just north of Xiengkhouang. This relatively infertile limestone plateau, surrounded by mountains, is the source of rivers flowing east, south, and west. The highest point in Laos — Pou Bia, 9,242 feet above sea level — lies just south of it. The only portion of Laos east of the main divide, draining toward and easily accessible from Vietnam, is east and northeast of the plateau.

The Annam Cordillera is a formidable and historic barrier to movement. A fairly continuous range with peaks rising to 8,000 feet, it is crossed by only three main passes, two in the province of Khammouane and one in Savannakhet. West of the divide the range is buttressed by a series of plateaus — the most extensive being the Khammouane plateau — from which the land falls off toward the alluvial plain of the Mekong. The Mekong most closely approaches the mountains here, leaving only a narrow area of level plain. In the south the plains are broader and movement is restricted only by the frequent streams. Rising from the plain east of Pakse is the fertile and generally rolling Boloven plateau, at an elevation of about 3,500 feet.

The Mekong marks the long boundary with Thailand and is the geographic key of Laotian life. The Mekong and its tributaries drain all of Laos except the Samneua province area east of the main divide. Its narrow flood plains form the wet-rice lands; its waters furnish fish, the protein supplement to the universal rice diet; and the Mekong and its tributaries carry the pirogues, sampans, and light barges that transport such freight as moves in this country. On or near its banks are all the larger towns, settlements of the dominant Lao.

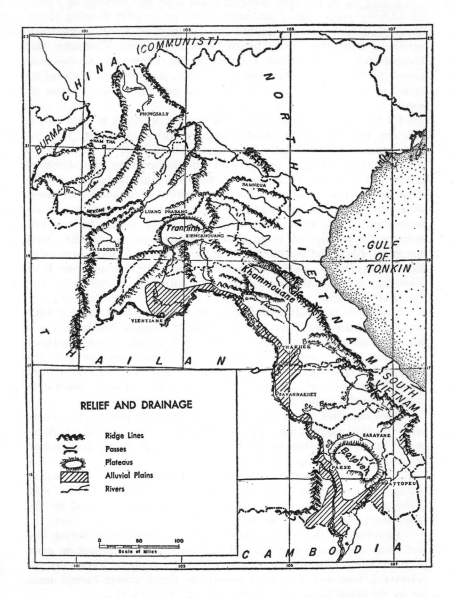

RELIEF AND DRAINAGE

〰 Ridge Lines
≍ Passes
🟡 Plateaus
▨ Alluvial Plains
〰 Rivers

0   50   100
Scale of Miles

Rising far to the northwest of Laos, near the borders of Tibet, the Mekong passes into Cambodia to the south after flowing along the entire length of the country. The river is wide but rapids are numerous over most of its length, except between Vientiane and Savannakhet, below which the formidable rapids of Khemmarat stretch another eighty miles or so. At the extreme southern end of Laos are the double Falls of Khone, impassable at any stage of water.

Of the northern tributaries, the most important are the Nam Tha and the Nam Hou, which, like the upper Mekong, flow in deep, narrow valleys. Both offer some possibilities of water communication by pirogue and afford alluvial pockets or intervales where wet rice may be cultivated. Below Vientiane, except in the bend where the Mekong turns south and the mountains closely approach the river, tributaries wind through broad mountain valleys and empty through nearly level alluvial plains for the last forty to fifty miles of their course. Among these are the Nam Ngum, Se Bang Fai, Se Bang Hieng, Se Done, and Se Khong, with their affluents. The Se Khong actually joins the Mekong south of Laos, but its middle reaches in Laos form an extension of the Cambodian plain.

The mean annual rainfall over practically all of Laos ranges from 50 to 90 inches (see the map, Mean Annual Rainfall). Only at places along the Mekong from Luang Prabang to the mouth of the Nam Nhiep does it average less, and only in the Boloven plateau and the highest altitudes of the Annam Cordillera is it greater. The Boloven plateau has the country's heaviest rainfall — over 160 inches annually.

Temperatures, never extreme, are tropical to subtropical, varying with altitude, latitude, and the monsoon. The highest temperatures, in the 90's, are reached in March and April just before the rains; the summer rains usually bring temperatures in the mid-80's; winter temperatures during the cooler part of the dry season (December to February) average in the 60's and 70's with perhaps a 20-degree daily range, although temperatures in the 30's have been reported in the northern mountains.

Flooding of the rivers, particularly the tributaries, during the wet monsoon assures enough moisture for wet-rice cultivation even in those areas where rainfall alone is not sufficient. There are no reservoirs, however, for impounding the flood waters except insofar as the small field dikes themselves accomplish this.

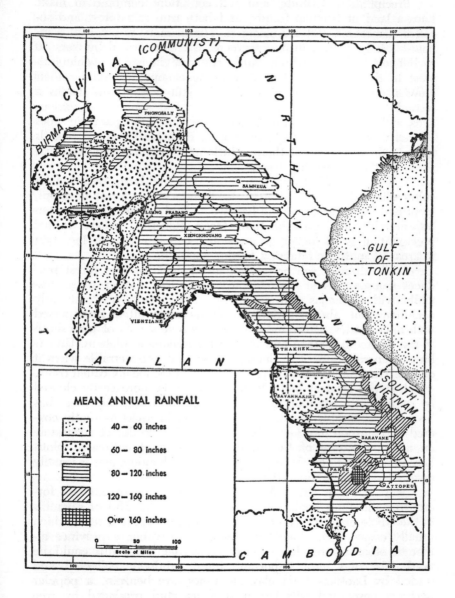

MEAN ANNUAL RAINFALL

- 40 – 60 inches
- 60 – 80 inches
- 80 – 120 inches
- 120 – 160 inches
- Over 160 inches

0   50   100

Scale of Miles

Precipitation, latitude, and soil conditions combine to make Laos a land of tropical forests, and both true rain forest and so-called monsoon forest are common. The primary rain forest, composed chiefly of broadleaf evergreens, is characterized by trees 80 to 100 feet in height whose trunks rise straight and branchless almost to their crowns. The fairly dense canopy formed by their crowns, overtopped here and there by still taller trees, shades a second level of smaller trees, seedlings, and saplings of various ages, and supports a luxuriant growth of lianas and parasitic vines as well as orchids and other air plants. Both hard and soft woods grow in these forests but there is little underbrush in the perpetual shade of these towering trees.

Where nomadic tribes practicing slash-and-burn, or *rai*, agriculture have deforested an area, a secondary rain forest develops, identified by fewer of the tall hardwoods and a much denser, often impenetrable low growth. Rain forest flourishes where annual precipitation is 80 inches or more but will develop on less rain in areas of moisture-retaining hardpan subsoil.

Easily drained soil or rainfall insufficient for rain forest produces monsoon forest — a more open stand of shorter trees, normally without lianas and air plants. This forest, predominantly deciduous but also containing evergreens, is often interspersed with open glades, as throughout the extensive stands of pine south of the Tranninh plateau and on the Khammouane plateau. Underbrush, generally absent, is dense, thorny, and impenetrable when it occurs. The usual ground cover is a coarse grass, locally called *tranh*, which stands six feet high. Monsoon forest is more easily cleared by *rai* agriculturists than rain forest, with the result that there has been a considerable change over the years in areas naturally covered by monsoon forest — a change impossible to depict accurately on a map because of the continual shifting of cultivated plots. Secondary growth on these plots after their abandonment is usually dominated by bamboo and scrub trees.

Most Laotians cut timber by hand from the surrounding forests to build their homes as there are only a handful of sawmills in the whole country. The only wood cut for export is teak, which usually comes from along the Mekong in Sayaboury province although other stands, less readily accessible, exist and could be used. The two most important forest products, collected and traded by Laotians from classical times, are benzoin, a popular perfume base, and stick-lac, a resinous gum produced by tree parasites and widely used in making varnish.

3. Population

Laos also abounds in wild life — from elephants, leopards, and tigers to cobras, lizards, and a relatively small kind of crocodile. The elephant, captured and trained as a beast of burden throughout the history of Laos, is the traditional symbol of Lao royalty and is depicted on the national flag. There is in addition a local breed of the water buffalo universally used by Laotians as a draft animal.

A dramatic possibility for the future of Laos is the projected development of the enormous water storage and power potentials of the Mekong and its tributaries, now broken by falls and rapids, to provide hydroelectric power and a water transportation network far superior to the natural system. This development project is, of course, dependent on foreign aid and technical assistance and is just now getting under way.

Population

There has never been a formal census in Laos, that is an actual, methodical count in the Western sense, and therefore it is impossible for anyone to state with certainty the population of the country. The most authoritative estimates range from about 1.5 million to well over two million (see Table 2). A figure of approximately two million appears most realistic.

In modern times the taking of a census by the Laotian government has consisted of sending questionnaires to all government officials, from provincial to village level, with the request that estimates be made of the population of their political areas. In the case of higher officials this means a coordination and evaluation of the estimates of their subordinates. This method, which is based on estimates rather than counts and which the officials know is primarily for apportionment of representatives in the National Assembly, is likely to produce inflated results. (A census by the Laotian government in 1955 gave a population of four million.) Demographers for the United Nations, on the other hand, have consistently estimated a much smaller population: 1953, 1,260,000; 1954, 1,360,000; 1955, 1,425,000. A thorough census is planned for 1962–63.

Based on the figure of two million and an area of 91,000 square miles, the density, country-wide, is somewhat less than 22 per square mile. In a country so largely dependent on subsistence agriculture, a figure for density per unit of cultivated land would be more informative but reliable statistics to support such a calculation are hard to find. It is known, however, that population density is highest in those provinces containing the largest proportion of the alluvial lands in the lower Mekong region — that is, Champassak, Savannakhet, Saravane, and Vientiane. In these provinces live more than half the population, and in their most intensively cultivated areas population density is reported to reach 180 per square mile.

Demographers view Laos as having a slowly growing population relatively unaffected by either immigration or emigration, nor have epidemic and famine caused a visibly disproportionate number of deaths in any particular age group. It is improbable that the depression years of the 1930's, the disruption of World War II, or even the recent Vietminh campaigns have had marked effect on either birth or death rates. Further, the climatic and economic environment of Laos is not given to extremes. Thus, the population is likely to be rather evenly balanced as to males and females, on the whole young, with a median age of around twenty and a life expectancy at birth of thirty to thirty-five (or a very small percentage of persons over fifty). Average family size is probably between five and six.

For want of specific statistics the ethnic composition of the population can only be stated in equally imprecise fashion. An official French estimate for 1921, apparently the only complete one ever made, omitted consideration of nonindigenous categories — Europeans, Vietnamese, Chinese, Indians, Cambodians (see Table 3). Official estimates in 1953 (see Table 4) were based on somewhat different ethnic classifications and excluded Phongsaly and Samneua provinces which were at that time under Pathet Lao control. A comparison of the tables indicates, however, that there has probably been no radical change in ethnic composition of the country as a whole in the last forty years despite some movement of ethnic groups between provinces.

There is no marked trend toward urbanization in Laos. Some 96 percent of the population is rural, living in nine thousand or so villages. Vientiane, the capital, is by far the largest town. Its population in 1959, as estimated by official Laotian sources (refer to Table 2), was 68,000; a United States publication of 1955 credited it with 45,000. The population is Laotian and foreign (Chinese and Vietnamese engaged in trade, and some foreign diplomatic representation).

The remaining few "cities" are all provincial towns along the lower Mekong — Thakhek (4,000-7,000), Savannakhet (7,000-

10,000), and Pakse (6,000-10,000) – and possess trade as well as governmental functions. Compared with the official atmosphere of Vientiane the royal residence and religious capital, Luang Prabang, has in many respects the appearance of a small town, though it may have as many as 15,000 inhabitants. The establishment of industry other than construction and road building has not been a major factor in the increase in town population.

There is today, as in the past, a considerable mobility of population groups within Laos. Kha villages may move a considerable distance within the space of a few years. The historic pressure of population from the north continues, and immigration from Yunnan, for example, has posed resettlement problems for the Laotian government. The Meo represent the last major immigration from the north, about the middle of the last century, and groups of Meo tribesmen within Laos are still moving southward. The only recent event resembling the historic migrations is the movement southward of some thousands of Black Tai from their lands near the border of North Vietnam during the course of the Vietminh troubles of the past few years. There is in recent history no pattern of voluntary mass emigration, but there is a constant movement of tribal peoples back and forth across the borders with Burma, Thailand, and Yunnan.

According to the *Bulletin Statistique du Laos* in 1958, there were at that time approximately 40,000 foreign Asians in Laos. An estimated 30,000 of these were Chinese, an increase from the 10,000 reported in 1953. The great majority of the Chinese in Laos are connected with commercial pursuits, including moneylending. There are in addition perhaps 1,000 individuals of Indian origin, chiefly merchants and moneylenders, and somewhat over 6,000 persons of European origin. The Americans in Laos number close to 500. The French, after their arrival in 1893, brought in numbers of Vietnamese, both as minor officials and as laborers: in the first instance, the need was for French-speaking employees already partially trained in French methods of administration; in the second, the French were influenced both by conditions of relative overpopulation in Vietnam and by the fact that Laotians were uninterested in labor for wages. The number of Vietnamese probably never exceeded 30,000 and is much reduced at present, probably to around 9,000.

There is no record available to indicate the enunciation of any government policy toward internal or external population shifts, although the government has sought in recent years to encourage resettlement of hill peoples on the fertile plains areas. There are evidences of dislike — both popular and official — for Vietnamese of whatever political views. Upon departure of the French, this general feeling seems to have shown itself only in informal discouragement of the presence of Vietnamese; so far as is known, no action leading to actual deportation was ever taken.

4

ETHNIC GROUPS AND LANGUAGES

THE LAOTIAN POPULATION COMPRISES a variety of ethnic groups, whose diversity and in many cases isolation make the realization of true political and cultural unity in Laos difficult. The historic rulers of the country have been the dominant Lao group and their leadership, although accepted by the other groups, has reflected the ideas and aspirations of the Lao elite rather than the activities and attitudes of the rest of the population. The concept of a multicultural society is foreign to the Lao, who seem convinced that all other groups should assimilate to Lao culture. For the Tai tribes, most closely related to the Lao, acculturation may be possible and those Kha groups in close contact with centers of Lao influence are already strongly acculturated. There is little evidence, however, that the more remote hill tribes in the north will ever surrender their tribal independence willingly.

Many important ethnic distinctions in Laos can be made on the basis of language, the major division being between those who speak Sino-Tibetan languages and those who speak Mon-Khmer languages. In the Sino-Tibetan group are the Lao, constituting about half the population, who speak Laotian Thai (Lao), a language in the Southwestern Thai branch of the Sino-Tibetan stock. Laotian Thai, closely related to Siamese Thai, has dialects but variation is minimal.

Differing in many ways from the Lao but sharing their cultural origins are the so-called Tai tribes, about a sixth of the population, which speak dialects belonging to the Central and Southwestern branches of the widespread Thai family. (The spellings *Thai* and *Tai*, which provide a natural and convenient terminological distinction, are based on the difference in pronounciation by some members of these groups of their original common name: *th* here indicates a sound more like the English *t* and the *t* in *Tai*, a sound somewhat similar to the English *d*.) In northern Laos, near the Chinese border, are the Meo and Man hill tribes, representing perhaps as much as a tenth of the population but probably closer to half that, who may be distantly related linguistically to the Tai tribes although their culture has incorporated a strong Chinese element. Added to these three ethnic subgroups are the few northern tribes speaking Lolo dialects of the Tibeto-Burman family of the Sino-Tibetan stock.

About a fourth of the population of Laos is made up of the so-called Kha tribes, which the Lao consider politically, socially, and technologically their inferiors. The Kha tribes are believed to be speakers of various Mon-Khmer languages. The Mon-Khmer language family includes Cambodian and languages spoken in Burma and the Malay peninsula but is unrelated historically to the Sino-Tibetan stock.

The rest of the Laotian population, a small but influential foreign minority, retain their own languages, learning Lao as a second language when necessary. This group of immigrants to Laos, many of whom come for business reasons, includes Chinese, Vietnamese, Burmese, Indians, Malays, and other Asians, as well as a few Europeans, mostly French.

There is considerable ancient literature in Lao, and the Laotians, proud of this heritage, have made Lao the official government language, although all publications continue to be issued in French as well. The universality of French and the facility in the language of almost all the Lao elite from its general use in education and government during the French protectorate make French a logical and convenient language for foreign and diplomatic communication. The growing importance everywhere of English as a commercial and diplomatic language is, however, rapidly changing the situation, and more and more Laotians are learning English as a second language.

The other native languages of Laos are for the most part unwritten and so local in use that most non-Lao groups learn some Lao for trading and other general purposes.

Ethnic Distribution

The Lao occupy the Mekong plains and the alluvial fingers ascending the tributaries, the only areas of fertile lowlands in Laos. Although the Lao areas appear straggling and tenuous on a map,

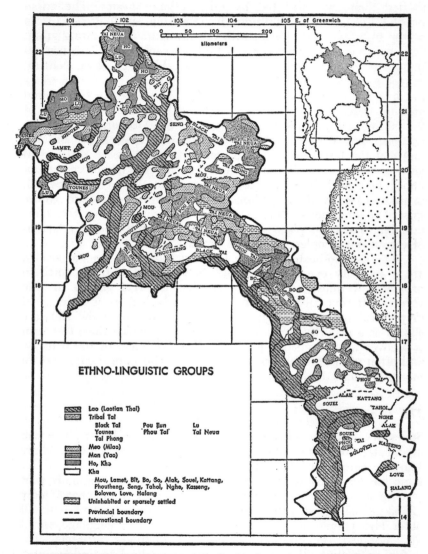

ETHNO-LINGUISTIC GROUPS

- Lao (Laotian Thai)
- Tribal Tai
  - Black Tai   Pou Eun   Lu
  - Younes   Phou Tai   Tai Neua
  - Tai Phong
- Meo (Miao)
- Man (Yao)
- Ho, Khɔ
- Kha
  - Mou, Lamet, Bit, Bo, So, Alak, Souei, Kattang, Phoutheng, Seng, Tahol, Nghe, Kasseng, Boloven, Love, Halang
- Uninhabited or sparsely settled
- --- Provincial boundary
- ——— International boundary

From the Carte Ethno-linguistique of the Service Geographique de l'Indochine, 1929.

38

they form a roughly continuous settlement, which is much more unified than any inhabited by other ethnic groups. The tribal peoples live at higher altitudes in relatively small groups, from hilltop to hilltop so to speak, with the lower land separating group from group and even parts of a tribe from each other. This vertical pattern of ethnic distribution has considerable bearing on political as well as geographic unity.

The map, Ethno-Linguistic Groups, shows clearly the limited area inhabited by the Lao, the scattered but wide distribution of the various Tai peoples, the limitation of the Meo and Man to the northern half of the country in small scattered enclaves, and the fact that the term Kha refers to many different groups distributed all over the country. It should be noted that the names are reproduced here without significant change from the French original; in many cases, variant spellings or even entirely different names exist. The limitations of the map preclude showing either the intermingling that takes place where groups join or the smaller islands of extraneous peoples within the zones shown.

The map indicates that the Lao together with the Tai groups are a majority everywhere except in two of the three northern provinces. It must be remembered that the Tai groups include several different tribal groupings among which there is little social or political unity. It is also to be noted that where the Kha are shown as a majority the fact is of little significance since the term is a cover for many small groups with no political or social unity, and often with little cultural resemblance. The Lao, then, are even more dominant than statistics would show.

The Lao

Sedentary wet-rice cultivators and Theravada Buddhists, the Lao are related to their neighboring Thai speakers, the Siamese. Many Lao live across the Mekong in Thailand, and the political border is no barrier to constant movement. The Lao were originally part of a widespread ethnic group that came south from what is now China and share with the Siamese and to a lesser extent with all other Thai peoples many aspects of their culture — language, social and political organization, agricultural methods, artifacts. Together with most other peoples in the area, the Lao underwent a long period of acculturation to Indic culture, which has provided a further series of cultural elements in common.

4. The Lao

But if differences from neighboring ethnic groups in material culture and even physical characteristics appear slight, the Lao are set apart by language. The Cambodians to the southwest as well as the Kha tribes of Laos itself speak languages of the Mon-Khmer stock; the Lao and the Siamese, as noted above, speak Thai languages of the Sino-Tibetan stock.

The Lao alphabet, in all essentials identical with the Siamese, came into existence about the thirteenth century and is written in several styles or forms — analogous to our roman, italic, blackletter, etc. Although the alphabet remains the same, the Lao in different parts of the country will use these different written styles according to their preferences, and there is no standardized spelling. There is, moreover, no one generally accepted system for transcribing the Lao alphabet into Latin letters, and several versions of a Lao word may be found in French or English publications, each quite at variance with a similar Siamese word.

In older literary Lao there was a large specialized vocabulary of religious and other technical terms taken from Pali, the ancient Indic language in which the sacred books of Theravada Buddhism are written. During the French protectorate technical terms of French and Cambodian origin were adopted in many instances, and since independence there has been a tendency to seek technical terms in Siamese. The latter are often Siamese adaptations or analogues of words in Western languages. As a consequence, the present Lao vocabulary, like that of the Siamese, includes words taken from Sanskrit, Pali, Cambodian, and French, as well as indirect borrowings from other Western languages. Most literate Lao will also have some literacy in French, but the literacy rate, although never accurately determined, is undoubtedly low.

Local variations in behavior and customs are known to exist among the Lao, but the extent and nature of the differences have not been studied in detail. The colorful traditional costumes are increasingly being forsaken by Lao men for Western dress — most popular being khaki shorts and short-sleeved shirts. Lao women for the most part continue to wear their traditional silk skirts and blouses away from the home, but dress less distinctively in their everyday lives.

Physically, the Lao are said to show less evidence of the Mongoloid eye fold than the Vietnamese and to be darker in color than peoples to the east and northeast. Many older Lao men are tattooed, the practice of tattooing magical symbols and sayings for good luck having been widespread even a generation ago. Today, however, tattooing is rapidly disappearing among the younger Lao males, particularly those in urban areas.

Western influence on Lao customs and behavior has so far been limited. During the French protectorate the Lao government elite were quick to adopt many aspects of French culture and most learned the French language. The rural Lao, whose only contact with the French was often through the few schools the French established, were little affected by these changes in the capital.

Since independence there has been a more noticeable Westernization, modeled, interestingly enough, on the adaptations to Western culture and technology of Thailand. The presence today of a growing number of technical assistants from the United States has put a premium on learning English with the result that there has been a remarkable jump in the last few years in the number of younger government officials, bonzes, and storekeepers who can carry on a conversation in English, and English has become the second most important foreign language taught in the schools.

The Tai Tribes

Living chiefly in the mountain valleys of northern Laos, the various Tai tribes are primarily wet rice growers, although corn, millet, sweet potatoes, and beans are often cultivated and the mountain slopes used for dry rice and wheat. Their religion is basically animistic, with vague Buddhist, Taoist, and Confucian additions. The tribes are in many respects self-sufficient — in their basic food and clothing requirements — but have always traded with the lowland Lao for some items.

The tribal groupings are referred to variously by different ethnologists, but the most common terms are Tai Dam (Black Tai), Tai Khao (White Tai), Tai Deng (Red Tai), as well as Tai Neua, Tai Phong, and Phou Tai. These names and others seem to be general designations by the Lao, who distinguish these "inferior" peoples roughly according to the color of their traditional costumes, their location, or some other real or imagined identifying characteristic.

Their widely scattered settlements (refer to the map, Ethno-Linguistic Groups) are too isolated for there to be any extensive sense of political or "racial" unity and political organization rarely extends beyond the immediate village area and its local social and trading relationships. But the Tai tribes everywhere, who reportedly regard themselves superior to the Lao, share a general suspicion and dislike of the Lao, which makes them susceptible to Communist divisive propaganda. There are an "autonomous" Tai district in southern Yunnan and a "Tai-Meo autonomous area" in Vietnam. These seem to have little political or other reality but their propaganda value to Communist agitators is self-evident.

The Black Tai are reported to be more conservative than any of the other groups and to have retained more of their traditional culture — probably because they live farther away from the Lao, at higher altitudes. They are said to have a strong feudal social organization, with commoners tied to the lord's land, at least in theory. Similar customs are reported for other Tai tribes.

The various Tai dialects are of the same general structure as Lao and are for the most part mutually intelligible. Speakers of Tai usually can understand Lao, at least partially, and they learn it with ease. Some of these dialects have writing systems, usually based on the same Indic source as the Lao and Siamese alphabets, but very few Tai speakers can read and write. With the spread of schools using only Lao, literacy in the Tai dialects, already small, will probably decrease.

The Meo and Man

The Meo (Miao) and the Man (Yao) are said by some authorities to speak languages related to those of the Tai tribes but are generally much more like their close linguistic and cultural relatives in Yunnan than they are like Tai or Lao. They exhibit strong evidences of influence from general Chinese culture.

The Meo are among the most recent migrants from China, first appearing in Laos about 1850. Their outstanding peculiarity is that they cannot or will not live at altitudes of less than 3,000 feet. They practice slash-and-burn agriculture to a more intensive degree than the other tribal peoples in Laos. It has been said that they habitually exhaust the soil to the degree that natural vegetation cannot return, though reliable observers deny this. They raise maize as well as rice, breed domestic animals for trade, and also raise most of the opium grown in Laos. Though hospitable when suitably approached, they are a proud people and disdainful of the lowlanders. Living in scattered small villages on the mountain tops the Meo have nevertheless apparently achieved some degree of political unity. The Meo are the only ethnic minority so far to have an elected deputy in the National Assembly.

The Man in Laos are few in number and there is little available descriptive information about them. Although the Man and Meo languages are related, they are not mutually intelligible. Each is said to have a writing system based on Chinese characters, limited in use to religious texts and known only by priests.

The Kha

Kha is the Laotian word for *slave* and though resented is applied by the Lao to some sixty different tribal peoples. The most numerous and perhaps best-known of these groups in northern Laos is the Kha Mou or Khmu. There is little sense of ethnic and no political unity among the various Kha groups.

Kha tribes live on mountain slopes above the Lao and subsist by cultivating rice, maize, tobacco, cotton, and other crops, largely by means of slash-and-burn methods. They also hunt and gather forest products. Their languages are said to be chiefly of the Mon-Khmer family. Some of these groups have in the course of time become acculturated to Lao culture, even adopting the Lao language.

The various Kha tribes are often distinguished by darker skin color and occasionally by kinky hair and broader noses, indicating a possible ancestral connection with various Negrito groups in Southeast Asia. In the past, Kha tribes, especially in the north, have been conquered and enslaved by Lao, Tai, and other groups. Some of them are said to have accepted inferiority, even rationalizing it by myths. From time to time, however, others have staged local rebellions. There is no evidence of any larger unity among these groups, and the degree to which they interact politically — with each other or with other groups in the country — is still small. In religion they are largely animistic, although Buddhism has been adopted by some Khmu villages near centers of Lao influence.

The various languages spoken by the Kha belong to the Mon-Khmer language family and are quite different in structure from Thai. No writing systems exist. Many Kha speakers know some Lao, and undoubtedly there are also many who know Tai dialects spoken by their close neighbors.

It can be assumed that assimilating the Kha tribes will remain a problem for many years. It is to be doubted that the Laotian government can have any effective plans for dealing with these groups except in terms of forced "civilization."

Other Tribal Groups

In northern Laos there are a number of groups originating in China, unclassifiable as Thai and locally called Ho and Kho. *Ho* is the Lao word for *Chinese,* and applies, it is said, as a group name for a few thousand Lolo-speaking mountain villagers descended from Chinese traders intermarried with Lolo women. The Kho (also called A'Kha) are even harder to classify; they are represented in small numbers in the same area, as well as in Yunnan and North Vietnam. Neither group is significant in numbers or political importance.

Foreign Minorities

There were in Laos in 1958 approximately six thousand Europeans, nine thousand Vietnamese, thirty thousand Chinese, and slightly over one thousand Pakistani and Indians. Most of these groups are concentrated in the urban centers, although many Chinese are found throughout the rice-growing areas as millers, moneylenders, and traders. Although there are sizable communities of Vietnamese craftsmen and merchants remaining in the larger urban centers, most of the Vietnamese brought by the French to fill administrative teaching and clerical posts have left the country. Their departure initially created real voids in the occupational structure, although these have for the most part now been filled by either Lao or Westerners. The few hundred Filipinos in Laos are a small but important minority; they have filled key engineering and clerical posts within the USOM and have been active in Operation Brotherhood, a medical aid program sponsored by the Philippine and Lao Junior Chambers of Commerce.

RELIGION

THERAVADA BUDDHISM (SOMETIMES CALLED Hinayana Buddhism) is the dominant and official faith of Laos. In practice Buddhism overlays a core of spirit worship deeply ingrained in the Lao as well as the Tai tribes, the Kha, and the other tribal groups. The cult of the *phi* (spirits) has assimilated itself to such an extent to the Buddhist faith that submission to formal Buddhist doctrine often appears perfunctory. Despite this mixture, however, Buddhism contains the ideal to which the Lao offers reverence. The people generally respect the Buddhist moral code and attempt to follow its more basic rules. Moreover, the importance of merit-making and the acquisition of merit in preparation for one's future existence remains a dominant theme in the lives of Laotian Buddhists just as it does among their coreligionists in neighboring Burma, Thailand, and Cambodia. In the day-to-day life of the average layman, the ascetic prescriptions of Buddhism are of relatively little importance when compared with the attention and effort expended on the acquisition of merit through such things as contributions to the support of the pagodas and bonzehood, sponsoring of religious ceremonies, and the like. As in neighboring Buddhist countries, much of the accumulation of capital and the expenditure thereof is directed to the attainment of essentially nonmaterial goals.

The Buddhist practices discussed in this chapter refer primarily to the Lao. Among the Tai, Kha, Meo, and Man tribesmen there exists a variety of faiths — Buddhism, animism, primitive Brahmanism, ancestor worship, and a weakened Confucianism — each combined to some extent with the all pervading *phi* cult. The foreign minority groups — Vietnamese, Chinese, Europeans, Indians, and a handful of Cambodians — on the whole retain the religious beliefs of their countries of origin.

The Cult of the Phi

Antedating Buddhism in Laos is an ancient and pervasive animism, a belief that certain spirits or *phi* with great power over the destinies of men are present throughout the material and nonmaterial universe. Despite sporadic attempts at suppression by the government, beginning with King Photisarath's decree in 1527, the cult of the *phi* is found today in some form everywhere in Laos, even among the highest levels of the Buddhist clergy. An indirect contribution to the persistence of the cult was undoubtedly provided by the Siamese war of 1826-28, which resulted in the temporary flight and deportation of many bonzes. The gradual absorption of elements of *phi* worship into Buddhist practice has continued for hundreds of years, however, creating a situation in modern Laos in which bonzes may participate side by side with village shamans in ceremonies to propitiate or exorcise *phi*.

The ubiquitousness of *phi* power can perhaps be judged by the bewildering number of kinds of *phi*, some borrowed from the vast Brahmanic pantheon. The earth, the heavens, water, and fire — the four universal elements — have their special *phi*; every moral principle is represented by its own *phi*; there is everyday familiarity with the *phi* of household, parents, relatives, village, roads, and streams.

In many parts of Laos the ancient doctrine of the thirty-two *phi* presiding over the thirty-two organs of man is still held. According to this belief, a form of metempsychosis, these immortal "souls" of the body fly away at death to be reincarnated in different combinations with the spirits from other bodies — except in the case of *phi phetu*, the particularly malevolent spirits of those whose death was from childbirth, accident, or any other violence. *Phi phetu*, which being evil are prevented from combining with other *phi* for rebirth in a new body, roam the earth tormenting the living.

The jungles and forests are inhabited and guarded by a particularly numerous and potent body of *phi*, whose existence makes wild or unknown areas fearsome places from which the unwary may never return or return so transformed as to be unrecognizable by family and friends.

Evil *phi* also cause disease, many Laotians believe, and must be exorcised by shamans — and sometimes bonzes — with special knowledge of *phi*. Such a ritual requires the exact determination of the *phi* inhabiting the sick person's body and the careful selection of music or offerings to induce these *phi* to leave. A less conciliatory attitude had to be adopted when cholera struck Luang Prabang in 1892: the desperate native chiefs and soldiers reportedly discharged volleys of musketry around the town to frighten away the evil spirits.

To succeed in any enterprise it is necessary to have the favor of the *phi*, and for this reason almost every house in Laos contains a small bamboo altar upon which offerings can be made. It is important, however, to know the desires of any particular *phi*. The tribal Tai, for example, believe the *phi* of tigers prefer a dog sacrifice, and the mountain *phi*, chickens and pigs. Goats are generally offered to the *phi* of roads, and buffalo and oxen to those of the village or ancestors. In fact, much of the livestock raised in Laos is intended as sacrifice to the *phi*.

Demons called *ho* sometimes take possession of people, according to a widespread belief, and these people, *phi pop*, are greatly feared for their power to cast spells and work magic. In addition to their ability to kill animals and men by incantation or an evil eye, *phi pop* supposedly have the power to reduce a buffalo hide to the size of a grain of rice, which when swallowed by the chosen victim swells to its original size, bursting his stomach. Possessed people were formerly tried by being thrown into a river, tied hand and foot, and were believed innocent only if they floated. The French forbade this practice, with apparent success, but villagers continue to banish suspected *phi pop*, compelling them to wander or to live in segregated villages. Foreign observers have reported that these so-called *phi pop* are often highly intelligent, attractive people.

Buddhism

Centuries before the birth of Christ, Brahmanism in India was already an old and elaborate sacerdotal and sacrificial religious system, its original vitality all but gone. Among the reformers who emerged from time to time was a young prince, Gautama (c. 563–483 B.C.), who renounced his high caste, his right to rule, his wealth, and his family to devote himself to religious study. Gautama, later to be called the Buddha or "the enlightened one," perceived the rigid Brahmanic caste system as a denial of all hope for individual spiritual and social improvement and set out to find, within the general Brahmanic philosophy, a way to escape the pain and sorrow of life and to attain a sublime state. His teachings, from which evolved the most meticulous, demanding, and durable asceticism ever known, were without claims of divine revelation or inspiration, being regarded by the Buddha as his discovery and interpretation of the truest way within the existing Brahmanism. The religious and philosophical system known as Buddhism was formed from the teachings of the Buddha by his disciples in the succeeding generations.

Buddhism is based upon three concepts: 1) dharma (in Pali, dhamma), or the doctrine of Buddha, a guide to right action and belief; 2) karma (in Pali, kamma), the retribution of actions, or the responsibility of a man for the sum of his actions in prior incarnations and to date in his present incarnation; and 3) sangha, or the religious community, the ascetic order within which a man can improve the sum of his actions. None of these concepts were original with Buddha, but to the Brahmanic doctrine of rebirth with its fatalistic determination of pain and sorrow in life after life Buddha added a hope of escape. There is no promise of heaven or of a life after death — Buddha did not preach the existence of a soul — but there is salvation in the form of a release from the cycle of births and deaths. That release is nirvana (in Pali, nibbana).

Though there is no Buddhist doctrinal concept of soul, the Lao, in common with the Siamese Thai, believe they possess a mobile "soul," or spirit, called by the Lao *khouan*. When resident in the body (usually in the head) it is the source of all well-being; should it wander, be startled out of the body, or driven out by a malevolent *phi*, the body sickens or dies.

The essence of Buddhism is contained in the Four Noble Truths taught by the Buddha: I, suffering exists; II, suffering has a cause, the "thirst" or craving for existence; III, suffering can be ended by extinguishing this craving; IV, there is an Eightfold Path by which a permanent state of peace can be attained. Simply stated, to follow the Eightfold Path requires: right understanding, right purpose, right speech, right conduct, right vocation, right effort, right thinking, and right meditation. Ascetic discipline though this may be, it is also an exercise in logic. Buddhism in the vast majority of its doctrines relies upon logic rather than upon revelation or divine inspiration. The element of divinity was not introduced until the Mahayana doctrine was devised.

Only minimal hope was offered the average layman. By following as best he could the doctrine's basic rules of moral conduct — the prohibitions on killing any living thing, taking what is not given, unchastity or incontinence, falsehood, and becoming intoxicated on fermented beverages — he could slightly improve his karma and gain a better condition in the next life.

For over two centuries Buddhism remained an ascetic ideal, a system governing the growing communities of monks who donned the prescribed robes of the order, begged for their food, and followed the elaborate rules of the sangha.

During the third century B.C., however, the complexion of the movement changed. Asoka (who died in 232 B.C.), ruler of the area in which Buddha had lived and worked, accepted Buddhism and proceeded to conquer most of the Indian subcontinent. Buddhism, as a system of practical morality, was spread far and wide, being superimposed upon the Brahmanism which was the pattern of Indian civilization.

But the Buddhist asceticism was too demanding and impersonal for the mass of the people, and in the second century B.C. there developed the Mahayana doctrines, those of the "greater vehicle." By reinterpreting what the Lord Buddha had taught about laymen, by incorporating into Buddhist doctrines many aspects of other philosophical schools, including the deification of Buddha himself, and by superimposing upon the entire doctrine a pervasive optimism, a broader ethic was created. Buddhism as interpreted in the Mahayana tracts offered hope and salvation — nirvana — to one and all, though continuing to teach that the ascetics could achieve it more readily.

A sizable number of Buddhists continued, however, to adhere to the earlier teachings which, being without the additions of the Mahayanists, came to be known as Hinayana ("lesser vehicle") Buddhism. While the Mahayana doctrines were gaining acceptance in the north of India, from where they would eventually spread to Central Asia, China, and Japan, the Hinayana teachings were perpetuated in the south — particularly on Ceylon which had been converted by one of Asoka's emissaries, the monk Mahinda, in 246 B.C. From Ceylon, Hinayana Buddhism — which its followers prefer to call Theravada ("school of the elders") Buddhism — was carried by the Singhalese eastward to the areas of modern Burma, Cambodia, Thailand, and Laos, where it is still predominant. The Theravada school offers the direct path to nirvana to only a few ascetics, while the Mahayana offers it to the many. Neither is prescriptive, authoritarian, prohibitive, or exclusive in its attitude toward its followers or other religions. Buddhism simply offers a way for those who will follow.

5. Buddhism as State Religion

Buddhism as State Religion

Although archaeologists have uncovered in Laos remains of carved Buddhas from the twelfth century, the earliest historical record of Buddhism dates from 1356 A.D., when the Wat Keo was built at Muong Swa (Luang Prabang). It is assumed that this is the year the Pra Bang Buddha, a Singhalese carving, was presented to the king by an official Khmer mission of Theravada Buddhists. The Pra Bang Buddha became through the centuries the very symbol of official Laotian Buddhism, but the conversion of the Lao was no simple matter and it took centuries even to make Buddhism the predominant faith. In the seventeenth century the kingdom achieved a political prestige never before equaled in Laotian history and during that golden era Buddhism triumphed within the kingdom.

Chao Setthathirath, King of Lan Xang (1548–71), with his capital at Vien Chang (Vientiane), made the kingdom a holy center of Theravada Buddhism. Souligna Vongsa, whose reign extended from 1637 to 1694, established the first official schools of the Buddhist faith in Laos.

The destruction of Laotian power and the consequent weakening of the official religion came in the eighteenth century. The Siamese were expanding eastward, and in 1778 the Thai general Maha Krasad (Chulalok) ravaged the country and captured the capital of Vientiane. Another sacred Buddha, the Emerald Buddha, originally taken by the Lao from the Thai kingdom of Chieng Mai, was carried off to Bangkok, where it has remained ever since. A subsequent Siamese conquest (1826–28) destroyed and looted scores of buildings in the major towns, and in 1873 Yunnan land pirates burned the That Luang, traditional holy center and depository of relics at Vientiane.

One significant aspect of Buddhism in political affairs has been the taking of the political oath of allegiance in a temple, an act first required by royal decree in 1824. The king had built the Temple of Sisaket in the capital, and it was there that all Laotian notables had to take an annual oath of allegiance. After the Siamese conquest the oath to Siamese suzerainty was taken in this same temple, as was the oath to the French after their assumption of the protectorate. Today the oath of allegiance is again to the king.

There are two Buddhist orders in Laos, the Mahanikay and the Thammayut. The former is by far the larger of the two, comprising many more monks and pagodas. The Thammayut, introduced from Thailand in the mid-nineteenth century, is largely a regional concentration, centering on the province of Champassak in southern Laos. There appear to be no basic doctrinal differences between the two sects, though there are differences of opinion concerning the proper observance of monastic rules. Thammayut bonzes, insisting upon strict adherence to all rules, lead ascetic lives in self-imposed isolation from the villagers and concentrate upon the holy writ; the Mahanikay bonzes are more lenient. The difference between these orders appears to have no effect on the beliefs or practices of the people in their everyday life.

The Buddhist clergy is organized into a well-defined hierarchy, and there are close connections between the religious and political spheres. The constitution of Laos designates Buddhism as the official state religion and requires that the king must be a "fervent Buddhist." The king is "Supreme Protector" of the faith and, subject to procedures involving the Ministry of Religious Affairs and the highest levels of the religious hierarchy, has the power to appoint the *phra sangkharaja*, who is the actual religious head of the church. The king's role in the church is more ceremonial than administrative, however, and is displayed through ritual and charitable merit-making acts rather than through direct wielding of power.

The political and religious hierarchies are parallel in structure and closely interdependent. The provincial leaders (*chao khana khoueng*) are appointed by royal ordinance, proposed by the *phra sangkharaja* and the Ministry of Religious Affairs after nomination by the religious heads of the districts within the province, in concert with the corresponding political chiefs. Below the *khoueng* the rule is that religious leaders are appointed by their religious superiors at the next higher level, upon the recommendation of a conference of religious and political officers of the area affected and with the concurrence of the political chief at the level of the appointing authority. Thus, the head priest of the district (*chao khana muong*) is appointed by the *chao khana khoueng*, being nominated and approved by the religious and civil officers of the *muong* (district) and *khoueng* (province). A similar procedure is followed in choosing the new *chao khana tasseng* of a canton, and the *chao athikan* (abbot) of a pagoda.

Church organization includes a system of advisory and disciplinary councils. At the cantonal level there is a Council of Discipline, presided over by the cantonal head priest and including the cantonal political chief, the leader of the pagoda, two bonzes, and a layman learned in Buddhist regulations. Each district has a religious tribunal over which the *chao khana muong* presides. Its membership includes the *chao muong* or his delegate, two bonzes, and one layman. At the top a Religious Council of five church dignitaries, called *chao rajakhana*, advises the *phra sangkharaja* on policy and personnel matters.

A royal decree of 1947 established a Buddhist Institute in Vientiane, and branches in each of the eleven provinces (now twelve). As of 1958 the Lao Bureau of Cults listed one hundred Pali schools affiliated with the Institute, with a total of 4,970 students, almost four-fifths of whom were in elementary courses. The Institute — and the increased governmental interest in the condition of religion — may point to improved standards within the clergy. Observers have often remarked the minimal doctrinal knowledge of most Laotian monks, who have never shown much interest in doctrinal disputation or speculation; the emphasis has been on obedience to the precepts and on performance of ceremonies and rituals. Often the bonzes do not understand much Pali and therefore do not grasp the import of the sacred texts. The populace understands even less. Except for the *Sip Xat*, a collection of ten tales from the *Jatakas* (the 550 tales of the lives of Buddha), and portions of the *Ha Sip Xat*, a similar collection of fifty tales from the *Jatakas*, there is relatively little popular knowledge of Buddhist sacred literature.

Despite criticism of the low caliber of some bonzes, and even though there is a slowly developing tendency for minor Buddhist officials to transfer to government employment — partly, perhaps, because promotion within the Buddhist hierarchy comes very slowly — the status of Buddhist bonze enjoys great prestige within the community. Government officials on tour show proper respect for bonzes of even the lowest degrees. Giving alms to the bonzes and supporting pagoda projects is still a basic part of the life of the common believer and an effective way to gain merit toward better reincarnations.

Nearly every sizable village supports at least one pagoda, which is the focus of the religious and social life of the villagers. There were an estimated 1,869 pagodas in Laos in 1957. A pagoda compound may contain a temple for lay worshippers and a sacred temple for bonzes, as well as libraries, votive shrines, dormitories, guest houses and reception halls. The entire collection of buildings, termed the *wat*, is commonly enclosed by a fence or wall. Since the bonzes depend upon the local population for all their material needs, the pagodas are always located near centers of population. Larger centers support a proportionate number of pagodas: Luang Prabang town, for example, has more than twenty.

According to Theravada Buddhist doctrine, every adult male should become a bonze. Traditionally this has meant at least three months of monastic life, entered into preferably before marriage. In Laos this practice still has significance though it is apparently less widespread than formerly. Both entrance into and separation from the status of bonze are at the choice of the individual. A person who has spent some time as a bonze accumulates merit and added prestige in his community. His family considers itself honored and is so regarded by others.

There are three categories of affiliation with the community of monks or sangha. In the first are the temple boys, from ten to fifteen years of age, called xieng or nen, who perform various personal services for the bonzes, assist at ceremonies, and help with housekeeping tasks while learning to read and write Lao and memorizing parts of the Pali litanies. In remote areas, where the government school system has not penetrated, this is virtually the sum of all education available locally. The next category comprises the student bonzes or novices, hatit, who may be as young as ten but are generally older and who undertake more advanced study of the sacred texts in Pali, led along the Eightfold Path by their elders. The full-fledged members of the sangha are the ordained robed bonzes who have taken their vows and renounced secular life for the period of their priesthood. There are six grades of bonzes — Nhotkeo, Loukkeo, Lakkham, Khrou, Sa, and Somdet — in decreasing order of their qualification in priestly learning and years in the bonzehood. The Lao Bureau of Cults in 1957 listed a total of 17,023 bonzes and novices, 10,209 of whom were classed in the former category.

The life of the bonze is bounded by numerous restrictions and prohibitions, beginning, of course, with the five basic precepts of Buddhist morality: do not take life, do not steal, do not break the vow of continence, do not lie, and do not drink fermented beverages. Additional regulations forbid the ordained bonze to use perfume, to seek personal adornment, to possess gold or silver, to buy or sell articles, to work for money, to eat or sleep to excess, to seek pleasure by looking at women or presenting them with flowers, to till the soil, to preach in other than Pali, or to consume food after noon. Every two weeks the bonze must have his head, eyebrows, and beard shaved. In his relations with the laity, the bonze must advise on spiritual matters whenever requested, but only if requested. His participation in political affairs is restricted to religious matters. This listing of rules is partial, being intended only to indicate their ubiquity and stringency: the ordained and robed bonze is subject to a total of 227 specific regulations on his behavior.

Bonzes are not productive in any material sense, but neither are they idle. A bonze is expected to be up by five each morning and by six, after his toilet and prayers, will set off to beg his daily food, usually accompanied on the expedition by a temple boy. The bonze gives no thanks for alms received; gifts of this kind are an act of merit and gratitude is thus neither expressed nor expected.

After completing the alms-collecting round, the bonzes return to the pagoda for a simple breakfast, then each turns to his duties for the day; some study, others teach; some perform necessary chores in the pagoda compound, others perform various ceremonies in village and pagoda. Shortly before noon they take their last meal of the day, followed by a period of rest and contemplation. At the close of the afternoon they return to their allotted tasks.

These prescriptions and obligations are not always all scrupulously obeyed. There are of course individual differences in behavior. Moreover, the Laotian bonzes are reported to be in general less rigid in their behavior and attitudes than their counterparts in some other Theravada countries. Some members of the political elite recently have complained of the indolent and undedicated men who become career bonzes. It is probably true that many of the sangha have low intellectual if not ethical standards.

The bonzes nevertheless perform a number of functions important in the life of the village. They officiate at all the formal religious festivals and ceremonies; their presence is indispensable at funerals; and they are often called in at the naming ceremonies of infants, since some of the bonzes specialize in the astrological lore essential to propitious naming. Also, as already noted, the *wat* serves as the chief institution of formal education for boys in many villages. Even where state-supported schools have been established, boys still go to the bonzes to learn many trades and practical arts.

Ordination actually is restricted to full-time bonzes; but many Lao males, having at one time or another been either students or novices, experience some form of the ordination ceremony. It is not elaborate. The presiding bonze, before two witness bonzes, accepts the novice's declaration of his desire to follow the rules of the Buddha. To these three men the novice is the "spiritual slave" until he is regarded a full-fledged member of the sangha. If he is a student, he cannot be such a member until after his twenty-second birthday. There is no evidence that this "spiritual slavery" has any confining meaning whatsoever; it simply makes three members of the religious community responsible for the novice's spiritual situation, if he needs help. The practice of Theravada Buddhism in a community is such a personal thing that the idea of "spiritual slavery" can be taken only figuratively.

Women may not take the vows of ordination but with this exception are accorded equal rights with men in the functions of the Buddhist religion. It is usually the women of the villages who give daily alms to the bonzes and who make the sacred offerings in the pagodas. There are some old women living within pagoda compounds, though not in the section of quarters reserved for the bonzes. Their duties include small religious tasks, such as decorating altars, and many light housekeeping chores. They shave their heads and eyebrows and lead a life of asceticism.

Religious Rites and Festivals

Theravada Buddhism as practiced in Laos has never developed prescribed, bonze-dominated ritual for the celebration or consecration of important events in the life of the individual, the family, or the society as a whole. Buddhism offers a way of life but prescribes rules only for its bonzehood. Consequently, while the bonzes are present as indispensable participants in virtually all the affairs of the people, it is the folkways that set the patterns; and these folkways contain as much of *phi* propitiation and popular custom as of Buddhist doctrinal practices.

The core of every popular festival or celebration — traditional, official, or spontaneous — is the *soukhouan,* the invitation and reception of the *khouan* (the mobile "soul" of man). Some venerable person, after invoking the mythological deities, invites the *khouan* of all present, if wandering, to return and bestow gaiety and well-being to their earthly hosts and feast with them from the *phakhouan* (repast of the soul) — the tastefully arranged and decorated platters of food and drink.

The bonzes play no role in the actual marriage ceremony, which is primarily a family affair presided over by an elder or village notable. The elaborate funeral practices do, however, involve the direct participation of Buddhist monks, but again the ceremonial aspects are fixed by custom rather than by religious prescription. Cremation being a principle for Buddhists, any family able to do so arranges such a ceremony. After the body has been prepared and placed in a coffin, a series of family ceremonies and feasts precede all public expression. If there is any show of grief, it is brief and takes place early in this private period of the obsequies, for the Lao believe that a family show of sadness would retard the rebirth of the spirit of the deceased in a better existence, or prevent its attainment of nirvana.

Bonzes are present during the entire period, praying and reciting. The burden of their recitals is the necessity of death as a prerequisite to rebirth in a better life. They assure the *khouan* of the deceased that his family takes account of his good fortune in being liberated from this life — that they await their own turn patiently and joyfully. "They are happy without you! Follow then your own destiny!"

After the family rites the body is placed on display at the home. The wealthier the family the more elaborate this display. A shelter is built in the compound or garden and the public feast begins. A constant stream of guests pours through the household day and night, viewing the body and partaking of food and drink. Cremation is delayed in proportion to the wealth of the family. For as many days as the festivities last the bonzes continue to recite the Pali litanies, singing and chanting endlessly as the laymen celebrate the death as a happy event in the cycle of existence. The *phi* receive the customary offerings. Finally the body and its coffin are transferred to the cremation pyre, away from the village in a field or on a river bank. As much intricacy of design and decoration in coffin and pyre as the means of the family permit is the rule.

Around this catafalque the celebration by family, friends, and bonzes may again go on for days. While the litanies continue to be intoned, both the feasting and the lauding of the deceased reach new heights. Many become inebriated and the praises of the dead man may begin to include ribald tales of his sexual prowess. The general festivity is also the occasion for courting among the young.

Finally, after the opening of the coffin, a last ritual washing of the corpse, and its exposure to the open sky, cremation takes place. All present contribute their bit of fire and those officiating make certain that the flaming mass falls in an auspicious direction. The pyre of an ex-official of the royal government should, for example, fall in the direction of the capital. After the cremation,

56

there may be many other activities: wrestling matches, buffalo fights, coin hunts, speeches, dancing, puppet shows. Formal Buddhist belief appears to assign no value to the preservation of the ashes of the corpse, though in the case of a high official or wealthy family a shrine may be built in the pagoda compound and the ashes placed therein.

If the family of the deceased is not able to afford this elaborate ritual, or even part of it, simple burial is resorted to. The body is placed in a roughhewn coffin, the bonzes recite the necessary litanies, and the body is buried in the forest. The grave is unmarked, and the sooner the evidence of the grave disappears the more auspicious it is for the deceased and the family; otherwise the spirit of the dead man may join the evil *phi phetu,* of which there are already too many to plague the lives of the villagers.

Whereas there are no Buddhist rites at childbirth and none corresponding to baptism, it is most often a bonze who is asked to suggest an auspicious name for the child.

The expression of public faith is most evident during festivals, both national celebrations and those innumerable occasions special to certain pagodas, villages, and administrative districts. The nationally celebrated festivals, which are at once both religious and civil in character, include the following:

The New Year. The Laotian lunar year begins in December, but the Lao prefer the fifth month (April) as the initiation of the chronological year. Then the astrological signs point to light and prosperity; also, this time of the year anticipates the end of the hot season and the coming of the life-giving rains. The departure of the old year is celebrated with a procession, prayers, and a long period of festivities similar in many respects to the Siamese Songkhran festival, also held in April. Houses are swept to symbolize the expulsion of any evil and marauding spirits which might have taken up residence. On the first day of the year the bonzes and the people cleanse the Buddha images with holy water. It is a time for visiting and all dress in their best. Votive mounds (usually of sand or stones) are erected in the courts of the pagodas and along the banks of the Mekong; streamers of colored paper bearing the signs of the zodiac decorate homes and buildings.

In Luang Prabang the festival is elaborately celebrated with the release of birds and animals, processions of royal elephants, and court gatherings. The king himself sprinkles the Buddhas with holy water. (The use of water in Buddhist ritual has never become formally prescribed, but it is important to the faith and universally used; in any ritual the participants, the Buddha images, and the altars to the *phi* are sprinkled.) Dances and masques all over the nation commemorate the legendary ancestors of the Lao, and offerings are made of fruits, flowers, new vegetables, and candles. (It is the new growing season, and many spring rites are incorporated into New Year celebrations.) The king gives a feast for the bonzes in Luang Prabang, and since 1941 there have been festivities especially for the children — who are "exposed" to the good omens of the new year.

Vixakha Bouxa (Boun Bang-Fay). This festival, which occurs in the sixth month (at the full moon of May), commemorates the birth, enlightenment, and death of Buddha. Bonzes are shown even more deference than usual. There are dances, processions, puppet shows, and general festivities even more jubilant than most Laotian celebrations. Children, young people, and expectant mothers are blessed and offerings made to the bonzes. The idea of pilgrimage and merit making plays a major role in these activities.

Often grafted onto this Buddhist rite are two local rites. The first, widely observed, involves the ritual firing of rockets. The second is a pre-Buddhist fertility rite which observers refuse to describe in any other way than as "licentious." The government insists such rites are disappearing and their observance today is confined mainly to Vientiane.

Khao Vassa, the beginning of Lent. This occurs in the eighth Laotian month (the full moon of July) and coincides with the beginning of the three-month rainy season. During Khao Vassa the *Patimokkha*, a confessional formula, is recited by the bonzes and extensive processions are held by clergy and laity alike. There is little rejoicing since for three months the bonzes will be in semi-retirement, somewhat less accessible to the villagers in whose lives they play such an important role.

Ho Khao Padap Dinh, the Feast of the Dead. This comes in the ninth month (August-September). Its origin is Buddha's commandment to honor the dead with gifts, prayers, and thoughts. There are as usual gifts to the bonzes.

Ho Khao Slak. The tenth month (September-October) brings the Ho Khao Slak, when offerings are made to the bonzes. The sources of the offerings are decided by lot. This has been also a traditional time for the feting of children with gifts of toys, sweets, and other good things to eat.

Boun Ok Vassa, the end of Lent. Boun Ok Vassa occurs in the eleventh month (October) and is the occasion of general rejoicing. The bonzes again recite the *Patimokkha,* confess their evil and careless thoughts, and leave the pagodas for pilgrimages. New living effects are given them: mats, robes, begging bowls, betel instruments.

The Festival of the Waters. Coming in the eleventh month (October-November), the Water Festival has become a time for decorating homes and pagodas, for processions, and for pirogue races on the riverways. Nominally, all is organized for the tutelary spirits, and there are ceremonies for the ousting of the evil *phi,* who have been lurking in the houses during the rainy season.

Makha Bouxa. This, in the twelfth month (November-December), is another festival originating in the Buddhist texts. It commemorates the calling together of Buddha's disciples before his death and entrance into a state of nirvana. Prayers, processions, offerings, and masques mark the ceremonies.

Boun Pha Vet. Another festival having its origin in the sacred texts is the Boun Pha Vet in the third month (February-March). This occasion is also marked by special national celebrations in the capital. These national rites, commemorating Lao origins and various historical events, are performed in the That Luang, the stupa about two miles from Vientiane purportedly housing a relic of the Buddha.

Tribal Religions

The various ethnic and tribal groups in Laos all have been influenced to some degree by Buddhism, but older pagan beliefs permeate virtually all ethnic groups in the society. One of the chief generalizations that can be made about religion in Laos is that while among the dominant Lao *phi*-worship has taken on an overlay of Buddhism, among the other groups worship of the *phi* has taken on a few Buddhist elements.

Belief in the *phi* is universal, for example, among the tribal Tai, who have added to it a strong element of ancestor worship. The spirits of the ancestors are ritualistically present at all important events and are deemed the true masters of family destinies.

The chief tribal Tai groups — the Black, White, and Red Tai — give a very special position to the *phi* of ancestors. Some Taoist and Confucian influences also are present.

These groups have no highly developed religious hierarchies, relying instead on local shamans and sorcerers. The Black Tai, owing to their quasi-feudal social structure, accord their nobility special religious privileges. The gods of the soil are considered the personal deities of the nobility, almost in the sense that the soil spirits are possessed and contained in the persons of the nobility. The nobility preside over the rites associated with rice cultivation.

Among the strongly Sinicized Man and Meo of the north, Taoist and Confucian influences are marked. The religion of the Man is a combination of animism and ancestor worship, presided over by local shamans and sorcerers. The shamans, however, must pass examinations, which entitle them to exercise various functions within the cult. An examination of the first degree, for example, empowers the individual to drive off evil spirits, while one of the second degree gives the holder power to select favorable burial sites.

Meo religion is much like that of the Man, though with a more evident Buddhist influence. The Meo have no pagodas or bonzes, however; elders serve as religious specialists. The religion basically is ancestor worship combined with animistic beliefs. The dead are buried and animal sacrifices are made to influence the spirits at births, marriages, and deaths.

Not very much is known about the religious beliefs of the Kha tribes, which together form about 25 percent of the total population. Basically animistic, they believe in many spirits and observe many taboos. Some of the tribes trace their ancestry back to particular animals. The Kha believe in a place of torment where the evil are punished. They believe too in reincarnation according to individual merit and in a vague sort of metempsychosis. Each house has its own spirits, like the Roman *lares,* and each individual his good and his evil spirits, locked in constant struggle.

Each Kha village has its own sorcerers who are highly respected and feared and who speak powerfully in local councils. Shamans are exempted from taxation and from the communal requirement of labor in the fields. Because of their ascribed powers of divination and geomancy they choose the new village site when the demands of slash-and-burn agriculture make such a move necessary.

The Kha are seclusive people who resent the intrusion of

outsiders at their rites and ceremonies. It is their custom to place bamboo arrows or woven wicker squares along the trail leading to a village engaged in ceremonies — to warn strangers that they are not welcome.

Christian Missions

Despite considerable missionary activity, the number of Christian converts in Laos as a whole remains small and the influence of Christianity on the social order slight. Laotians have in general been more inclined to apathy than hostility in their attitude toward efforts to introduce new religious beliefs. Content with their deeply ingrained Buddhism and *phi* worship, they have shown little desire to adopt a new faith or religious disciplines without roots in their own historical and social environment. Missionary efforts in Laos have been continuous, however, since shortly after the opening of the twentieth century.

In 1902 the first missionaries of the Swiss Brethren established themselves at Song Khone, to be followed over the years by more missionaries from Switzerland. The Swiss Brethren have been aided by a few French and American missionaries.

The Presbyterians also entered the field, later turning their work over to the Christian and Missionary Alliance, which operates mainly in northern Laos.

A Protestant translation of the Bible into the Lao language was made in 1926 and five thousand copies of the New Testament printed. In 1928 the Old Testament was also printed in Laotian. Despite more than fifty years of activity, however, the Protestants have gained only a few thousand converts, largely among the Meo tribes.

In some areas their work ran counter to official restrictions imposed by the French, who wished to limit missionary activity to the Roman Catholics. Catholic missionary effort has for this and other reasons enjoyed somewhat more success. In 1901 the number of converts was estimated at three thousand. By 1953 the *Annuaire des États Associés* listed thirty-two thousand. Most of the converts have been made among the Kha and Vietnamese of southern Laos, with lesser numbers among the Man. The Roman Catholics established their headquarters in Thakhek and divided their surrounding sphere of action in the southeastern part of the country into seven districts. There is a church and a priest in each of these districts.

SOCIAL STRUCTURE

EACH OF THE COUNTRY'S ETHNIC GROUPS do to a degree preserve a distinct social system or subsociety and each tends to view the others as foreign. Before the present century many of these peoples were enemies among whom armed clashes were frequent, and for the most part they continue to resist intensive contact and intermarriage.

What political and cultural unity the kingdom possesses is provided by the largest group, the Lao. Their society, with common language and traditions, is dominant throughout the lowland regions and directly or indirectly articulates with all the others, binding the kingdom into a loose system of economic, political, sometimes religious ties.

The diverse, tribal peoples of the highlands are at the bottom of the social scale in Laos. Above and barely outnumbering them are the Lao peasant villagers. Perched above these is the small Lao elite, composed of royalty and the wealthy official class. Distributed between and among the officials and villagers are other minorities, chiefly Vietnamese, Chinese, and Europeans, who occupy special foreign statuses and usually perform quite specific services.

Despite the gradual blurring of borders between the social strata in the last fifty years and the many indications of an acceleration of this process in the future, Laos remains a highly stratified and heterogeneous society. Although the elite at one end and the Kha at the other have moved toward each other in terms of mutual dependence and legal status, this has been offset by other less obvious factors that make for increased social distance. The most important of these is the veneer of European culture that has been taken on at the upper reaches of society. The new value placed on literacy, higher education, material wealth, and improvement in health and sanitation, and, more than anything else, the identification of these things with the notion of progress have only magnified the internal cultural differences. A gap of almost unimaginable immensity still separates a widely traveled, multilingual member of the Lao elite, highly educated in both Eastern and Western traditions, from a primitive rice cultivator in the highlands — yet these two are part of the same society. It would seem that Laos will remain for some time to come a very loosely integrated society with most of its people's needs, activities, and sentiments concentrated within the boundaries of the family and the village.

The Lao Family

Many of the basic sociological facts concerning Lao family life are at present unavailable or contradictory in nature. In lieu of adequate information it is frequently necessary to generalize from what is known about the closely related Thai of neighboring Thailand, particularly those agricultural villagers living in northern and northeastern Thailand.

As in rural Thailand, the overwhelming proportion of all activity — political, social, and economic — begins with the family. The household is the basic economic unit, and all productive property and family labor are combined for collective use and mutual gain. No one farms a plot of land for himself only, to the exclusion of others, or raises a buffalo for his own individual benefit, apart from his family.

To the outside world, the household is represented by its single male head. It is he who sits in village meetings; it is in his name that the census is taken and taxes collected; he makes loans, decides when and how to sell most of the surplus, works out labor exchanges with other households, and lends buffaloes or rents land. It is possible, however, that the Lao wife and mother, as is the case with her counterpart in Thailand, may have considerable say within the family circle concerning family finances and the management of the family income.

The composition of the Lao household is variable. The ideal arrangement among the rural Lao would appear to consist of a nuclear family similar in composition to that found throughout the United States. The extended form of the family, including unmarried adults and married sons or daughters, is not, however, uncommon and may tend to be the rule rather than the exception among the official and well-to-do families in the urban centers. Because the range, variety, and amount of labor required to maintain comfortably even a small group is more than a young married couple can manage alone, a new household will not usually be founded until the couple has children old enough to be productive, or until other kinsmen can be included, or unless there is some supplementary food or income from the outside to make up the labor deficiency. A young couple therefore normally begins married life as part of either the husband's or the wife's parental household, leaving to set up their own residential unit when economic circumstances permit. As in Thailand, an exception is made, apparently, in the case of a youngest married daughter, who normally remains in her parental household and inherits the house site on the death of her parents.

Within the household, labor is divided along the lines of sex and age. Men do most of the heavy work in the preparation of the fields though at planting, transplanting, and harvest time women and children also help. Men fish, build canoes, make and repair fishing gear and tools, hunt, and go to the hills to gather forest products or to trade. Women are responsible for practically all the domestic tasks. These include carrying water and wood, pounding rice, cooking, tending kitchen gardens and livestock, spinning, weaving, and making clothes. Women also go to market to sell or exchange household surpluses. Old people and children are assets rather than liabilities in this kind of economy. The children learn early to help in the garden, haul water, and do small jobs around the house. If the old people are not able to assist in regular adult activities, they can always look after the children and thus release the mothers for other necessary tasks. Others devote their time to religious meditation.

The typical Lao house is a rectangular dwelling raised from three to seven feet off the ground on piles. Across one side, the front, is an open but roofed veranda that can be closed with screens at night. The entrance to the house is always by railless steps or inclined ladders leading up to the veranda. The inside of the house is divided by a partition with doors that separates a large front room from the sleeping rooms in the rear. In the front room is a hearth for heat and light and an altar where images of the Buddha are placed. There may be additional altars or offering places for household spirits. The kitchen may be a small area to the side or another open platform on the end of the house.

The household congregates on the veranda and in the front

room, this being the "public" part of the house, where visitors are entertained and where the women may work during the day. The bedrooms in the back are private. Each family in the household has its own bedroom. Young unmarried men, however, are apt to sleep in the front room or on the veranda rather than in the bedrooms with their parents and sisters.

The space beneath the house, often latticed, is used as a stable or pen for the household livestock and for storing dry firewood. During the day the women sometimes use it as an additional work space.

At a short distance from the house stands a raised granary or mat bin in which unmilled rice is stored, and nearby is a foot-operated mortar-and-pestle rice mill. The house is almost invariably set in a yard among fruit trees and palms; farther out there is usually a kitchen garden. Dwellings are seldom crowded together; around Vientiane, for example, the average size of a house site is one-eighth of an acre.

Chickens, ducks, and pigs are usually kept, both for consumption and for sale, and those who can afford it will own a buffalo to use in the paddy fields. Wealthier households will own several buffaloes, sometimes renting them out or selling them.

As long as there is a house site and a dwelling, the household continues. It can even endure without owning rice lands, for these can be rented or farmed in tenancy. The house site is always in a village and is usually separated from its agricultural plots. These plots can be divided and redivided through sale and inheritance and can be added to by purchase or by rent. The household group that lives off this land is flexible enough to adjust its size and composition to the varying amounts of productive land available to it.

The Life Cycle

The first significant event in the life of a Lao is the naming ceremony, held in the household shortly after birth, with relatives present. Frequently a bonze with some knowledge of astrology is asked to select a propitious name. Then, following the brief ceremony — and depending on the wealth and position of the family — there will be a feast to which the village as a whole is invited.

The given name is usually descriptive, referring to such objects of everyday life as flowers, colors, metals, or trees. Family names have been used by the Lao only since 1943 when a government decree made their adoption mandatory. Titles indicating hierarchical position are added by priests and government dignitaries, and women, too, often have status titles. The Lao continue, however, the practice of changing their names at will: to signify a new occupation or location; to ward off evil spirits from the sick or old; to mark the stages of growing up. During his first years, for example, a child is almost always known only by an affectionate nickname.

For a boy, the next important event is the ceremony marking his transition from childhood to pre-adult life, held when he is about thirteen. This is nonreligious and consists of the ceremonial cutting of the boy's hair. A feast with kindred and villagers participating follows. Formerly young men were tattooed at this time, the decoration constituting an indispensable mark of manhood that no self-respecting male could be without. It also had magical value, offering protection against harmful supernatural agencies.

Preferably before marriage, and usually at about age twenty, a boy's parents organize a ceremony of ordination marking the occasion of his entry into the village monastery for a period of a few weeks or months (ideally for one Lenten period, July to October). At this period in his life the boy dons the saffron robe of the sangha and participates for a time as a novice in the life of the monastery, thus accumulating merit both for himself and his family. Although apparently less widespread than formerly, the ordination ceremony is regarded as a deeply spiritual experience and a family may expend considerable money and goods in order to assure that the occasion will be as meritorious as possible.

Although marriage of one of its members is important to the household, few marriages are actually arranged by the parents or household heads, considerable freedom of choice being allowed. When the decision to marry has been made and both households concerned are agreeable to the possibility of such a match, a go-between is engaged to make the final arrangements. These negotiations center around the amount and kind of bride price the bridegroom must pay, the future residence of the couple, and any inheritances either may eventually expect to receive. When agreement is reached a bonze will be asked to name an auspicious day for the ceremony.

On the day before the wedding the bride price is delivered to the bride's house where it is counted and publicly witnessed, the amount being recorded on the government marriage certificate. This portion of the bride price is usually paid in currency; the average payment in Vientiane province a few years ago, for example, was about 2,000 *kip*. At the same time a procession of the bridegroom's relatives bring small gifts, traditionally one hundred or two hundred in number, consisting of betel, tobacco, fish, meat, and cakes. At last the official request for the bride's hand is made through a long ceremonial dialogue during which the bride's relatives make great show of reluctance. This dialogue successfully concluded, the bride and groom are publicly betrothed in the presence of a bonze or a village elder.

The actual wedding takes place the next day at a formal feast (*soukhouan*) preceded by a ceremonial procession of the groom and his relatives who, symbolically and with much horse-play and broad humor, fight and bribe their way into the bride's house enclosure. The groom must pay the bride's servants or sisters to wash his feet before he is permitted to ascend the ladder of the house. Elopements without this ceremony and the celebration do occur, especially when the man's household cannot pay the bride price demanded by the girl's father. If an elopement marriage lasts it is later legitimized.

The marital bond seems quite firm, although divorces are not unknown. The stability of the union is reinforced by pressures from the two parental households, which, in addition to being made up of kinsmen, are concerned about the bride price involved. Laziness and adultery are the two complaints most often mentioned in terms of divorce and either is sufficient grounds for separation. Husband and wife both are expected to mold their ambitions to those of the household and to work industriously toward its ends. If they do not, either can be rebuked by their own households and by other relatives, who will attempt to bring the deviant into line.

Concerning adultery, sanctions and pressures are differently applied. If a wife is guilty her husband can immediately divorce her, and he may mobilize his own kin and demand damages from the offending man. If the husband is guilty he need fear no rebuke or divorce threat from his wife or her household, but if another married woman is involved he can expect demands from her husband.

It is possible for a man to take a second wife, but owing to the compulsory bride price polygynous marriages are restricted to the few wealthy and important men. In terms of the household, a second wife is always subordinate to the first wife and, at present, has no legal status within the country. No distinction seems to be made, however, between their children. Among royalty and the very wealthy, polygyny was at one time almost universal and numerous wives were a mark of social distinction.

From the point of view of kinship, the largest and most important ceremony for the individual is his final one — the funeral. More than any other ceremony pertaining to the cycle of life, the funeral is marked by participation of the bonzes, who pray and recite litanies from beginning to end of the proceedings (for fuller discussion of funerals as religious ceremonies, see Chapter 5). The funeral is more than an assemblage of friends and relatives who have come to pay their respects. It is a ceremony where all the important relationships of the deceased are formally acknowledged and then one by one severed.

Kinship and Inheritance

The Lao distinguishes relatives on both sides of the family mainly by their age, sex, and genealogical distance from himself. As distance of relationship increases, the prerogatives and sentiments of kinship decrease. For example, an uncle, cousin, and nephew are referred to by kinship terms similar to those for father, brother, and son respectively but the relationship in these cases is less intense.

In many ways the Lao kinship system is similar to that in the United States, but in the Laotian system the behavior between persons of different age, sex, and generation is much more formal. The Lao system furthermore recognizes ancestral and lineage relationships to a lesser degree, emphasizing rather the lateral extension of kinship ties to include age mates and cousins.

Toward the Lao father one is obedient and always respectful, and by extension to all other men of his generation. The same deference is expected toward the mother and other women of her generation but is less formally expressed. In these relationships the Lao roles are more reserved than similar American roles. Respect is given also to an older brother, for the society regards the elder as having more authority than the younger. Between brothers and sisters age is not as important as sex; the relationship is informal and easy but neither must touch the other or be overly friendly in public for this can be interpreted as sexual interest. Restriction on behavior between sexes is extended to all personal encounters in public between a man and a woman. Even a husband and wife do not publicly show affection.

In principle at least, property of all kinds is divided equally among all children; in practice, sons seem to be favored over daughters in the case of agricultural land, and the reverse appears to be true in the case of the house site. As in northern Thailand it is often a daughter who inherits the house and house site, giving the continuity of the group a strongly matrilineal bias. It is unfortunate that so little is known about land tenure and inheritance, particularly as it relates to the household, but in what is known, the flexibility of the inheritance system, like the composition of the household group, is the main characteristic.

With the possibility at least of inheritance to both sons and daughters and the variability of households, land and wealth can quickly be dispersed, so that what was once owned by one person may be owned in a few generations by many who have only a vague feeling of kinship to one another. This possibility is compensated for by preferential marriage with second cousins, however, so that property tends to move within a restricted set of kinsmen rather than be dispersed indefinitely throughout the population.

The rights and obligations that exist between an individual and the relatives who constitute his "spatially extended" family, or kindred, are extremely important. A man borrows money and rents land from a relative, because he can expect to pay less interest and less rent than he would to a nonrelative. When parental households disintegrate or are no longer able to accommodate the grown children and grandchildren, a man or a woman may look within the kindred for a relative whose house group he can join. Although they may be dispersed the members of an individual's kindred will always assemble to join the ceremonies and festivities honoring his passage from one stage to another in the life cycle. A person's kindred are bound to him and to one another by common obligations of mutual help and support.

Thus while the individual's kinship ties and obligations ramify outward in both directions, there is a tendency for the practical usages of kinship to operate within a group of closely related households located in one village or in adjacent villages.

The Lao Village

With an average population of somewhat over two hundred, most Lao villages are located just above flood level on a river or tributary, often at the confluence of the two, or sometimes along a main road. The village, usually founded on a matrix of families related to one another by blood or marriage, forms a self-conscious and strongly self-sustaining unit. Kinship ties of the villagers are reinforced by reciprocal labor exchanges, a sense of participation in village political councils, vested interest in the local pagoda, and village ceremonies in honor of common ancestral spirits.

Within the traditional Lao village there are few formal associations or groups to which an individual can belong and relatively few positions which carry with them the automatic ascription of social status. More important is a man's demonstrated moral and personal character and it is this, rather than inherited status, which has in the past determined his position in the village. As government organization and private enterprise penetrate into the rural areas it may be expected that these traditional aspects of village society will change and that social differentiation based on such factors as secular education and wealth will become increasingly important.

Although villagers are free to leave and outsiders sometimes move into a village, the preference in marriage for relatives — beyond first cousins — as against outsiders makes marriage even within a small village both possible and in many respects desirable. Additional if indirect impetus for village marriage comes from the traditional Lao attitude of permissiveness toward premarital sexual relationships, which tends to precipitate rather than postpone marriages. Young people are allowed considerable sexual freedom as long as they are discreet about it, but should a girl become pregnant both families characteristically insist on an immediate marriage. This permissive attitude extends to the frequent village and family celebrations known as *ngan*, when young people engage in a kind of institutionalized courting. Sitting in sex-segregated rows facing each other, they engage in witty exchanges and sing love songs. A young man and the young woman opposite him never touch one another or openly suggest there are any intimate feelings between them — but, in rural areas at least, seem to be free to wander off casually into the dark to be alone.

There is thus considerable opportunity for courtship and marriage within the corporate entity of the village, and most marriages do in fact occur within the village. Outside liasons are by no means excluded, however. Persons residing outside the village frequently visit relatives during celebrations, and this brings together marriageable boys and girls from different villages.

Every village that can support one has a Buddhist pagoda, or *wat.* Sermons are preached for the villagers in the pagoda's public building, which may also double as a school, village-affairs meeting hall, guesthouse, and dispensary. In poorer villages the *wat* will be of wood and bamboo; in more prosperous communities it may be of brick and tile, with elaborate carvings and murals and many memorial shrines erected by individuals to honor their dead. Responsibility for maintaining and supporting the temple and the mendicant clergy falls directly upon the villagers. The obligatory daily food contributions and the frequent monetary and labor requirements draw everyone in the community into participation in a common set of activities — not only allowing individuals to earn merit but also contributing toward a development of local sentiment and pride. A village too small to maintain its own pagoda looks to the nearest one in the region as its center, but for this same reason is not really a complete community.

The bonzes, although concerned primarily with their religious duties, perform important social functions. Their presence at naming, betrothal, and cremation ceremonies is considered indispensable even when specific religious rites are not involved. The honor and respect accorded the bonze as a religious figure reflect, however, only one side of his role in village life. His superior education and moral stature make him a natural leader whose advice is sought on a wide variety of subjects.

Villages may also have a sacred place or structure where the *phi,* or spirits, are honored for the general welfare and prosperity of the entire community. Included are the spirits of the dead, the "soul" of rice, and spirits of special localities such as village, fields, and household.

In the political hierarchy the village is the smallest unit. Its headman, *pho ban* or *nai ban,* chosen from among the most respected heads of households, is generally elected for life or until he chooses to retire. He is usually one of the most well-to-do men, respected among the other householders for his community and religious activities and for the lavishness of the feasts he gives, the elegance of his house, and his contributions toward the temple and clergy. The important criterion is not the possession of wealth but rather the use of wealth as a revelation of character, but since the headman is, next to the head of the pagoda, the most important person in the village, he must be able to maintain the dignity of his position — for which he is not paid. Consequently, a poor man, however highly respected for his industry, piety, generosity, and knowledge, would rarely be chosen headman. In some villages the title tends to be hereditary, or nearly so; a retiring headman designates his son or some other close relative to succeed him, after which the villagers elect his choice.

The headman's authority, limited both by statute and by custom, is mainly directed toward organizing and supervising work groups, settling disputes between households, welcoming strangers, announcing government directives, and referring matters that are out of his jurisdiction to the proper authorities. There is little overlap between the activities of the headman and the bonzes, for the latter are forbidden to take an active role in secular matters.

Some villages — especially those near Vientiane — elect another of their most respected men to serve as "keeper of the temple." It is his duty to initiate and manage all money contributions and labor for the construction and maintenance of the temple. Occasionally this and the office of the headman are combined.

A further dignitary of a village is the male (occasionally female) shaman, or spirit doctor, who uses his skills and powers to cure disease. The shaman is a full- or part-time specialist, and any man showing adeptness in divining what spirit is causing the trouble and handling spirits in general can become a shaman. Since anxiety about the unknown and unpredictable spirit world is common, a skilled shaman can entrench himself firmly in the regard of the community.

Nowadays the village school teacher, although resident in relatively few villages as yet, is a highly respected individual, ranking with the abbot and headman as an influential village leader.

Although exhibiting a high degree of self-sufficiency, the Lao village is by no means a discrete and isolated entity. In three fundamental areas — religious, political, and economic — the village also acts as a unit in a larger structure. The Buddhist hierarchy provides an organizational structure ultimately relating all villages, as does the national government. In the economic sphere the dependence of villagers on outside sources for manufactured goods as well as various foods and raw materials gives rise to an intricate system of intervillage trade which extends even to the most isolated hill group.

Ultimately centering in a few large river towns, this network of trade relationships constitutes a means of intervillage relationship and a channel for information and ideas often more effective than the agencies in the formal government structure.

72

The Hill Tribes

Village social structure and organization vary considerably among the hill peoples. Although practicing shifting rice cultivation, the Lamet, a group closely related to the Khmu of northern Laos, live in about one hundred permanent villages, ranging from two to thirty-eight households. Though lacking much of the advanced technology of the lowland Lao, their productive organization is much the same. The household is the basic unit of production and consumption, each maintaining its own rice field, vegetable garden, and livestock. The division of labor by sex is not unlike that of the Lao. Each village has a communal house with sacred sacrificial locations adjacent; under the direction of the priest the house is the center for all community activities. Although each household clears, plants, and harvests its own field, groups of households join together to clear and plant contiguous fields. Labor is exchanged unit for unit (and sometimes hired) only within this planting group, which otherwise has no function.

Among the Upper Lamet, each village has its own fixed lands. Every villager has the right to use what he needs for planting, hunting, and gathering, but nonresidents may not use lands. The Lower Lamet have similar village territories but do not altogether exclude outsiders from them.

In a Meo village each household plants its own fields, and there is an exchange of labor between households. Land is used until it is exhausted — within one to three years — and when all lands near the village site have been used up the villagers move as a body to another site, with fresh and available land. This movement is always under the direction of the headman.

The A'kha, or Kho, another northern hill tribe, live in villages consisting of forty to fifty households. Here the hereditary village headman has very limited powers and prerogatives; he is advised by a council of household heads and wealthy men who make the important decisions among themselves. The household is quite autonomous and there is no concept of village territoriality or communal ownership of fields. When lands are exhausted, households move out individually and establish new sites. The headman has practically nothing to do with the selection of the new site or laying out the new village; it is worked out in council by the heads of households.

Among the hill tribes there is generally no formal political organization beyond the village level. Most of the people are not

Buddhists and so lack the unification of a formal religious structure. In the past, before pacification was complete, the armed revolts of some groups revealed that some informal political organization, capable of being put to military use, did exist. The Meo of northern Laos, for example, usually living in small villages of eight to twenty-five households under a headman, pass on stories, perhaps fanciful, of former times when there were chiefs, elected by warriors, whose authority extended over as many as twenty villages. During their last uprisings, in 1919–21, the Meo organized an elaborate chain of command, headed by a supreme commander, and including "high leaders" and "low leaders." Even a "low leader" had three "officers" who each commanded sixty to a hundred warriors.

The linkage through trade of hill villages and the lowlands has already been mentioned. Some of the northern hill people descend to the lowland markets; others come down to work as laborers. There is also some travel to Thailand to seek work in the various extractive industries; each hill man, however, expects to return to his home village as soon as he has made his "fortune."

The Laos government uses local headmen to integrate the hill villages into the national administrative system. In villages that are accustomed to a headman the system works, but where no such position has ever existed difficulties arise. Among some Kha tribes, for example, the only village official is the hereditary shaman whose authority does not extend beyond his religious duties; secular power is vested in a group of nonhereditary "wealthy men." If the shaman is one of this group he can act as a village headman; when he is not, he is ineffective as a headman when it comes to the requisitioning of labor and enforcing government orders.

Social Stratification

This brief survey of family and village patterns should indicate the cultural disparity between the Kha, unquestionably the lowest group on the Laotian social scale, and the Lao villager. Although their political and legal status has improved somewhat and their rights to territories have been recognized in some places, the majority of the Kha continue to be regarded by the Lao as second-class citizens, little different from the savages seized, sold, and held as heritable slaves by the Lao up to the arrival of the French. Slavery and forced labor were prohibited by the French and this prohibition was carried over to the Laotian constitution after independence, but the Kha of northern Laos remain subject to corvée draft even today.

Another great social gap separates the mass of Lao villagers from the official classes in the larger provincial towns, and the official classes are in turn manifestly lower on the social scale than the Lao nobility and quasi-nobility.

These different social strata have all been affected, though to a limited extent only, by the political and social changes since independence. Each stratum is becoming a little less homogeneous within itself and offering some new possibilities for individual social mobility. Even at the lowest level, among the Kha, social distinctions and a new social mobility are evident. A nonhereditary elite is recognized, made up of local "wealthy men" and their households. Formerly, a man advanced to this elite by slowly building up and mobilizing the labor of a household, then skillfully directing its combined efforts toward the accumulation of the requisite wealth. Nowadays, however, a young man without any status whatsoever can leave his village and work for cash in the lowlands, return to his village, establish his household, and then take up his position as a "wealthy man" far more quickly than was possible in the past. Where they live in close contact with the Lao, as in parts of Luang Prabang province, the Kha tend to become Laotianized, in some instance even acquiring a veneer of Buddhism.

Among Lao peasants there is also increasing economic and social differentiation. In some areas peasants have become tenants without land, and must rent, sharecrop, borrow money at very high rates of interest, and occasionally even pass into debt slavery to wealthier persons. The wealthy are further able to mobilize capital to invest in trade and other businesses to advance their position. Owing to the establishment of more government schools, more and more young men, having become literate, are able to assume positions as village teachers, traditionally reserved for Buddhist monks.

The social gaps between groups remain, however. The villager, generally a farmer, still knows little of the world outside his own province, is illiterate or has rarely had more than three years of schooling, speaks only Lao, and tends to be distrustful, resentful, and sometimes fearful of townspeople. But his knowledge of government affairs although meager is increasing through participation in general elections and extension of government services into the rural areas. The townsman, on the other hand, particularly in the larger provincial capitals, works in an office or store, has traveled moderately in Laos and may have been abroad, has had six or more years of schooling, has a fairly good speaking knowledge of French and perhaps English, listens to the radio and attends movies, has considerable interest in government and politics, and tends to adopt a disdainful or condescending attitude toward the villager.

At the top of the social scale, with undisputed prestige and power, are the Lao ruling elite, the nobility and quasi-nobility. Along with the evolution of the Lao kingdom itself this group became ordered into the most formal and rigid class system in the country. Noble rank could be inherited only by members of the king's family, although it could be granted others for one generation, and even in the royal family junior lines resulting from plural marriage are said to have lost their rank after five generations.

A quasi-nobility, the so-called mandarinate, a rather complete and highly integrated government service, surrounded the royal house. Its members were directly associated either with the palace or with the administration of constituent principalities and territories. Strictly speaking, this official class was not hereditary, for a son, though awarded an honorific of address, did not automatically inherit his father's office, title, or status. In practice, nevertheless, the mandarinate tended, through the obvious avenues of favor and opportunity, to be self-replenishing. At the same time it was open to entry from below, since any person demonstrating the requisite qualifications could be appointed to it and positions were also awarded to those who had earned the gratitude of royalty. The careful distinctions between the various grades of princes and high officials were marked by titles, and differing vocabularies were to be used in addressing them. Complete prostration was formerly the rule before royalty, and all commoners squatted as a high official passed. Such exaggerated forms of respect have been done away with but differing modes of address are still used.

The coming of the French did little to change the structure of the hierarchy of the mandarinate, but its functions were changed considerably since French administrators held all real power. Many in the lower and middle grades, especially at the larger centers of government, were replaced by French-speaking, French-trained Vietnamese. Nevertheless, those in the highest grades constituted the wealthy class of the country — the only ones (aside from the princes of royal blood) wealthy enough to afford a Western education at the University of Hanoi and in France. Consequently, when events during and after World War II brought first a measure of self-government and then independence to Laos, it was these mandarin families who had the education, the outlook, and in varying degrees the training to step into important positions in the new constitutional government. The present elite class, then, is the outgrowth of the higher mandarinate and is composed of no more than a few hundred persons of from twelve to twenty great families. No longer solely concerned with duties at the royal court, government administration, and the management of their lands, this class is branching out into the professions and engaging in international banking and commerce. It thus shades off and merges with what might become an emergent middle class.

There is, however, as yet very little that could be called an indigenous middle class. Lesser government functionaries, schoolteachers, and perhaps some of the officer grades in the army and police can be considered a middle class in the economic sense. The urban Lao have until very recently left the field of commerce to the Chinese, Indians, and Vietnamese. Only with the advent of foreign economic aid have Lao of the elite entered this field, and their entry has been at the top, in directive positions. Professional persons, because of the wealth required to aspire to the necessary foreign education, are all from the elite.

Any acceleration in the pace of political and economic change in Laos could contribute to the growth of a true middle class, provided the current expansion of educational facilities and economic opportunities, the prerequisite of such growth, continues.

EDUCATION

WITHIN A BUDDHIST COUNTRY SUCH AS Laos the bonze, representing the highest human virtues, has traditionally been regarded the best teacher a boy could have, and up to the arrival of the French the only formal education in Laos was to be found in the local *wat*.

Following the establishment of secular schools by the French, a gradual blurring of functions occurred as these schools multiplied and education for government service assumed greater importance under French influence. In the autonomous government set up following the *modus vivendi* of 1946 the pagoda school system and the secular school system were in fact placed under a single ministry of education. There has since been an increasing definition of functions and today, although both systems remain under government control, religious and secular schools are administered by separate ministries.

Secular education has in principle been compulsory since 1951. Laos still faces major practical problems, however, such as the inadequacy of funds for expansion, the scarcity of trained teachers and administrators, the very limited opportunities for higher education, and the country's ethnic diversity. Statistics on rural schools and school attendance are incomplete and unreliable; it has been estimated that of approximately 300,000 children in the compulsory age bracket (6-14 years) only some 100,000 are presently enrolled. Of this number about 7,500 are enrolled in secondary or private schools and the remainder in upwards of 1,500 secular elementary schools and an estimated 750 monastic schools.

Despite these somewhat discouraging statistics, the increase in educational facilities has been impressive when it is realized that as late as 1946 there were only 175 elementary schools in all of

Laos. Rural schools are continuing to increase in number and educational facilities and teacher training will continue to receive a large share of the economic and technical assistance being made available to Laos by the United Nations, France, the United States, and other countries.

Traditional Education

As in the neighboring Theravada Buddhist countries of Thailand and Cambodia formal education in Laos has traditionally been centered in the village *wat*. Although secular schools are increasing in number it is still true that in a great many rural villages the only education available is of this traditional type.

Though conducted by bonzes and containing much religious content, monastic education has been and still is oriented primarily to practical needs — specifically the skills and knowledge needed to participate in traditional Lao village society. To this end boys are taught manual arts and reverence for their religion and their king, but above all the monastic schools teach discipline, morality, respect for elders, all within the larger context of the Buddhist way of life.

Usually at the age of nine or ten a boy is "given" by his parents to the abbot of the local *wat*, where he will continue to live and where, in the service of the monastery and the monk who will be his *khru* (*guru*, master, teacher), he absorbs the sacred scriptures and the Buddhist precepts which in later life he is expected to put into practice as a meritorious man — a respected and responsible member of his village.

While resident in the pagoda, the boy is subjected to a strict discipline and placed completely in the hands of the bonze, who according to a traditional formula is told in effect: "Do what you like with him and treat him as you please, so long as you do not cripple him." Discipline is tempered, however, by the Buddhist regard for human dignity. Although corporal punishment is still used on occasion, reproaches and abusive language are avoided.

Although every male is supposed to enter a pagoda during his youth, residence is not compulsory and there is no set term for those who do enter. A boy may or may not continue his studies to the extent that will qualify him for ordination. Family needs at home most often determine when a boy will enter and leave the monastic school.

Following a tradition as ancient as the kingdom of Lan Xang, the full monastic school curriculum should ideally include the study of Pali religious texts, especially the *suttas*, the sermons and teachings of the Buddha; study of the Lao language, including the rules of versification; religious ethics; domestic ethics, as exemplified by maxims and sayings; basic law, divination, medicine, and politics; commentary on history and legend; geography; calligraphy, to permit the copying of ancient texts with style and distinction; and manual training in the utilitarian, artistic, and religious fields.

Not many monastic schools are equipped to pursue the traditional program in its entirety. It is probable that the majority teach little more than the basic elements of Pali (and in fewer cases Lao) and some arithmetic, along with traditions of origin, an oral grounding in Buddhist doctrine, and much practical manual training. Instruction is preponderantly oral, with emphasis on memory training, recited verses, and singing.

Attainment in the monastic schools, even when the student does not join the bonzehood, is recognized by the granting of the traditional titles or honorifics — for instance, *Maha* for one qualified in Pali, and *Nak Tham* for one who has passed an examination in dharma, the body of Buddhist doctrine.

Despite their shortcomings, these pagoda schools have supplied candidates for both the ordained bonzehood and the traditional mandarinate, though in the latter cases candidates more often than not owed their chances of obtaining a post to family status rather than to advanced education alone. Because the vows of the sangha are not binding for life, many bonzes have left the pagoda or monastery for government posts, and, conversely, government officials have, at times, entered the bonzehood.

French Secular Education

As soon as the French protectorate was firmly established, the French administrators, in part to fill the need for secretary-interpreters and, later, minor functionaries, established two schools of adult education (1902 and 1905). This system was subsequently expanded to include the elementary grades for children. The first teachers were French, soon supplemented by imported Annamese (who had already learned French). In 1909 a teachers college to retrain Laotian bonzes as teachers in the secular system was founded at Vientiane, to be followed in 1911 by three more: at Luang Prabang, Savannakhet, and Pakse. The introduction of the traditional teacher, the bonze, into the secular school system pleased the people but turned out to be impractical. Too many bonzes, after their course at the college, sought civil service posts, where pay and the opportunity for advancement were better.

With all these handicaps, the secular school system spread slowly. Where the schools existed (principally in the provincial towns and an increasing number of larger villages) they competed with the pagoda schools and, because their curricula offered preparation for government employment, tended to overshadow them in importance despite the smallness of their enrollment. They actually reached very few, registration ranging from about 1,000 in 1920 to some 7,000 through the 1930's.

By a French decree of 1917 the Laos schools were made part of a common Indochina education system in which every *commune* was to have one official primary school. The five courses offered in this "primary cycle" were subsequently increased to six and after 1938 were divided into an elementary primary cycle (1-3) and a complementary primary cycle (4-6). In addition to these schools a 1939 order authorized "village schools," the school building and a house for the teacher to be provided by the village and the teacher and school materials to be provided by the government.

The beginning of World War II brought a resurgence of national pride and a reawakened interest in education soon replaced the apathy and discouragement that had characterized the depression years of the 1930's. Elementary schools were set up in increasing numbers and, in the period between 1939 and 1946, enrollments jumped from 6,700 to 14,700. Secondary schools were also expanded at about this time. The Pavie Collège at Vientiane, first opened in 1925, was supplemented by provincial secondary schools located at Pakse (1945), Luang Prabang (1946), and Savannakhet (1947). A very few Lao (usually members of wealthy elite families) left the country for higher education abroad.

In addition to the expansion of general educational facilities a revival of interest in the traditional arts resulted in special schools at Khong for silversmithing, at Vientiane for iron- and woodworking, and at Pakse for the weaving of traditional designs and lamé. Selected students were sent to other countries — to the School of Asiatic Mechanics in Saigon, for instance, and the Technical and Industrial School at Hanoi or the School of Cambodian Arts at Pnompenh.

To bring education to more isolated groups in the population there were formed such institutions as the "tribal schools" for sedentary hill peoples — six such schools with an enrollment of about

250 were reported in 1944 — and, claiming about 600 students, "mobile schools" which moved with seminomadic tribes. Meo children in the vicinity of Xiengkhouang were encouraged to attend the schools in the provincial capital and in those cases where medical orderlies with some teacher training could be found a "hospital school," half school and half hospital, was established.

This proliferation of educational opportunities had various effects. Realizing the changing educational pattern, the monastic schools attempted to modernize their curricula by adding such subjects as French and arithmetic only to find the bonzes in most cases inadequately trained or too preoccupied with religious duties to do the teaching. The special nature of the educational problem in Laos became clear in other ways as well. The Lao, who in the villages formed the majority, were outnumbered in the schools of the chief provincial towns by the Vietnamese (in one school in Vientiane, for example, there were 1,150 Vietnamese students to 850 Lao in March 1945). The result was that the Lao, poorly prepared in academic terms, were seriously handicapped in schools where formal standards were already rigidly in force.

The experience gained during this period, the building of schools, and the extension to large parts of the population of the advantages of formal education were, however, to provide the basis for postindependence educational development.

Present Education System

State administration of education is divided into three categories. General education is under the jurisdiction of the Ministry of Education, which is composed of four directorates: Primary Education, Secondary Education, Higher Education, and Sports and Youth. Technical education is provisionally under the director of the Ministry of Public Works. Religious education falls under the administration of the Ministry of Cults (Religion).

Although curricula are set by the Directorate of National Education, in other ways the administration of education is decentralized. The provincial governor receives general instructions from the national ministries, but the management of all administrative affairs is his responsibility. Inspection of the school system is carried out by provincial primary inspectors, one for each of the twelve provinces, who are required to turn in monthly and annual reports to the director of primary education. The primary school inspector of the province represents the Ministry of Education but works in close contact with the provincial governor, who coordinates the functions of the governmental departments. For instance, recommendations for scholarships to be awarded in accord with government policy are made by the inspector to the governor, who acts on them as the executive agent for the central government.

Elementary schooling is traditionally the financial responsibility of the local communities. The local financial support of primary schools was continued under laws of 1951 and 1952; all citizens within five kilometers of a school are liable for the materials and labor needed for the building and maintenance of the schoolhouse and teacher's residence. The national government supports all other aspects of the public education system, including construction and maintenance of secondary and higher public schools, teachers' salaries at all levels, books, and basic supplies. Exercise books and writing materials are also provided for the elementary primary schools. Draft estimates prepared yearly by the primary inspectors are incorporated by the Ministry of Education into "draft national education estimates" and submitted to the Ministry of Finance, which has the final word as to inclusion of items in the national budget submitted to the National Assembly for adoption. Since 1952 approximately 17 percent of each annual budget has been spent on education. Private education does not receive any regular support from the national budget but the Director of National Education may include amounts for such subventions and scholarships in his annual draft budget if he wishes. In 1954 a total of 98.8 million *kip* were spent on public education from the national budget, which does not include some 11 million additional *kip* contributed by the American economic aid mission. Over 80 million of this went to current expenditures, primary education receiving 75 percent, secondary education, 15 percent, higher education (scholarships) 10 percent, and central administration, 2 percent.

Organization of the School System

Education in Laos is ordered in the French pattern, with primary schooling in two cycles of three years each — the elementary and complementary. Secondary schooling is provided in *collèges* for the first three years, in a *lycée* the fourth year.

Although officially the French educational regulations of 1917 to 1939 have been abandoned, the present system and curricula actually correspond very closely to those of that early period. The subjects taught now are of similar scope to those taught in the public schools of France: ethics and civics, history and geography, arithmetic, drawing or manual work, singing, and physical culture. Lessons are given in Laotian in the first cycle, French in the second.

English has been a relatively recent introduction into the curriculum and knowledge of English is spreading, not only among the Lao but also among Chinese and Vietnamese storekeepers in the provincial towns. English is taught in the secondary schools, in some cases by French teachers, in others by persons brought in by UNESCO or sent by Colombo Plan countries. English is also being studied in a few of the schools for Buddhist monks.

P R I M A R Y   S C H O O L S .   A law of 1951 made the elementary school cycle compulsory in principle but the enforcement of the law, which is tied to the requirement that all villages must construct their own schools, is lax — probably realistically so, since many communities are poor and remote and in any case the government is unable to provide teachers in sufficient number.

Elementary schooling is given in three types of institution: the elementary primary school, the pagoda school, and the rural education center (see Table 5). All of these cover the first cycle of three years. The rural education center also functions as a dispensary and information center and gives special courses for young people and adults as part of the rural self-help program. Besides separate complementary schools, there are some full-course schools which provide both of the three-year cycles. Complementary schooling is not compulsory and only about one-fifth of the elementary graduates enter the second three-year cycle, but the certificate of graduation from the complementary school is much prized.

The secular elementary school is likely to be a one-room affair of thatch and bamboo with a dirt floor. The teacher is usually a Lao, sometimes from the same village, who has had a six- to nine-year schooling plus a brief period of instruction in teaching methods. The curriculum and procedures in these schools are said to be not unlike those prevailing in the monastic schools at the same level.

The number of schools available to Khmu, Meo, and other hill peoples is today negligible, although those Khmu, for example, who live in proximity to urban centers are not unaware of the value of an education and have in a few cases requested the services of a Lao teacher.

S E C O N D A R Y   S C H O O L S .   Secondary schooling is very limited, only a small percentage of the primary students going on to higher grades. There has, however, been a remarkable rise in enrollments since 1945 when no more than 200 students were registered: by 1955 a total of 652 were enrolled in secondary schools, although it was reported that five times that many sought admission, and in April 1959 the figure stood at 2,396 (see Table 6).

Five *collèges* provide a three-year lower secondary education, those in Luang Prabang, Thakhek, Savannakhet, Xiengkhouang, and Pakse. Only at Vientiane is the final fourth year of secondary education available. Here the former Pavie Collège, opened by the French in 1925, has been greatly expanded in the last four years as part of the French aid program and by October 1959 had an enrollment capacity of over 2,000 students.

The curriculum of the *collèges* includes ethics and civics; French, Lao, and English; history and geography; mathematics; physical culture; drawing; music; and manual work. All lessons are given in French in the *collèges* and the Lycée Pavie. The curriculum of the Lycée Pavie in Vientiane is virtually the same as in a French modern and classical *lycée*.

Students graduating from the *collèges* can continue at the Vientiane Lycée or the National Military School for Officers in Laos; or go to the Medical Officers' School, the Public Works Clerks' School, the School of Agriculture and Stockbreeding, or the Forestry School in Cambodia; or go to France to complete their secondary education.

Graduates of the Vientiane Lycée can go directly to higher studies in Vietnam or other foreign countries. Higher education is possible only outside Laos, but scholarships are awarded on a rather liberal scale. Between 1955 and 1959 the French provided scholarships for 171 students in France and the Lao government sent another 104 students to various countries in the period 1950–59. There are at present about 400 Lao students studying at the college level outside the country.

Vocational training is ordinarily a family matter, although some attention has been given by the government to the problem of supplying the country with the technicians needed in modern life. A special section of the Ministry of Education, the Inspectorate of Technical Training, was created in November 1955. "Apprenticeship centers" were instituted in Vientiane and Savannakhet for the purpose of training in hand skills.

In addition to the official schools there are more than thirty private schools in Laos authorized by the Lao government, including sixteen Catholic schools, three Chinese schools, seven French schools, four privately owned schools, and one school for children of American government personnel in Vientiane. These schools had a total enrollment in 1959 of about 5,000.

Teacher Training

Teachers in Laos have suffered in the past from having little prestige or hope of advancement, while corresponding civil service jobs enjoyed social prestige deriving from honorific titles or decorations bestowed by the king. Teachers held none of those coercive powers which tended to make a governmental employee feared and respected. Above the village level the teaching staff was divided into a few rigid categories with little upward mobility as compared to the civil service where officials could transfer from one classification to another and advance to high rank.

Since the coming of independence Laos has attempted to make teaching an attractive career. Recruitment bonuses of 2,000 to 5,500 *kip* are paid. A series of professional examinations are offered as a means of allowing teachers to rise from one rank to another. In 1954 the total teaching staff was reported at 1,436, a pupil-teacher ratio of about 29 to 1. As enrollment increased, the consequent need for teachers brought about a lessening of standards, which had in fact never been too rigidly applied. An attempt to correct this situation was the establishment in 1950 of a normal school at Vientiane, with a four-year course and a stipend of 400 *kip* a month to student teachers.

At present the qualifications for teachers are modest. The staff of the teacher training school must hold the *baccalauréat* from the *lycée*. Primary teachers must have attended a teacher training school and hold the lower-cycle secondary school certificate. Assistant teachers must have the complementary (second-cycle elementary school) certificate. Pupil-teachers are those who have finished only the primary course. Secondary school teachers must be either licentiates in education or *agrégés* (professors) who have received their training in France. Since French is still taught at all levels along with Lao, and since it is the primary language of instruction in the secondary schools, the recruitment of French-trained secondary school teachers will probably continue for some time. The present emphasis on accelerated technological, political, and social development also encourages the retention of French and French teachers.

A new Buddhist Institute under the Ministry of Religion has as its purpose the coordination of Theravada Buddhist studies in

Laos. The Institute publishes religious works in Pali and Lao, directs the religious instruction at the Pali schools, and preserves religious and historical documents. Buddhist libraries and museums in Luang Prabang, Vientiane, and Pakse are under the direction of the Buddhist Institute. It also operates the Higher School of Pali in Vientiane (with 155 students), four secondary schools (in Vientiane, Thakhek, Savannakhet, and Pakse), and approximately ninety elementary schools. Elementary instruction is divided into two sections: dharma (doctrine) and Pali, which together accounted for 4,293 students in 1958. The graduates of the Pali section are qualified to go into the secondary schools (which had 522 students in 1958).

The intent of the Institute is to produce Buddhist bonzes who will be trained in both religious and lay matters. Instruction is given in civics, history, geography, drawing, mathematics, applied sciences, the history of religions, and the Lao, French and English languages. According to a prospectus, "the bonzes will learn in the Higher School of Pali the duties of the citizen and the importance of religion which is the basis of all social activity."

Prospects

The determined efforts of the Laos government to speed economic and social development have resulted in the last few years in a visible increase in the number of primary schools, student enrollment at all levels, an expanded and better paid and trained teaching staff, and more school supplies. In all this the government has been aided by the economic and technical assistance programs of the United States, France, UNESCO, and the Colombo Plan countries.

Through its own "project assistance" activities the United States Operations Mission has paid and trained primary school teachers to assist in the rural self-help program, assisted in the construction of 400 village schools, sent teachers to Thailand, the Philippines, and the United States for training, completed two technical education centers (Vientiane and Savannakhet), and completed the first unit — a Teacher-Training School — of what will eventually be a National Education Center near Vientiane. In addition UNESCO and the United States aid mission have jointly undertaken to set up a press in Vientiane to reproduce school books.

French aid pays the salaries of some 125 teachers, most of

whom staff the secondary and vocational schools. The French also provide textbooks and other supplies and sponsor and finance the *lycée* in Vientiane. Scholarships for higher education in France are supplied through the French aid mission and the French have also provided funds for vocational and technical education both in Laos and abroad.

UNESCO and the Colombo Plan countries have contributed technical personnel, including teachers, and UNESCO sponsored a survey of education in Laos completed in 1956.

Despite these encouraging advances, it is apparent that the Laotian school system is inadequate in terms of present national goals and aspirations. There can be no doubt that the governing elite at the highest levels recognize the shortcomings of the system, but it is questionable how far down the social scale this perception of need extends. At the rural level, generally, there appears slight disposition to show preference for a more modern school system over the traditional. Exceptions can be cited, however, in which rural villages have gone ahead and built their own schools despite lack of government funds.

Obstacles in the path of developing even a modest approach to furnishing a modern, universally applied elementary school system are very real. First and foremost is the fact that the economy cannot generate the necessary funds. Entirely aside from the question of paying teachers (if there were money to educate enough teachers), the mere problem of supplying textbooks and other school materials is a strain on the budget, since most such materials must be imported.

The larger and long-range problems of Laotian education are closely tied to the whole socioeconomic problem. The social demand for broad educational opportunity does not exist, because the economic system does not as yet provide the impetus to social mobility. And for the economic system to advance to the point where the advantages of such social mobility are apparent, a more broadly educated population is one of the most important prerequisites. The time when Laos can arrest the motion of this vicious circle is probably not in the near future. The best that can be said is that apparently some of the country's more advanced leaders are conscious of the situation and are attempting a reasoned and moderate approach to its solution.

8

ART AND LITERATURE

THE INCLINATION OF THE LAO TO ADJUST to rather than change his environment is reflected in his artistic and intellectual heritage. The Lao does not habitually engage in philosophical explorations, nor seek new explanations of life: Buddhism provides a complete and systematic answer to all his questions—and art a means to demonstrate his reverence for the divinities.

The utilitarian and functional aspects of Lao art, even in religious art, are its *raison d'être*. Art as conceived by the Lao has a limited and practical purpose and therefore does not represent a creation for public admiration and preservation for posterity. In funerary art for ritual consumption, elaborate structures are built to be burned down as a part of the death ritual. Many art objects are made to celebrate religious festivals only to be later crumpled and consumed by fire as offerings to the spirits.

But an artistic sense pervades the daily lives of the people as well. The Lao have a natural instinct for music. Courtship is conducted by means of love duets, sometimes improvised under romantic stimulus. Often the girl will listen to the songs of her suitors while sitting at her loom, but weaving and basketry, though essentially domestic occupations with practical purposes, reach the level of folk art as practiced by the Lao.

In addition to its religious function, art may have a social and utilitarian value. Jewelry, for example, is purchased as a form of family investment and may be worn as an indication of wealth as well as an adornment. The carving of pirogues, the presentation of artistic objects at religious festivals, the elaborateness of funeral pyres all to some extent serve as a gauge to social prestige in addition to serving the specific purpose of the particular ceremony.

The Fine Arts

In ancient Laos all artistic activity was closely linked to religious devotion. Architecture was, however, regarded the principal religious art, and Buddhist edifices such as pagodas, stupas, and temples dotted the landscape, their interiors enlivened and peopled with images by painter and sculptor. But these ancient monuments, often built under the personal sponsorship of a Lao prince, were constructed of perishable materials subject to the ravages of weather, fire, and invading armies, with the result that very few have survived to bear witness to the religious and artistic efforts of the people.

Pagodas in modern Laos vary greatly in style, size, and ornamentation. The pagodas in the villages are built of wood and thatch; those in the cities are mostly brick structures plastered together with earthen mortars. City pagodas as a rule are elaborately decorated with multicolored tiled roofs, gilded or lacquered carved woodwork, and frescoes of religious, legendary, and realistic scenes. The latter are usually the work of foreign artists as few Lao have attained mastery in this art, but negligence and inclement weather have worked havoc on many once beautiful frescoes.

As a whole, Laotian religious edifices are simpler in architectural design than Cambodian ones, which have an intricate complex of intertwining eaves and fragile fretwork. Those in Laos are rectangular whitewashed structures with high roofs that drop steeply. Siamese influence is quite pronounced, but there is also a distinct archaism typical of native art that characterizes, for instance, the temples in Luang Prabang.

The stupa, called *that*, is bulbous and elongated into a sort of spire. The most splendid of these is the French restoration of the That Luang in Vientiane, originally built about 1567 to house a relic of the Buddha. Though Lao architecture lacks originality, it has a charm and elegance of its own, particularly noticeable in the decorative details of the doors, panels, pillars, and statues.

Sculpture is also a religious art in that the statues in temples and pagodas are the images of Buddha. In the course of time, different foreign influences have given rise to a variety of set postures of the Buddha statue, but there is one common trait that dominates all Laotian Buddhas: a serene and contemplative look inspired by the Theravada concept of the deity. The materials with which the artist works comprise stone, brick, and bronze, sometimes gilded. The Lao seem to have learned early the art of bronze-casting and their bronze statues are remarkable for stylization and immense size. Though now in ruins, the original statue of the Buddha in the Wat Manorum in Luang Prabang, before it was carried off by the Siamese to Bangkok in 1827, is said to have stood more than eighteen feet high without its pedestal. Some of the wooden statues are also of huge dimensions.

The Lao practice a well-developed art of wood and ivory carving and show special skill in making jewels and silver and gold ornaments such as bracelets, necklaces, and earrings. Decorative designs based on religious traditions adorn betel services, vases, cups, boxes, knife handles, and sword hilts. Weaving, an exclusively feminine occupation, is learned traditionally by every young girl. Scarves, skirts, and other clothing are woven of cotton or silk, often with gold or silver threads in a variety of designs.

Music, Dancing, and the Theater

The Lao are born lovers of music, especially vocal music. Everywhere in the country the people — farmers in the paddies, lovers, boatmen along the rivers, songsters at feasts and festivals — give vent to their feelings in songs, remembered or improvised. Depending on the occasion the song may be about love or heroic adventure or be a song of prayer and prophecy. The typical love song consists of alternate parts sung by the male and female in the form of questions and answers. But the greatest vogue is apparently for the improvised — sometimes bawdy — ballads of the traveling folk singers, who reportedly may sing without intermission for as much as ten hours to an appreciative audience.

Being without a system of musical notation, Lao musicians depend on their memory and an improvisatory skill derived from constant practice, and there are very few formal compositions. The most popular instrument — and the usual accompaniment for love songs — is the *khene,* a kind of bamboo harmonica made of tubes of varying lengths which, having been paired and arrayed in rows, are joined by two half gourds whose cavity forms an air chamber. Also popular and played everywhere is the flute.

A small Lao orchestra for the accompaniment of choral or solo singing may include, in addition to the *khene* and the flute, violins and several percussion instruments. The most common violin is a two-stringed instrument with a neck of carved wood and a sound box made by sealing a half coconut shell with a thin piece of wood. Percussion instruments range from drums and xylophones to the *khoung vong*, a horseshoe-shaped instrument on which are mounted sixteen small bronze gongs sounded by wooden mallets. Some small orchestras will also include recently introduced Western violins and accordions.

For royal or religious processions there is a more formal orchestra, similar to the above but excluding violins and the *khene* and augmented by large drums and a kind of clarinet.

Among the Kha gongs assume even greater importance although a Kha orchestra will also have flutes, clarinets, single-stringed violins, and xylophones. The Kha make deafening music to influence the *phi* — for example, when illness strikes a household — and use loud and stirring music for their war dances.

Although dancing as a social activity is not popular, the Lao like to watch professional dancers. A few professional dancing troupes, all male, continue the traditional court ballets based on episodes in the Indian epic, *Ramayana,* and popular traveling troupes perform indigenous dances at pirogue regattas or at funerals and festivals. In most cases the dancing is accompanied by singing and music.

In the theater, ballet dancing, music, and pantomine constitute the main attractions. The play itself is to a Westerner often longwinded and dull and lacks real interest in life; stories are taken mainly from Indian sources like the *Mahabharata*, the *Ramayana*, and the *Vedas.* The Laotian repertoire consists of dramatizations of romantic tales, warrior legends, and religious stories — some of pure Khmer or Cambodian origin, others adaptations from the Burmese and the Siamese. Gorgeous costumes and colored lacquer masks take the place of scenery and stage properties and give splendor to the performance. Like dancing, acting is an exclusively male profession with female parts played by boys.

In their shadow and puppet theaters, the Laotians extend their borrowings to the Javanese and through them to the Chinese. But in spite of their foreign origin, the marionettes represent local types and customs, while the animated shadow figures are skillfully manipulated in life-like gestures and movements to the delight of the audience.

Literature

Lao literature can be divided into the sacred and the profane. Sacred literature includes both formal canonical Buddhist treatises like the *Tripitaka* and the more entertaining Buddhist tales in a moral, satirical, and allegorical vein. The most famous of the latter, the *Jatakas,* consist of some 550 tales of Buddha's former lives in the various cycles of his reincarnation from animal, human, and divine existence. A special collection of the last ten tales, called *Sip Xat,* provides material for many sermons and edifying images.

There is also a noncanonical literature that contains stories of the saints and gods, among whom especially well-beloved is the Vedic god, Indra. Hymns, chants, invocations, sermon songs, and magic formulas complete the list of minor religious literature. In all these, poetry is regarded as a kind of word magic used to expel or cajole recalcitrant spirits. Sermon songs which originally developed and flourished in the sixteenth century to ward off evil influences have gradually assumed the form of admonitions and instructions to the listeners. The power to protect human beings from sickness, fire, and other dangers and evils is vested in the magic formulas, usually in rhythmic Pali verse.

In Laos, even the profane literature is imbued with religious overtones suggestive of Buddhist and Brahmanic inspiration. Folklore, prose and verse romances, epics, and apologues are all influenced by Indian traditions. A Lao version of the *Ramayana* follows closely the Indian epic in general outline, but with the scenes laid in Laos and some episodes of pure local invention; a Laotian collection of animal fables is taken from the *Panchatantra,* enlivened by native wit and humor.

While almost all Lao literature is anonymous, the *Sin Xay* (*Sininjaya*) has the distinction of having a known author, Pang Kham. The *Sin Xay,* unlike most other long epics, whose texts are corrupt and whose contents are similar and monotonous, has been preserved in its entirety in fifteen chapters and is noted for its literary and philosophical excellence. The greatest poem read by every educated Lao, it is taken from an Indian source with important local variations. There is also a Cambodian version of the poem, differing somewhat in poetic style, plot, and characterization.

Verse and prose novels constitute another important part of the nonreligious literature. Prose novels, based on Buddhist writings, have given place to verse romances; some of the modern works are derived from ancient Lao legends and poems. Typical characters in these romances include the gallant and brave hero, the beautiful and faithful heroine, the benevolent hermit magician Rishi, the ferocious giant monster Yak, and the almighty Indra, who also acts as the *deus ex machina*. Although love and adventure are the themes of these romances, they abound in religious teachings and moral reflections.

In addition to the *Panchatantra* fables, the Lao have numerous prose tales, some of them comic and others judicial. Codes of law and chronicles of semilegendary and real events constitute the last category of secular literature. Among these, the most popular are the comic tales, which deal with all classes of society and their activities. They are more representative than the romances of the life and sentiments of the Lao. Despite the satire, the social order is not challenged, but merely wittily and astutely commented upon.

The literary products of the Lao provide clues to an understanding of Lao culture and Lao personality. In the novels and tales, social structure and interpersonal relationships are not questioned. Man is a constant. The variegated patterns of life change and revolve around him, affecting his conditions and affairs but leaving unchanged his personal traits. There is no development of character and events have no catalytic effect. The prevailing mood of the Lao, whether expressed in prose or verse, seems to be an unconditional resignation to life, however unpleasant it may be. Melancholy and languor coupled with an implied inevitability are the underlying motifs of poetry, even in love songs that might sound risqué and saucy to foreign ears.

VALUES AND PATTERNS
OF LIVING

ALTHOUGH THERE IS AN OVERLAY OF modern technical and administrative method in government and increasingly in the economy,
the basic pattern of Lao values has been relatively unaffected by
the years of French colonial administration and the more recent
contact with other foreign nations. A general satisfaction with
their traditional way of life makes the Lao reluctant to change.
In fact, given the still great difficulties of transportation and communication, only a small proportion of the people have actually
been exposed to foreign influence to any effective degree.

Life for the rural Lao, making a living from agriculture, di-
vides roughly into the rainy season and the dry season as dictated
by the monsoon regime of Southeast Asia. The coming of the
southwest monsoon rains in May means the busy planting time,
accompanied by village ceremonies and rites to propitiate the
guardian *phi* of the rice fields. Throughout the growing season,
to the end of the rains about October, the villagers are free from
intensive work in the fields. This season is also the period of *vassa*,
a kind of Lent for the bonzes, who retire for contemplation and
commemoration of the Buddha's annual retreat during the rainy
season.

The dry season brings more intense activity, beginning with
the harvest and the accompanying ceremonies and celebrations.
Harvesting, threshing, winnowing, and storing of the rice complete, the villagers turn to building, repairing, and the refurbishing
of farm tools. The bonzes are once again in evidence and, the dry
season being the only season when much land travel is possible,
the traders, pack-peddlers, and ballad singers begin their village
rounds.

9. Values and Patterns of Living

Even politics bows to the monsoon. Elections are impossible to hold in the wet season when traveling by the candidates is too difficult, and the National Assembly's annual five-month session begins just before the rains start in May and adjourns as the rains slacken in October.

Because the monsoon seasons follow each other with great regularity and consistency there are seldom bad crop years for the wet-rice farmer. This fact contributes to a conservatism and satisfaction with life characteristic of the rural Lao except in those areas near the larger towns. The dry farmers of the mountains in some parts of northern Laos are, on the other hand, more subject to climatic variations and because of poorer soil are more affected by them; consequently they have less grounds for feeling secure in their existence.

Laos has lived, since the coming of the French, by two calendars: the Gregorian, as used in the Christian world, and the ancient Lao calendar which combines the solar and lunar systems. The Gregorian or Western calendar is now used for dating the business of government and in all contact with the modern world but is little understood or used outside of the capital and the provincial towns.

The Lao solar year, very closely calculated by astronomical methods centuries old, is within seconds of both the mean solar and sidereal years in length and, as compared with the Gregorian system, loses only one day every sixty-one years.

The ordinary year, composed of twelve lunar months of thirty and twenty-nine days alternately, is brought into conformance with the solar year by means of a system of intercalary days (one or two each year and one additional in some years) and months (a thirty-day month called the "second eighth month"). The intercalary month is added every two or three years in such a way that seven such months are inserted into every nineteen-year period.

The months are numbered, the first beginning in late November or early December of the Gregorian calendar. This, however, is not considered the beginning of the new year. Finding the zodiacal signs unpropitious at this season, the Lao astrologers fix by intricate calculation a time for the opening of the new year in April. The exact day varies but is always "between the sixth day of the waning moon of the fifth month and the sixth day of the waxing moon of the sixth month." The New Year is a great period of celebration and feasting, comprising a three- or four-day holiday: the last day of the old year, one or two intercalary days, depending upon astronomical calculation, and the first day of the new year.

The Lao also give numbers to the days of the week but when referring to events will usually say, for example, "the fourth day of the waning (or waxing) moon"—in effect, a reckoning by fortnights. The holy days are the eighth and fifteenth of each phase of the moon, marking its quarters. Notorious for casualness about time and appointments, the Lao value leisure and love to organize feasts, *boun*, that almost invariably are followed by all-night entertainments, *ngan*. At the *ngan* the young engage in formalized courtship in the so-called "courts of love" and their elders are entertained by ballad singers, reciters of legends, and experts at repartee. Religion and enjoyment are mixed in the celebration of all holidays, whether official or private.

Accepting man's mixed nature in his capabilities for good and evil, Theravada Buddhism is largely nonprescriptive and nonprohibitory in relation to the individual, especially the layman. Suffering in life is ascribed to man's struggles to fulfill his own desires but there is a way or method — the Eightfold Path — by which one may avoid or cancel out suffering in this life or future lives through the acquisition of merit. Man is in this way treated individualistically and shown that he may progress or regress through his own efforts.

The way, a middle path between the extremes of conduct, is characterized ideally by gentleness, acceptance of nature, avoidance of conflict, and respect for all life, but within these bounds there is freedom of choice and, by implication, the right to have this choice respected by others.

Full compliance with Buddha's teaching means virtual asceticism so only the bonze is expected to avoid the demands and compromises admittedly necessary in life and give full time to observance of the doctrine, to study and teaching, and to contemplation. But in Laos, as in all Buddhist countries, it is a tradition, and of immense value in acquiring merit and prestige, that every male spend some time in the priesthood. Despite these well-recognized factors, the Lao seem to be somewhat ambivalent about taking the robe. Some enter for only a few weeks or for the duration of a rainy season, others not at all. This attitude with respect to an ideal of behavior is typical of the individual deviation permitted by the Lao scale of values. While he who remains in the monastery for a more extended period acquires greater prestige and is forever after addressed by a title which places him in the exact position he earned by his religious studies, there is relatively little disparagement of one who exercises his individual right not to enter the priesthood or gives the custom only perfunctory observance. Even the bonzes honor the individual's right of choice in the matter, holding to the Buddhist prohibition on exercising moral judgment.

In his attitude toward death the Lao most strongly shows his acceptance of Buddhism. While he does not welcome death, he accepts its inevitability in the belief that he will be reborn, and in the hope that a later life will be more enjoyable than this one. Funeral ceremonies are an occasion of feasting, gaiety, and enjoyment, apparently even among the family of the deceased, who believe that a show of grief would reduce the chances of the departed for a favorable rebirth.

Man and Man

The pervading individualism of Lao-Buddhist life and its implicit emphasis on personal responsibility for self is reflected in the lack of overt guidance the young child receives. He is not pushed or even encouraged in learning to walk or to swim (a skill learned among the lowlanders almost as soon as walking) nor is he given any mark of approbation when he does learn. The child is presumed to gain the idea that the acquisition of these skills is its own reward. Apparently the only attention he gets is a watchful eye lest he hurt himself seriously.

By the time he is three the child freely alternates between the family environment of permissiveness, protection, and deference to seniority and the play-world of his age-mates of the village. Here at an early age he has to find his own way and learn the relationships of competition, compromise, and cooperation. In this way his self-reliance is further developed and adjustment to the absence of protection comes at an age of great flexibility.

Parental permissiveness apparently continues throughout childhood. Children are not pressed into performing household and farm tasks. It is said of girls, for instance, that they learn rice-hulling, food preparation, and weaving mainly by association with and observation of their elders, picking up first the simpler tasks, and these very much at their own volition in their own good time. The same is true of the boys, but their introduction into family tasks is said to come later, with, for example, minding the family buffalo when it is not at work, taking it to the wallow, or gathering forage for it.

Physical punishment is not unknown but probably rare. Admonition is said to take such forms as to produce shame rather than guilt-reaction: "no child of mine would behave thus" (you should therefore be ashamed) rather than "this conduct is wicked" (you have sinned). This is seen to be entirely consonant with the Buddhist teaching concerning wrong conduct and the judgment of one's fellow man.

Although individual responsibility for self is high in the Lao scale of values, it is not a goal to be pursued regardless of the welfare of others. The Buddhist doctrine emphasizes the gentle virtues of self-restraint, modesty, generosity, and serenity, and by extension the subsidiary values of careful good manners, hospitality and respect for others — particularly elders. Respect patterns are learned early, and the child finds that deference is given to seniority — to his older brothers and sisters, and most of all to his parents — regardless of sex.

The great exception to the rule of respect for the elder is that the bonze, regardless of age, is accorded greater respect than anyone else, and this applies regardless of lay status. Highest officials are said to observe the traditional forms of respect in meeting a bonze of any degree or age.

Manners, hospitality, and respect are expressed in Lao behavior in numerous ways. There are different styles of speaking for different classes of people, and special vocabulary items designate or refer to the social relations between persons of different status. Personal pronouns vary with rank and relative status. Respect is also shown by joining hands, smiling, and bowing slightly. Deferential bowing, prostration, and crawling on all fours were at one time proper procedures before a person of high rank but are gradually going out of practice. Restraint in gestures and quiet speech both are considered desirable. Brusqueness or offhandedness in such matters is practically unheard of, particularly in the rural areas, and to copy Western casualness in polite expression is considered misguided.

Physical contact in social greeting is not liked. Western handshaking is reluctantly accepted in the capital, but anything like back-slapping is considered coarse familiarity. There is one particular taboo of such deeply felt significance that it constitutes a real danger point in relations for well-meaning Westerners: it concerns touching or even pointing to the head of another. The belief is that the *khouan*, the independently mobile "soul" whose residence is normally in the head, would consider this an aggression and take flight from the body. To point the foot at the head, even inadvertently, as in carelessly crossing the legs, is taken as both injury and insult. Relative height of the head is also important. One should never, for example, raise his own head higher than that of the king.

The extension of hospitality is an almost universal value of the Lao. The guest, whether expected or not, is greeted courteously and ceremonially and done all honor that the host, or sometimes the entire village, can afford. Almost inevitably, occasion is made to give a feast, for which the Lao have the significant term *soukhouan*, or "invitation to the soul." When the *soukhouan* has particularly formal connotations, as in entertaining an official or specially honored guest, it is termed a *baci*, but the underlying idea of the *soukhouan* remains, and a spirit of gaiety and generosity prevails.

Another highly regarded value in interpersonal relations may be described as serenity, equanimity, or imperturbability. It is characterized by moderation in speech, lack of argumentativeness, and the concealment of any displeasing emotion. It is not clear to what degree these ideals are put into practice in and between all classes of society but the general reputation of the Lao as being polite to a fault argues for an extensive belief in the virtues cited. Western observers have noted that such polite behavior has its negative side in that it is often difficult to get a Lao to give a frank opinion.

In view of the apparent distaste for face-to-face disagreement, it might be expected that Lao culture would furnish numerous examples of the use of intermediaries, but such is apparently not the case. Intermediaries appear in connection with the marriage gift, which in Laos is paid by the groom's family to the bride's, but even here the use of the intermediary appears to be only a vestige of old custom since later practice has tended to standardize the amount within well-understood limits. Courtship itself appears to dispense entirely with intermediaries, although when the young couple's intentions become fixed the actual demand for the girl's hand is made by elderly female relatives of the groom.

The negotiations in 1957 for the reintegration of the Pathet

Lao rebels into the nation were conducted in direct, face-to-face meetings between the prime minister and the Pathet Lao leader, who were half-brothers. The value set upon the common interests and harmony presumed to exist within a family evidently outweighed any consideration of the use of intermediaries to avoid embarrassment and disagreement.

Another aspect of the distaste for open conflict in interpersonal relations is a readiness to compromise, which is entirely consonant with the Buddhist concept that people should follow a "middle way" and with the esteem in which serenity and moderation are held.

There is little information about the value placed on truth and integrity in personal dealings. An oral contract is reportedly as binding, if not more so, than a written one, not surprising in a country of extremely limited literacy. It is worth noting, however, that great value is attached to having witnesses to such an agreement. Little information is available about such matters as the relative moral values inherent in speaking the truth within the family, between friends, or to strangers.

Man in Society

The positive valuation within Lao culture of individual responsibility, and the working out of one's own future existence within the framework of a prescribed ethical and moral code, finds expression also in institutions which transcend the level of purely interpersonal relationships. The meritorious man — the individual who by virtue of age and demonstrated behavior — best embodies these cultural ideals is likely to be accorded a position of political or religious leadership within the village. The village headman is chosen by essentially democratic processes for his personification of the virtues of moral and ethical excellence and generally serves for life or until he chooses to retire. He is supported by a more or less informal council of respected heads of families and such slight initiative as exists for joint projects of the village as a whole probably comes from this group after extensive discussion. The headman finds no need to assume a directive position except insofar as he transmits infrequent orders from above.

The respect for the individual bonze as the exponent of the teachings of Buddha and the unquestioned exemplar of the virtuous life translates easily into the village support of the pagoda and its community of priests. A sure way for the village — as well as the individual — to acquire merit is by donations of money or labor to repair or embellish the pagoda.

The Laotian is willing to work hard — but only as hard as necessary. Growing a larger crop merely to increase one's wealth is not within the Lao scheme of values. Prestige or merit are not gained by mere acquisition or hoarding. The family which works as hard as necessary and manages wisely is respected for those qualities. The girl who willingly does her share of the work acquires the reputation of being a good prospective marriage partner, but the man who acquires a surplus and saves it would lose rather than gain prestige.

The worth of surplus goods to the Lao lies in the potential it gives him for satisfying his two foremost concerns; religious merit and pleasure. At the heart of both is giving — expending — surplus lavishly. The acquisition of a sufficient surplus for the daily gift of food to the bonzes is mandatory to the degree that to the Lao it is not a surplus at all but a necessity of life. Over and above this are the recurring contributions, in company with all others of the village, of materials, labor, flowers, candles, robes, and the whole furniture of living to the bonzes and the pagoda, at the many appropriate and designated occasions, all entered into with generosity and joyfulness. The same combination of expending for pleasure and merit is seen in the ceremonies that mark the stages of life from birth to death, every one of which is marked by shared feasting and gaiety, even — indeed especially — cremation ceremonies, the celebration of the beginning of a new and happier life for the deceased. Giving, feasting, and gaiety are not only pleasurable to the Lao but eminently logical as well, for to him the most readily grasped of the Buddhist tenets is its central purpose of eradicating suffering, and pleasure is evidence of success in this pursuit.

The congruence of religious, personal, and social values no doubt explains why throughout the literature — largely French — written about the country the Lao are invariably described as "gentle and carefree." There are evidently few underlying conflicts of values to mar this surface — at least in traditional rural Lao society.

Everything written about the family environment of the Lao in his early years — the security given him, the lack of factors which might produce resentment or frustration, and the early introduction to respect relationships with his elders, especially parents — confirms the thesis that his primary loyalty goes to the family.

Next after family the tie to the precepts of the Buddhist religion and its ideal practitioners, the community of bonzes, is most binding. The forms and practices of this religion surround the child before the age of reasoning and the lack of dogmatic demands and prohibitions makes Buddhism easy and logical to accept as a philosophy. Its very lack of intolerance and exclusiveness is its own protection against competing religions.

Loyalty to one's village is probably a strongly developed trait, although there is relatively little information available upon which to base such an opinion. Most rural Lao have little contact with the world beyond their own village. The fact that the partners to a marriage tend to come from within the same village, the fact that most disputes are settled within the village, and the involvement of the entire village in the religious life of the monastery are all factors which would tend to strengthen the individual's psychological identification with his own village.

It is somewhat difficult to generalize concerning the degree to which beliefs, values, and patterns of living may differ between classes within the society. Rural-urban differences appear to be developing on an increasing scale and there are indications that the traditional homogeneity of rural agricultural life is giving way in the face of improved communication networks and the influx of Western goods and ideas. The more extreme ways of showing respect, for example, are falling into disuse or have been officially abolished. Such omissions, however, cannot be taken as evidence that the difference in status, or the respect due such status, has disappeared with them. There is nothing in Buddhism which proclaims the equality of all men; in fact, the contrary is held, since rebirth may be as prince or servant according to one's accumulation of merit in his previous existence.

Regard for family unity and solidarity may be intensified in the official (mandarin) class; at least, it seems more conspicuous to most Western observers. In the short life of independent Laos, political affairs have tended to be handled on the basis of the interests of only about a dozen great families and their supporters. The Lao elite have sought, too, to become controllers of various commercial fields opened up through the handling of foreign aid funds, thus entering a field which has historically been the preserve of the foreign minorities. To this degree, differing values seem to exist between classes, and the acquisition of wealth has assumed importance. Yet it remains doubtful whether this difference creates a friction point in Laos, since the privilege of acquiring wealth as a perquisite of office is a time-honored practice, having existed since the absolute monarchy when reportedly all property was deemed to be the king's, and subjects, no matter how high in favor, had no more than the right of usufruct.

POLITICAL DYNAMICS

IT HAS BEEN ALMOST IMPOSSIBLE to hold high office in Laos without belonging to the royal family or the handful of prominent families surrounding the court. In government after government the key ministerial posts have been assigned to men who were related in some way to King Savang Vatthana through either the reigning Luang Prabang royal family or a junior line. Other ministers have often been descendants of the nobility in the formerly independent princely states of Vientiane, Xieng Khouang, and Champassak.

An illustration of the power of this ancient Lao nobility is the domination to an important degree of the postwar period by three royal half-brothers, cousins of the late King Sisavang Vong — Prince Petsarath, who died in retirement in 1959; Prince Souvanna Phouma, who has served repeatedly as prime minister; and Prince Souphanouvong, leader of the Pathet Lao movement. Strongly opposed to King Sisavang Vong's decision in 1945 to rely on some form of relationship with France, Prince Petsarath rallied his supporters and in 1945 organized the Lao Issara (Free Laos) movement, whose existence was a powerful factor in propelling Laos to independence. Only with the granting of full sovereignty by France four years later did Prince Petsarath agree to dissolve his Lao Issara, although he himself returned from self-imposed exile in Thailand only after the Geneva cease-fire.

Prince Souvanna Phouma assumed a major role in the new state, advocating with decisive effect neutrality for Laos on the model of Switzerland.

The third brother, Prince Souphanouvong, originally joined Prince Petsarath in the Lao Issara but, with the encouragement of the Communists in North Vietnam, established in 1950 the rebel Pathet Lao (Lao Country), which — in the form of the Neo Lao Hak Sat political party — continues to harass the royal government.

At all but the lowest (i.e., village) levels of government there reigns a traditional ethnic exclusivity which leaves all government operations in Lao hands. Although now and then there will be reports of incidents or clashes between arrogant Lao local officers and the tribal populations, the Laotians by and large do not express any concern about the Lao monopoly in government or the conduct of national affairs. Pathet Lao political activities in the northern provinces, where the Lao are a minority, have played on latent ethnic resentment to stir various minorities to a greater interest in their political rights and even to outright disaffection for the administration in Vientiane. This has created a situation where representation of these minorities in the royal government has become a political necessity. It must be considered a significant step in that direction that the Lao government constituted in June 1960 contained a secretary of state for information and social affairs, Touby Lyfoung, who is of Meo ethnic origin. In all probability this move was designed to assure the minorities that they too are considered an integral part of the Laotian nation.

The greater part of the population remains, however, only vaguely aware of the constitution, political rights, the concept of the state, or the role of the king. The repeated staging of elections with campaigning by candidates among the population will eventually bring changes in this situation but, for the present, government and politics continue to be primarily the concern of the educated Lao elite.

Role of Political Parties

The close interrelationship of the majority of political leaders together with the influence of French political education and relative newness of independent political action in Laos are reflected in the fluid nature of present party organization. Parties tend to be the personal organizations of strong personalities rather than groups distinguished by their special interests or ideological commitments. Up to the formation in 1957 of the legal political arm of the Pathet Lao, the Neo Lao Hak Sat, platforms among the various political groupings differed only superficially if at all. But the emergence of effective antigovernment leadership brought division in progovernment circles concerning the best method for dealing with the opposition and has produced appreciable variation in pro-government party programs in recent years.

Membership statistics being nonexistent, the numerical strength of any given party is difficult to ascertain. There is, further-more, a tendency on the part of candidates for the National Assembly to switch to the majority party after election, either from an independent position or from another party. These shifts in affiliation explain the difference between election results and the subsequent official list of National Assembly party distribution.

In the 1955 election, for example, the distribution of the thirty-nine Assembly seats among the four legal parties — Progressive, Independent, Democratic, and National Union — which had put forward candidates and the nonaffiliated winners changed in the first few weeks after the election as follows:

	Election	Postelection
Progressive	19	22
Independent	10	7
Democratic	4	3
National Union	2	2
Nonaffiliated	4	5
Total	39	39

Conduct of Elections

The present constitution provides for the election every five years of the members of the National Assembly in accord with the electoral law. This law states that all citizens of Laos twenty-one years old or older who have been resident in the country for five years may vote.

Women, excluded from the first general elections in 1955, became eligible to vote as the result of a constitutional amendment in 1956. Voting fraud, bribery, and coercion are punishable under a royal ordinance of 1951 by fines, imprisonment for one month to three years, or deprivation of voting and officeholding rights for five to ten years, but the ordinance has thus far not been enforced and the 1960 elections gave rise to widespread charges of corruption and fraud.

The National Assembly has fifty-nine members, one for every fifty thousand people based on the government population estimate of three million, and the country is divided for election purposes into fifty-nine single-member districts. The distribution of these districts by province is:

Luang Prabang	9	Saravane	6
Vientiane	6	Sayaboury	3
Savannakhet	9	Nam Tha	3
Khammouane	5	Xiengkhouang	3
Champassak	6	Phongsaly	3
Attopeu	3	Samneua	3

Whoever wishes to run can file his candidacy as much as seventy-five but at least forty-five days before the elections. A plethora of candidates in earlier elections led to the inclusion in the revised electoral law of two restrictive clauses. The first states that a candidate receiving less than three hundred votes must forfeit his filing deposit. The second requires the candidate to resign any government job — most candidates come from government ranks — forty-five days before the elections, or at the time of filing, and at the same time prohibits for a year after the elections the employment in the government of a defeated candidate.

The official campaign period is forty days but, because electoral lists are posted only thirty days before the elections, active campaigning is more likely to run from that time. Geographic and educational factors dictate a highly informal and personal kind of campaign for most candidates. In a country where the storyteller and balladier still reign and illiteracy remains high, campaign literature is relatively useless. Other media such as radio, though increasingly important in the towns, are practically non-existent in the countryside. Travel from village to village with reliance on face-to-face talks and large picture posters is therefore the most effective way to campaign.

There have been charges that government actions in encouraging the vote and protecting polling places amount to intimidation of the voter. The 1955 elections took place without serious incident and the government claimed the victory of Bong Souvannavong, the National Union party leader, in Vientiane attested to their fairness. The Pathet Lao strongly protested the elections, however, and Radio Hanoi broadcast a number of "reports" from the Pathet Lao of arrests by the royal government of opposition candidates and their supporters. The 1960 elections, which resulted in a decisive progovernment victory, again brought charges of "rigging" from the Pathet Lao.

108

The First General Election

The results of the first general elections in December 1955, in which candidates from four political parties as well as several nonaffiliated candidates had been entered, provided the following distribution of the thirty-nine seats in the National Assembly:

Progressive	22
Independent	7
Democratic	3
National Union	2
Nonaffiliated	5

The victory of the Progressive and Independent parties, which had agreed not to oppose one another in the election, was a victory for the government as both were progovernment with platforms calling for peace, unity, higher pay, and better standards of living. The larger Progressive party, most closely resembling a Western political party, was led by the late Katay Sasorith, former prime minister and influential political figure. His nationalist convictions had led to his voluntary exile with the Lao Issara in Thailand after World War II and following the 1955 election he renamed his party the Nationalist party. The leader of the Independent party was Phoui Sananikone, staunch supporter of the monarchy.

The other two parties — Democratic and National Union — were more regional in character and amounted to little more than campaign alliances for the promotion of unrelated opposition candidates. Their influence in the National Assembly, however, was to be of great importance: under the constitution a cabinet could hold power only with the support of two-thirds of the Assembly and the major parties could command this majority only with the help of the opposition. The Democratic and National Union members had in effect veto power over any cabinet and for the next year and a half were able to provoke cabinet crises or block legislation at will. To remedy the situation the constitution was amended in 1957 to permit approval, as well as dismissal, of governments by an absolute rather than two-thirds majority.

The Pathet Lao Agreements

Another, perhaps more fundamental, change in the political picture in 1957 was the emergence of the Neo Lao Hak Sat party as a re-

sult of the agreements between the royal government and the
Pathet Lao. Prince Souphanouvong and his fighting units, trained
and largely supported by the Vietminh in North Vietnam, had been
in control of Phongsaly and Samneua provinces in northern Laos
for four years (for a discussion of the formation of the Pathet Lao
and the role of North Vietnam, see Chapter 13). On November
18, 1957 the royal government concluded a series of agreements
with Prince Souphanouvong and the Pathet Lao for the return to
the royal government of the two provinces, for the integration into
the royal army of two battalions of Pathet Lao forces, and for
Pathet Lao representation in the royal government through legal
political activity.

The formal resumption of control by the royal government in
the two provinces took place without untoward incident in December 1957. In Phongsaly a Pathet Lao member became *chao khoueng*,
or governor, with a deputy from the royal side; in Samneua, the
situation was reversed. Pathet Lao armed forces were assembled
and those not designated for incorporation into the national army
turned in some of their arms and were permitted to return to their
homes, many of which were in southern provinces. Only after the
completion of this process in February 1958 were national army
units able to enter the area and assume military dispositions.

Ratification of the Pathet Lao agreements by the National
Assembly cleared the way for full and legal participation of the
former dissidents in Laotian politics — at least for a time. Prince
Souphanouvong was appointed minister of planning and of reconstruction and urbanization, a portfolio which offered wide scope
in deciding where and how foreign aid should be spent. A close
adviser to Prince Souphanouvong, Phoumi Vongvichit, was made
minister of cults (religion) and fine arts, a less strategic post.

On the parliamentary scene the former Pathet Lao launched
a political party, the Neo Lao Hak Sat or United Lao Patriotic
Front, and put forward National Assembly candidates for the supplementary elections called for May 1958 to provide twenty new
deputies for the two northern provinces.

1958 Supplementary Elections

A second, less formally organized, political group, the Santiphab
or Neutrality party also emerged in time to participate in the election so that by May 4, 1958 when the elections were held there
were candidates from six different parties. A vacancy caused by

death had meanwhile raised the number of seats at stake to twenty-one.

Bong Souvannavong, firebrand of Laotian politics, was the leader of the neutralist Santiphab party, regarded an offshoot of the antiroyalist National Union party. The Neo Lao Hak Sat, exhibiting a political strategy closely resembling the Communist popular front, backed the Santiphab candidates and, to concentrate voting strength, put forward only thirteen Neo Lao Hak Sat candidates for the twenty-one seats.

The multiplicity of government party candidates weakened the position of the older groups and the two progovernment parties — the Nationalist and Independent — together won only eight seats. Nine seats went to the United Lao Patriotic Front and four to the smaller Santiphab group. Alarmed by this showing of strength and unity in the opposition the Nationalist and Independent parties decided to close ranks and a month later, in June 1958, merged to form the Rally of the Lao People, or Lao Luam Lao. This realignment of progovernment forces and the shift of three previously nonaffiliated members to the Santiphab party were reflected in the National Assembly seat distribution announced in July by the government:

Rally of the Lao People	36
Neo Lao Hak Sat	9
Santiphab	7
Democratic	3
National Union	2
Nonaffiliated	2
Total	59

Having received the largest personal vote in the elections, Prince Souphanouvong was further acclaimed by selection as session president of the National Assembly. Prince Souvanna Phouma continued as prime minister and was also made chairman of the new government party. A statement by the RLP (Rally of the Lao People) chairman, explaining the merger of the Nationalist and Independent parties, announced that "the fundamental objective of the new party is to defend the kingdom against an extremist ideology contrary to the customs and traditions of the Lao country and to maintain the true unity and independence of the kingdom against subversion from within or without."

Souvanna Phouma had by this action made public the growing

apprehension among government leaders regarding the true character of the Pathet Lao movement and foreshadowed the end of the uneasy peace between the Neo Lao Hak Sat and the royal government. His personal leadership had been weakened, however, by an accumulation of charges related to the management of government finances and the graft and corruption among government officials. As a result his government fell in late July. Opposition to the Phouma government had been led by the young reformers of the RLP who, loosely organized as the Committee for the Defense of the National Interest, were beginning to be an important political force.

Phoui Sananikone, taking office as prime minister in August 1958, excluded all former Pathet Lao members from his cabinet — though Bong Souvannavong was retained — and began their quiet elimination from the civil service. An immediate protest from the Neo Lao Hak Sat, echoed by Communist China and North Vietnam, charged that this policy constituted persecution of the Pathet Lao and a flagrant violation of the 1957 agreements. Phoui Sananikone was adamant, countering at one point with the observation:

> Like all Buddhists, Laotians have the habit of practicing tolerance to a very high degree. . . . However, events have made it clear to us that what matters is no longer philosophic considerations but the defense of our cultural traditions and our love for freedom, which are being endangered by a subversive proselytism.

Although the Neo Lao Hak Sat party continued to participate in national political affairs, a significant number of former Pathet Lao members in government resigned, one by one, either to join progovernment parties or to disappear from public view. Laos' first experience at "coexistence" was about to end.

Renewal of Fighting

The beginning of the dry season in Laos at the end of 1958 brought new disturbances in Phongsaly and Samneua provinces. Alarmed by the resurgence of the Pathet Lao, Phoui Sananikone in January 1959 asked the National Assembly for decree powers for a year to deal with the rebels. Growing fear of support for the rebel forces from North Vietnam led to an appeal to the United Nations for observers (see Chapter 13) and, as the intermittent fighting continued through the summer, there was increasing evidence of Phoui Sananikone's desire to return to a neutralist policy.

In July 1959 Prince Souphanouvong and the other Neo Lao Hak Sat members of the National Assembly were put under "house surveillance," a move intended to reduce the effectiveness of their leadership and end Pathet Lao terrorist tactics. The legal status of the Neo Lao Hak Sat party was, however, unaffected.

The arrival in October of a United Nations team finally brought a lull in the fighting but opposition to the Sananikone government had been mounting, led by three cabinet members — Khamphan Panya, foreign minister, Sisouk Na Champassak, secretary of state for foreign affairs, and Colonel (later General) Phoumi Nosavan, secretary of state for defense. Following the coronation of King Savang Vatthana, advocate of a firmer policy toward the Pathet Lao, this opposition group, which had been tentatively organized a year earlier as the Committee for the Defense of the National Interests (CDIN from the French), became even more openly critical of government policy.

A crisis in December, technically over the right of the National Assembly to vote to stay in power beyond the terms of the members (elected for four years in December 1955) until the new elections planned for April 1960, resulted in a reshuffling of the cabinet to exclude all CDIN members. Quickly rallying the support of the army high command, the CDIN in a bloodless *coup* forced the resignation of Phoui Sananikone two weeks later on January 1, 1960.

After a brief period of military junta administration, King Savang Vatthana announced the appointment of an elderly non-political royal adviser, Kou Abhay, as caretaker prime minister with the primary task of preparing for the new elections.

The 1960 Elections

A total of 149 candidates, including for the first time several members of the armed forces, filed for the April 24 elections. The Rally of the Lao People, which had been represented in the outgoing National Assembly by thirty-six deputies, had only twenty-four avowed candidates, a reflection of the division in progovernment political circles as the influence of the CDIN grew. The CDIN, without status as a political party, formed the National Front party for the elections but only two candidates ran officially under this designation. There were, however, a number of candidates normally associated with the RLP or the CDIN who ran as independents, postponing their commitment to a party until after the elections.

The opposition parties, Neo Lao Hak Sat and Santiphab, put forward a total of sixteen candidates despite the fact that most of their first-line leaders were in jail in Vientiane on charges of treason and sedition. Other candidates from less extremist leftwing parties included Bong Souvannavong, running as a National Union party candidate.

The elections were held in an atmosphere of calm. The movement of Pathet Lao troops just before the elections, particularly in the southern part of Laos, and threats of election disturbances from the Neo Lao Hak Sat leadership had led the government to take strict security measures at all polling places and the presence of the army prevented any serious incidents even in places where Pathet Lao guerrillas had attacked just days before.

The progovernment parties and candidates won a landslide victory and the Neo Lao Hak Sat party paper promptly charged the elections had been "rigged" and accused the CDIN of having ordered the military units to ensure the election of progovernment candidates. Western sources also stated that some of the incredibly high progovernment majorities had been obtained fraudulently.

The RLP paper countered with another analysis of the decisive government victory, citing the case of a northern constituency:

> The statement by an opposition candidate who promised, if elected, to halt the "civil war" and to "recall the combatants fighting in the jungle back to peace" provoked a contrary reaction. Through such a confession of responsibility by the opposition for the troubles which threaten security in rural areas, the voters in the constituency voted en masse for the national candidates who thus benefited from the unexpected shift.

The elections had proved the strength of the CDIN and Phoumi Nosavan, CDIN leader, guided the organization of the newly elected CDIN deputies and their supporters into a new political party, the Paxa Sangkhom or Social Democrats, with Tiao Somsanith and Khamphan Panya as vice chairmen. The Paxa Sangkhom party promised, in addition to a firm attitude toward the Pathet Lao, a number of social improvements to raise the standard of living for the people and lead to a more democratic political life for Laos. The new party gained thirty-five seats in the National Assembly making the political distribution:

Paxa Sangkhom	35
Rally of the Lao People	17
Nonaffiliated	7

The Neo Lao Hak Sat and Santiphab parties were no longer represented in the National Assembly, having lost even the sixteen seats won in 1958.

The selection of Tiao Somsanith, a leader of the new majority party, as prime minister was announced in June 1960. The Somsanith cabinet, nine ministers and four secretaries of state, was with the exception of two members from the Independent party and one from the RLP, drawn exclusively from the ranks of the Paxa Sangkhom party. Included were Phoumi Nosavan as minister of defense and Khamphan Panya as minister of foreign affairs.

As far as could be judged in the summer of 1960 the Paxa Sangkhom appeared to be more of a defensive reflex against the Pathet Lao danger than a regular political party destined to become a permanent feature of Laotian politics. The flight from Vientiane prison on May 22, 1960 of all the arrested Pathet Lao and Neo Lao Hak Sat leaders — including Prince Souphanouvong — left the government parties faced with a strong pro-Communist movement which had regained its full leadership. In early August a *coup d'état*, led by a politically unknown captain of a paratroop battalion, Kong Le, brought down the government of Tiao Somsanith. The *coup d'état*, the political complexion of which could not immediately be determined, underlined the instability of the political solution that followed the April election and the need for a political base that would reach beyond the traditional power elite.

11

THEORY AND STRUCTURE
OF GOVERNMENT

PROCESS AND STRUCTURE OF GOVERNMENT in precolonial Laos were already highly developed and so well adapted to conditions in the country that the French found it to their advantage to rule through the existing government by means of an overlay of *résidents* and commissioners. French interest in changing the government seemed to be limited to the gradual introduction of more modern administrative methods and some modification of the harsher aspects of absolutism.

Lao royalty from earliest times enjoyed an absolute power of the kind common to other Hinduized states of Southeast Asia. The king's personal powers extended to every area of government and life: all land, at least in principle, belonged to the king; officials held office solely at his pleasure; only the royal family had hereditary titles, other titles being given or annulled by his personal command. These absolute rights were in theory unquestioned and immutable; they were tempered, however, throughout the precolonial history of Laos by the benevolence and paternalism of the majority of Lao kings. Lack of adequate communications and the remoteness of many parts of the kingdom in addition tended to limit the effectiveness of absolute rule. There was, in practice, rarely any interference in the lives of the common people. Personal possessions and usufruct rights to land tended to be respected so long as the proper taxes and gratuities were paid. It was the elite — members of the court, royal officials, and others — who ran the risk of royal disfavor under a capricious king.

Their long acceptance of monarchy and inexperience in any other form of government led the Laotians logically to constitutional monarchy in establishing Laos as an independent modern state. The transition was accomplished easily *pro forma* but Laos has faced a continuing problem of selecting, indoctrinating, and training persons capable of operating its new and modern government in accordance with the principles inherent in the constitution. As a matter of policy the French colonial administration did not do much to train Laotians to meet the problems of modern government, preferring "government at one remove." There was no true unification of Laos and no development of a general government, even in French — much less Laotian — hands, since Laos was administered as an unimportant part of a vaster entity: French Indochina.

The fact that only a small elite has had any experience or education in modern governmental concepts has resulted in a government in which the popularly elected legislature tends to follow the lead of the executive rather than to exercise its own initiative and the judiciary operates as much in accordance with old tradition as in conformance to modern ideas of jurisprudence.

Preconstitutional Government

The basic patterns of governmental organization in Laos derive from the establishment of Hinduized states in what is now mainland Southeast Asia as early as the second century A.D. In the case of Laos, the basic structure of the system remained substantially the same from the commencement of written record, about the middle of the fourteenth century and generally coincident with the establishment of Lan Xang, until the adoption of the constitution in 1947.

There were three levels of officials in the traditional Lao government, functioning in executive and judicial capacities. The first of these, and the most unusual, was a "second king" or *maha oupahat*, who was the king's most intimate consultant and performed any and all tasks as the sovereign might decide. It is perhaps significant that French writers seldom translate the word as *vice-roi* — he was evidently more than this term in its conventional Western sense implies. At different times he has been the king's alter ego in matters of routine government, the leader of the king's troops, or his negotiator in international relations. He might or might not be crown prince, another of the king's sons, or a collateral relative of royal blood. At times he was even a commoner. There was always a *maha oupahat*, down to the time in 1946 when the last one, Prince Petsarath, chose self-exile in Thailand. The institution of the *maha oupahat* was not, however, continued under the present constitution.

11. Preconstitutional Government

The second level of traditional government was a council of ministers chosen from princes of royal blood and arranged in a definite hierarchical order: the *ratsavong*, or first prince and "minister of the right hand"; the *ratsabout*, second prince and "minister of the left hand"; and two other prince-ministers, the third called the "minister of the center" and the fourth in charge of the government service. Apparently the ministers worked in consultative, planning, and executive capacities, together and as individuals. Though under a complete autocrat, they had, as members of the royal family, a very real power themselves and tremendous prestige. There were also lesser officials of royal blood.

This royal body of governing personalities was supported by a third level — an extensive and well-integrated class of high officials (the so-called mandarinate) who filled all the remaining government posts from councilors and judges to tax gatherers, bookkeepers, and storehouse keepers. Carefully graded from top to bottom, jealously guarding their titles of address, these officials formed the backbone of government. Although their titles and positions were not hereditary, favorable environment tended to make the class self-replenishing. There was opportunity to acquire wealth from pay and perquisites as well as from the "gifts" presented by petitioners and claimants. Retaining a percentage of taxes collected was regarded a legitimate practice. So also could a judge properly retain a portion of the fine or judgment awarded in criminal cases and in litigation.

A rudimentary system of elections developed in the provinces, though just when is not known, in which the responsible heads of family chose their village chief. There was a corollary system whereby chosen delegates of the villages met to elect the chief of the canton, *tasseng*, and so on up the line to the officials of the province, *khoueng*. When the *chao khoueng*, the governor of the province, was not a royal appointee, he too was chosen by the delegated notables and "responsible" commoners. The administrative mandarinate was, however, always appointed from above.

When the French first became firmly established in Laos the area had been passing through a long "time of troubles," characterized by division, weak kings, wars with the Burmese and Siamese, and incursions by Chinese bandits from the north. The Siamese, who by 1893 occupied most of the area except small parts tributary to Annam or Tonkin, permitted affairs internal to Laos to be administered as usual, under the supervision of Siamese commissioners backed up by a few detachments of troops.

Basing their policy largely on the studies and recommendations of Pavie, the French followed the Siamese pattern. In northern Laos, *i.e.*, the kingdom of Luang Prabang, the king was officially confirmed and continued to rule as before, but under the supervision of a French *résident supérieur*. In southern Laos, French rule from Khammouane southward was necessarily more direct as there had been no supreme native authority for generations. The princes of Champassak, however, were confirmed as hereditary governors, though the mass of their people and even their capital, Bassac, on the right bank of the Mekong, remained subject to the Siamese until 1907.

By the turn of the century a French *résident supérieur* had been established at Vientiane as the principal representative of French interests, but as much as possible of the administration was left in Laotian hands. Basic law and customs remained largely undisturbed except for the suppression of slavery and the institution of a system of mixed courts supervised by the French to try cases where French criminal law was violated. The French also regularized the tax structure and oversaw tax collection and accounting procedures.

The basic and most obvious change in the scheme of government was the loss of absolute power by the rulers, whose acts were in the last analysis subject to the approval of France however little the French *résident* might interfere in the normal course of government. In addition an increasing number of the princes and other members of the elite were being educated in France, and French schools in Laos and Vietnam (particularly the University of Hanoi) had begun to produce government interpreters and minor civil servants with some Western orientation. In this manner European notions of government became known to a numerically small but dominant section of the population.

Whatever plans the French may have had for gradual political evolution in Laos were upset, however, by World War II. The French protectorate had failed to protect and the prestige of the French suffered from the fact that their administrators were forced to yield to Japanese control. The Laotian elite were furthermore not unaffected by the Japanese propaganda for the Greater East Asia Co-Prosperity Sphere. Loyalty to France ended in the minds of many with the Japanese declaration of March 1945 that French colonial status was terminated, and pressure was put on the king to proclaim independence under the Japanese aegis, which he refused to do.

It was during the rapidly developing sequence of events following the defeat and departure of the Japanese that the idea of a constitutional monarchy was first publicly advocated. The motivation for this formal limitation on the king's power was more the reaction to the external royal policy of King Sisavang Vong, who favored return to a protectorate status, than any overt objection to the social implications of absolute rule. A provisional constitution and government established by the Lao Issara resistance movement in October 1945 were rejected by the King and he was deposed, forcibly but without bloodshed. The King reconsidered his stand, however, promulgated the constitution, approved the government, and was, after some delay, reinstated with due pomp and ceremony.

The French reoccupation of the country, complete in May 1946, drove the Lao Issara into exile in Thailand. Although this exodus involved a considerable proportion of the guiding elite of the country, including the former *maha oupahat*, Prince Petsarath, and his half-brothers, Prince Souvanna Phouma and Prince Souphanouvong, the precedent of a constitutional monarchy had been established.

A joint commission to draft a provisional agreement on the status of Laos, promptly convened by the French authorities, resulted in the *modus vivendi* of August 27, 1946, which among other things proclaimed the sovereignty of Laos under the King of Luang Prabang. Appended was a protocol by which Prince Boun Oum of Champassak renounced his sovereign rights in favor of unity of the kingdom. As a concession, he was entitled Inspector General of the Kingdom for life. At the same time a constituent assembly to draft a constitution was authorized. While in theory and intent the delegates were to be elected by universal adult male vote, unrest within the country, the poor state of communications, and the lack of informed public opinion limited the exercise of the franchise to the principal towns and the few politically conscious citizens. Most of the forty-four delegates elected had been serving as public officials. With the help of French advisers, they produced a constitutional draft which was accepted by the king and promulgated by him on May 11, 1947. After more than two hundred years, Laos was again unified — and for the first time a constitutional monarchy.

The Constitution

There is a strong element of tradition in the Laotian constitution as exemplified by the striking reference to unity in the first words of the preamble:

> Laos, conscious of the role reserved to it by its history, persuaded that its future can only be assured through the reunifi-

cation of all provinces of the country, solemnly proclaims its unity and independence.

Implicit in this proclamation is the concept of a state adhering to the traditions of the ancient kingdom of Lan Xang under the leadership of the dominant and politically more sophisticated ethnic Lao.

Traditional concerns and values are reflected in the care with which the royal succession is detailed in the constitution and in the provision for an upper house with mixed executive-legislative-judicial powers. The Laotian national anthem, *Phing Xat Lao*, and national flag — the conjoined heads and forequarters of three white elephants facing front, right, and left, standing on a five-tiered platform under a nine-tiered white parasol of state, all centered on a red field — recall symbols of ancient Lan Xang. The amount of decentralization contemplated in regard to local self-government in the provinces probably results as much from traditional values as from adaptation to a country with inadequate communications facilities.

More modern in tone is the general enumeration in the preamble of civil rights guaranteeing equality before the law, legal protection of the means of existence, liberty of conscience, and "other democratic liberties as defined by law." Although freedom of the person, freedom of speech, and freedom of assembly "subject to law" — all specifically asserted in the original constitution — were omitted in the 1956 version, the National Assembly subsequently passed a very particularized bill of rights which conforms generally to the guarantees in force in most occidental countries.

A general statement of the duties of the Laotian people includes service to their country, obedience to the laws, and the fulfillment of family responsibilities.

Following the preamble are seven sections entitled General Principles, Royal Powers, Council of Ministers, National Assembly, King's Council, Administrative Provisions, and Final Regulations.

General Principles

Foremost in importance in this section is the clearly stated affirmation of sovereignty:

> National sovereignty emanates from the Lao people. The king exercises this sovereignty in accordance with the provisions of the present constitution.

11. The Constitution

Other articles declare Buddhism the state religion, prescribe Lao as the sole official language, and accord Laotian citizenship to all permanent residents of Laos regardless of "race" who are not already citizens of another nation.

A stipulation here makes certain provisions — those pertaining to the permanence of the monarchical form of government, the representative character of government, the definition of Laos as an indivisible unitary nation, and the principles of liberty and equality as set forth in the original document — immutable. These general principles have in fact gone unquestioned in the course of the debates on constitutional amendment.

Royal Powers

The powers and prerogatives of the king are spelled out in eleven articles of the constitution that begin with the declaration that the person of the king be "sacred and inviolable" and are permeated with respect for ancient tradition. The king, who must be a "fervent Buddhist," is empowered to appoint his heir, either to ascend the throne within his lifetime or to succeed him, the abdicating king retaining in the former case the right to annul the appointment. (This was the procedure adhered to in the transfer of royal powers from King Sisavang Vong to his son Savang Vatthana in 1958.) Proclamation of a new sovereign comes from the National Congress of the King's Council and the National Assembly meeting jointly.

As in traditional Laotian dynastic rules, the heir need not be the king's eldest son but must be a male of the direct royal line, a stipulation also binding on the King's Council which proposes an heir if the king has failed to do so. A regent appointed by the King's Council with the assent of the National Assembly rules in the event of royal minority or incapacity.

The king's executive powers under the constitution range from the signing of all treaties approved by the legislature and the titular command of the armed forces to the right to confer military and civil rank and to grant pardons or commute sentences. The king also declares war although two-thirds of the National Assembly must concur. His most important right, however, is the right to select and appoint his prime minister who in turn proposes for royal appointment the rest of his cabinet, the Council of Ministers.

Council of Ministers

The prime minister and the Council of Ministers, of which the prime minister is president, comprise the government in the European sense of the term (see the plate, Structure of Government in Laos). All problems related to national policy and the functioning of the administrative machinery devolve on the prime minister and his cabinet, which is made up of the ministers of the various executive departments. The Council of Ministers has ultimate responsibility for the implementation of the laws passed by the National Assembly, with power to issue decrees and regulations for this purpose, and may itself recommend legislation to the National Assembly.

As in the French model of the Laotian government, a motion of censure or nonconfidence by the National Assembly causes collective resignation of the government. A government thus under motion of nonconfidence remains in charge of "current affairs" — and without the right to propose new legislation — until a new government has been formed and received the National Assembly's vote of confidence.

A cabinet minister may be simultaneously a member of the National Assembly, in which case he is prohibited from votes of censure and confidence. The minister who is also a member of the Assembly enjoys all other rights and privileges of a delegate, however, including his individual right to introduce legislation and parliamentary immunity in his legislative capacity. Outside the Assembly a cabinet minister has no special immunity and is personally responsible for any crimes, misdemeanors, or malfeasances in office.

EXECUTIVE DEPARTMENTS. Although there has been a recent tendency to use the term "department," Laotian executive departments are generally called "ministries." Their number may vary from government to government but in any case a single ministerial portfolio may combine several departments. These combinations, which may sometimes seem incompatible, result from the very small number of Laotians qualified for such administrative duties. In the government of Thao Kou Abhay, for example, which took office in January 1960, the nine portfolios were:

  Minister of National Education, Fine Arts
  Minister of Justice, Culture, Sports and Youth
  Minister of Foreign Affairs
  Minister of Finance, Agriculture, National Economy

STRUCTURE OF GOVERNMENT IN LAOS

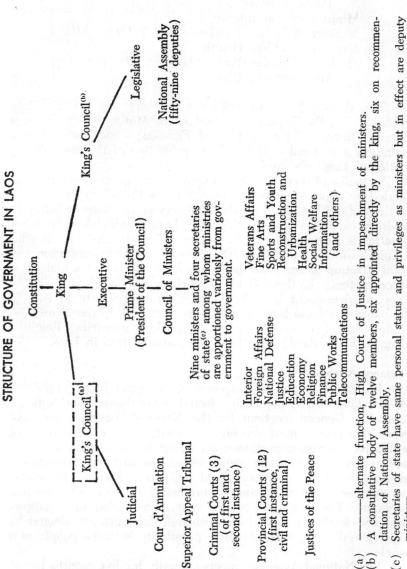

Constitution

King

Judicial	Executive	Legislative
	King's Council[a]	King's Council[b]

Judicial

[King's Council[a]]

Cour d'Annulation

Superior Appeal Tribunal

Criminal Courts (3)
(of first and
second instance)

Provincial Courts (12)
(first instance,
civil and criminal)

Justices of the Peace

Executive

Prime Minister
(President of the Council)

Council of Ministers

Nine ministers and four secretaries
of state[c] among whom ministries
are apportioned variously from government to government.

Interior   Veterans Affairs
Foreign Affairs   Fine Arts
National Defense Sports and Youth
Justice   Reconstruction and
Education   Urbanization
Economy   Health
Religion   Social Welfare
Finance   Information
Public Works   (and others)
Telecommunications

Legislative

King's Council[b]

National Assembly
(fifty-nine deputies)

(a) ———— alternate function, High Court of Justice in impeachment of ministers.
(b) A consultative body of twelve members, six appointed directly by the king, six on recommendation of National Assembly.
(c) Secretaries of state have same personal status and privileges as ministers but in effect are deputy
ministers.

Minister of Information, Tourism, Propaganda,
Public Welfare
Minister of the Interior
Minister of National Defense and Veterans Affairs
Minister of Public Health
Minister of Public Works, Planning, Transports and
Telecommunications

The diverse functions within a ministry are grouped into
bureaus — *i.e.*, the *Direction du Budget du Ministère des Finances*
(Budget Bureau of the Ministry of Finance) — and each minister
maintains a personal staff for the coordination of the multiple activities of these divisions.

Virtually all executive departments in the government are now
headed by Laotians although in many cases French experts remain
on the staff, either filling regular civil service positions or acting in
advisory capacities side by side with Laotian officials. The latter
situation is particularly true in technical departments such as education, health, and telecommunications where the inauguration and
administration of ambitious programs have demanded a high level
of competence in these fields. French personnel serving in the
Laotian government have been under strong pressure to stay in
the background and have by and large complied. In recent months,
United Nations experts from French-speaking countries (Belgium,
Canada, Switzerland) have been increasingly used in Laos.

National Assembly

The legislative branch is composed of an upper house appointed
by the king and a popularly elected lower house, the National
Assembly. General elections for the National Assembly are held
every five years — most recently in April 1960 — on the basis of
legislative districts apportioned according to the number of registered voters as opposed to population. A constitutional amendment
in 1956 created twenty additional legislative districts, increasing
the number of delegates from the original thirty-nine to the present
fifty-nine. The additional twenty seats were filled in a supplementary election in May 1958. Although delegates are elected by
legislative districts, their stated responsibility is to the people as a
whole.

The National Assembly meets annually for five months beginning in May, electing a session president and vice-president and

determining the rules of procedure by vote. The king may prolong a session for good cause and has the right to call a special session on advice of the cabinet, on petition of one-half the Assembly members, or on request of the Interim Committee.

The provision in the constitution for the Interim Committee, which is composed of five Assembly members chosen by the Assembly at the beginning of each session to sit continuously through the rest of the year, specified three functions: to keep Assembly members informed on cabinet activities; to grant decree powers to the king in an emergency, subject to later ratification by the full Assembly; and to itself act in a legislative capacity, also subject to later ratification. This "little Assembly," in addition to the obvious value as a legislative check on the executive, has beneficial effects from the resulting continuity of relations between the two branches, a continuity made difficult by the short Assembly sessions and the primitive condition of communications in the country.

Proceedings of the National Assembly are usually public and a weekly publication by the Ministry of the Interior, *Journal Officiel du Royaume du Laos* (Official Journal of the Kingdom of Laos), makes available in French the official record of all laws, ordinances, regulations, and other official transactions of the National Assembly as well as the executive and judiciary. Although under no obligation to carry Assembly debates verbatim, the *Journal* has done so on occasion, *e.g.*, the debates on constitutional amendment. Parliamentary immunity is extended to all persons printing or distributing official records, as long as these are not declared secret, an important free-speech guarantee where statements in heated debate often fall within the scope of libel laws.

The constitutional powers of the National Assembly include the exclusive power to enact legislation, the authority to initiate legislation — shared with the cabinet which at present actually proposes most laws — and the power to dissolve the government by refusing a vote of confidence. The resemblance to the French National Assembly is perhaps greatest in this provision for the vote of confidence but this power is somewhat balanced by the power of the king to dissolve the National Assembly on the proposal of the Council of Ministers acting with the concurrence of the King's Council. Elections must take place within ninety days of such dissolution and the new Assembly must meet within thirty days following these elections.

King's Council

Acting as advisers to the king are the twelve members of the King's Council, six appointed directly by the king, six nominated by the National Assembly for royal appointment. The members are appointed for five years during which holding any other government office is prohibited.

Although without true legislative powers, the King's Council is in effect an upper house of elder statesmen who examine all bills passed by the National Assembly and recommend signing, veto, or request for amendment by the king. In addition legislative proposals by the king are generally drafted and finally presented to the Assembly by this group of advisers. The King's Council is also empowered to act in behalf of the king or his regent in case of absence or incapacity and sits as a high court of justice in impeachment proceedings against cabinet members.

Administrative and Judiciary Provisions

The French colonial court system provided for two separate jurisdictions — one for native Laotians and one for French and other nonnative residents of Laos. The court system for Laotians comprised a first-instance tribunal in almost all district capitals, a court of appeals in every provincial capital, and a supreme court of appeals in Vientiane. The other court system, applicable to nonnatives, consisted of "justices of the peace with extended competence" established at the provincial level. Appeal could be made to the higher courts of Saigon or Hanoi, and final appeal to the Court of Cassation in Paris. Between 1949 and 1953 a French Union court system replaced the French colonial court system for non-Laotians.

A single court system for all residents of Laos, except those having diplomatic immunity, became a fundamental objective in planning a judicial structure for independent Laos, as was a guarantee of the independence of the judiciary from the executive and legislative branches of government. These principles were written into the constitution but, in realization of the extent of preliminary legislation to be enacted before Laos would have the basis for a modern judicial system, the one article on judicial organization was deliberately phrased only in general terms. Following the model of the French constitution of 1946, the Laos constitution, with the exception of a provision for a Superior Council of Magistrates to determine the rights and duties of the judiciary and to "ensure their discipline," merely states that laws for a complete judicial structure would be formulated.

The Laotian court system has been substantially expanded since independence and a total reorganization of the judiciary was undertaken in 1954. At the district level there now are some forty "justices of the peace with extended competence," their jurisdiction extending to all the village groups within their *muong*. There is a first-instance tribunal in each provincial capital to hear both criminal and civil cases plus three special criminal courts — at Pakse, Vientiane, and Luang Prabang — each with responsibility over several provinces. The criminal courts also act as appeals tribunals for cases tried before the lower courts.

At the national level is a Court of Appeals, and final appeal can be made to the *Cour d'Annulation* (Nullification Court), which has supreme court powers in nonconstitutional cases.

Although the theoretical basis for a modern judicial system in Laos has been created, implementation and actual operation still fall far short in many cases of modern judicial standards. A shortage of trained personnel makes the administration of justice slow and inefficient in most places and the legal code, partly traditional and partly borrowed, retains archaisms, duplications, and minor contradictions. By continuing to bar the languages of the ethnic minorities from the courts, for example, the judicial process becomes all but inaccessible to these minorities.

A concerted effort to codify existing laws and recommend additions and changes where these would be beneficial has recently been undertaken by a commission composed of the minister of justice, the attorney-general, the president of the Higher Appeals Tribunal, three French advisers, and a counsel from the army's justice department.

Provincial, Local, and Tribal Government

National unity is regarded by Laotian rulers the key to their independence as a nation and any great degree of decentralization is discouraged. The constitution leaves latitude for political development, merely providing that each province shall be under a governor responsible to the central government. Without affirming or denying the principle of election, the constitution states that provincial governors will be assisted by elective councils whose powers will be increased from time to time. In addition some of the larger towns are given virtual self-government under the central authority. Thus a precarious balance has been struck in the present government between the desire for effective centralized authority and the strong tradition of regional autonomy.

The numerous historical divisions of Laos are clearly reflected in the country's present territorial organization (see the map, Provinces of Laos). Divided for nearly two hundred years into three separate kingdoms, the country was redivided by the succeeding French colonial administration into the protected kingdom of Luang Prabang, several provinces under direct French civil administration, and one area — now the province of Phongsaly — under French military administration.

Independence brought unification of the country, the former kingdom of Luang Prabang forming four provinces. There are at present twelve provinces, each headed by a governor appointed by the Minister of the Interior. In some cases hereditary leadership patterns are respected and traditional local leaders are appointed as provincial governors: in southern Laos, for example, a member of the former royal house of Champassak is usually appointed governor of Champassak province.

A province is divided into districts or *muong*, each headed by a *chao muong*, and cantons or *tasseng*, which group several villages, *ban*. In many cases the district head is a traditional leader who is simply confirmed in office. In sparsely populated areas there exist satellite administrative units, known by their French name *postes administratifs*. The small villages have headmen called *pho ban* in the south and *nai ban* in most tribal areas and in the north. The Meo and certain Laotianized Kha tribes have chieftains that occupy specially created administrative posts called *naikong lao-theung* which correspond to the office of *chao muong*. The national administrative capital, Vientiane, and a few other towns are administered as *muong* by a *chao muong* assisted by elective municipal councils.

Still very much self-governing are the many tribal areas which have retained their local chieftains and accept control from central Laotian authorities only conditionally. The provinces of Phongsaly and Samneua were, from 1954 to 1957, under control of the Communist-dominated Pathet Lao, which had its own type of local administration based upon people's committees set up in the villages. The reintegration of these provinces into the national administration is presenting the Laotian government with special problems.

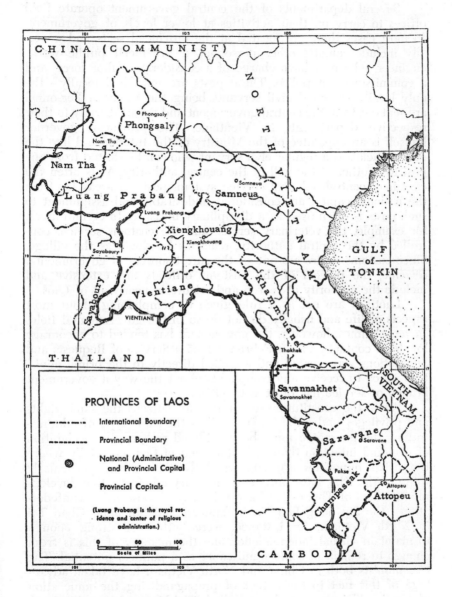

CHINA (COMMUNIST)

THAILAND

NORTH VIETNAM

GULF
of
TONKIN

SOUTH VIETNAM

CAMBODIA

O Phongsaly
Phongsaly

Nam Tha
Nam Tha

Luang Prabang
Luang Prabang

Samneua
Samneua

Xiengkhouang
Xiengkhouang

Sayaboury

Vientiane
VIENTIANE

Khammouane

Thakhek

Savannakhet
Savannakhet

Saravane
Saravane

Champassak

Pakse

Attopeu
Attopeu

PROVINCES OF LAOS

— · — · — · — International Boundary

— — — — — — Provincial Boundary

◉ National (Administrative)
    and Provincial Capital

○ Provincial Capitals

(Luang Prabang is the royal residence and center of religious
administration.)

0   50   100
Scale of Miles

Several departments of the central government operate field offices to carry on their activities at lower levels of government. In most cases these are located at the provincial seats and generally include, among other personnel, a provincial public works engineer, who may have charge of a considerable labor force, and a commissioner of police. These posts are not filled locally — the only locally recruited civil servants being the teachers. Personnel are sent out from the central government and report directly to their respective departments in Vientiane. The provincial governor himself is an appointee of the Ministry of the Interior and like the other officials is a regular civil servant who can be shifted from one post to another at the will of the central authority. As is often the case in a centralized civil service system, posts in areas far from the national capital are considered undesirable and assignment to such posts is often used as a disciplinary measure. In certain areas, for example, the veterinary service and the customs service, controlled by the central authority, reach as far down as the village. Since customs duties are one of the surest sources of governmental revenue, the powers of the customs officials are extensive and include the authority of search and seizure in nearly all of Laos.

Laotians are not as a rule given to complaining about most aspects of life and usually do not do so in the governmental field. In recent times, however, the government has tended to encourage low-level contacts, and in February 1955 a Service of Requests and Suggestions was created and attached directly to the prime minister's office to receive any complaints about the way a government branch or service has dealt with citizens.

While the constitution guarantees all citizens the same rights and privileges under the law as well as the same type of administration, the guarantee must be considered rather as a declaration of eventual intention than as a statement of fact, especially where the tribal minorities are concerned. Certain tribes, particularly those of the Kha, have only a rudimentary administrative development; others of Thai origin have a history of loose tribal confederation — the Sip Song Pan Na in Yunnan and Sip Song Chao Tai in North Vietnam, for instance, were both once strong enough to maintain virtual independence and the memory of this is fresh enough to remain of some significance as a political potential. The Communists both in China and North Vietnam have taken advantage of this fact to the extent of propagandizing the annexation of Laotian Tai areas to the so-called "Tai-Meo autonomous area"

of Communist North Vietnam, whatever political or social validity
this may have. The Laotian government, on the other hand, has as
yet made no marked effort to bring the tribal peoples to more
conscious participation in state affairs.

In the case of the exclusive, wary, and independent Meo, certain concessions have been made. In the province of Xiengkhouang,
where the Meo form nearly a quarter of the population and have a
degree of unity under their leading families, they are granted virtual
local autonomy and, at the national level are represented by delegates to the National Assembly and a cabinet member in the new
government.

Government Personnel

A career in the government commands prestige and often offers as
well an opportunity to acquire wealth, with the result that most
educated Laotians will seek a government position. In theory,
appointment to the civil service is open to any Laotian national,
or resident of Franco-Laotian parentage, who is eighteen years old
or over. In practice, education and experience requirements present major obstacles to any but the elite class whose wealth and
position ensure privileged status in these respects.

The particular requirements vary from ministry to ministry,
but the categories of civil service in the Ministry of the Interior
may be taken as typical. Here there are four grades, each with as
many as nine pay scales: *maha amat*, general (the highest grade);
amat, superior; *long amat*, secondary; and *naikong*, special. Candidates for the *maha amat* grade must have university and graduate
law school degrees or equivalent experience at the rank of provincial governor. A secondary school certificate is required for
appointment at the *amat* and *long amat* levels, although there are
special provisions for army personnel without this certificate. An
army officer with ten years' service in the commissioned ranks is
eligible for a special examination for *amat* positions or, in the non-
commissioned officer ranks, for *long amat* positions. The *naikong*
or special category comprises those engaged in administration in
tribal districts. Promotions, below the top administration level, are
made on the basis of competitive examinations, a civil service officer becoming eligible for such promotion every two years in the
lower grades and every three years in the higher grades.

The number of government employees (including schoolteachers but excluding the armed forces and police) was estimated by the government in 1960 at about 8,000. This figure also included the 150 to 200 French and Vietnamese advisers and technicians in the government, again excepting the military. The shortage of trained personnel is felt most keenly in those departments where technical competence is especially needed and in ministries such as foreign affairs, defense, and justice formerly administered almost exclusively by the French. At the top administrative level all positions are appointive and almost without exception occupied by Lao from the elite class.

The class and ethnic exclusivity which characterizes the government poses one of the most difficult problems Laos faces. Another problem is that of continuing corruption in the government. Practically nonexistent under the French, corruption among government officials began making inroads in the administration after World War II. Although this is in part a reversion to tradition, Laotians tend to blame the example of Thailand, whose administration Laotians commonly refer to as "utterly corrupt." The returning members of the exiled Lao Issara supposedly brought back the notion that government office carries an implicit right to "squeeze" the people. A government campaign in 1956 to eradicate corrupt practices resulted in the suspension and transfer of a number of high officials.

In addition the government is plagued with the occasional reports of malfeasance in office of Laotian officials in tribal areas. Arrogant behavior rather than fiscal peculation is the usual complaint. In Xiengkhouang province, for example, a column of thirty Lao soldiers was reportedly cut to pieces by the Meo, infuriated because a Lao official had been exacting "the right of the first night" from non-Lao brides.

Although the number of young officials from lesser families who have been educated mostly in France is steadily increasing, there is the unmistakable fact that for the foreseeable future the Lao elite will remain the primary source of qualified government personnel for top administrative and policymaking posts and will therefore continue to be to a large degree a self-replenishing class. A significant expansion of educational and economic opportunities will have to precede any real change in the situation. It is interesting to note in this connection the movement of the elite into positions of control in the commercial enterprises emerging under the impetus of foreign aid and government encouragement.

Law Enforcement

Because the police force was staffed during the years of colonial administration almost exclusively by the French, few Laotians were prepared for police administration when the Lao government assumed full charge of police functions in 1953. Recognizing the need for a wholesale reorganization and consolidation of what police and security forces remained the government passed in November 1955 a royal ordinance creating a single national policing administration, the Tamrouat Lao or Police Corps, into which were absorbed the former Royal Gendarmerie and the National Guard.

The present Police Corps comes under the direction of the Minister of the Interior, who is responsible generally for the maintenance of law and order throughout the country. For purposes of territorial organization Laos is divided into four police commands, each staffed with one police "legion." There are within these commands provincial and district level subdivisions of the regular police and certain areas of Laos in which the road system is still inadequate have been or will be provided with mounted police or police units equipped with pack animals. Other police units along the Mekong have been equipped with power launches.

Members of the police force ordinarily undergo training at the National Police School in Vientiane, which has been expanded into a full-fledged police officer academy that trains all the commissioned officers of the national police and all of its senior enlisted personnel. In addition, several hundred personnel have been sent annually for training in regular patrol and traffic work to Thailand police schools and, more recently, one hundred officers completed an eight-weeks special criminal detection course at the Manila Police Academy.

The intent to create an organization of high prestige and morale is evident from several measures taken to make service in the police highly desirable. The Tamrouat is equipped and organized as a lightly armed paramilitary force with a full-fledged system of military ranks. Six different types of complete uniforms have been assigned, from a white and a khaki parade dress and a special evening dress to a full infantry combat kit including steel helmets with camouflage cover, jungle boots, and submachine guns. The Laotian government has made a definite effort to transform its police into a special elite force by making admission fully competitive and by raising admission standards to compare with those of the Laotian army. This elite status is also reflected in the pay scale, which corresponds generally to that of army personnel, making the Laotian force one of the highest paid police in Southeast Asia. The maintenance of such a high pay scale is made possible only by foreign aid.

MASS MEDIA

IN FEW OTHER COUNTRIES IS THE STATE of public information more primitive, more embryonic, than in Laos. The effectiveness of the printed word is severely limited by the fact that probably well over three-quarters of the population is illiterate. Only a few persons besides the governing Lao elite — and these few often Chinese, Vietnamese, European, or American — are able to read the country's newspapers and other publications. There is a single broadcasting station — Radio Vientiane.

All formal information media are controlled by either the government itself or persons closely associated with high government circles, the only exceptions being the scattered publications of opposition politicians and their factions or parties. The use of all media for propaganda purposes is accepted and generally practiced, but here again the high rate of illiteracy restricts the effectiveness of any propaganda.

For the present, however, word-of-mouth communication is by far the most important source of news for the majority of Laotians.

The Traditional Newscarriers

Along the Mekong and its tributaries itinerant bonzes, boatmen, and ballad singers are always greeted eagerly by the villagers, who look to these travelers for their news of other villages. Laotians living near provincial towns, along popular trade routes, or close to army posts keep fairly well informed on local matters in this way. Tribal groups living high in the mountains, on the other hand, will see far fewer travelers and are accordingly apt to be totally ignorant of affairs other than their own.

The reliability and nature of the news carried by these travelers will of course vary with the person and his position. Bonzes, particularly those who have assumed the robe for years or for life, often move from one temple to another over the country, bringing news from other regions, but as their active participation in non-religious affairs, specifically political decisions, is forbidden their conversation normally centers on spiritual and philosophical subjects. Traders and boatmen bring both news from the larger towns and gossip from neighboring villages, but their news may be weeks old. In addition, traders and boatmen, being uneducated men as a rule, are rarely in a position to talk to those who know and could interpret the news of the capital and the world and therefore pass on highly personal versions of any news. The many festivals attract a third kind of news bearer, the ballad singers, who follow the festival rounds from village to village, skillfully weaving into their traditional songs impressions of recent events and important people.

There is no evidence to indicate that any party, governmental or other, had ever attempted consciously to use these traditional newscarriers until the entrance into the political scene of the Pathet Lao, after the reintegration of 1957. During the subsequent election campaign of 1958, it is reported that their newspaper and that of the Neutrality party were distributed free, in quantity, to the bonzes in and near Vientiane. It is not known whether the bonzes then gave them wider distribution, but it is interesting to note that the Pathet Lao proceeded on the theory that they would.

Pamphlets and leaflets have on occasion been used by the government and by political candidates, but the low state of literacy makes it necessary for such material to be largely pictorial in content.

The lack of electric power precludes the use of radios and loudspeakers in most places, although portable speakers are known to have been used. Gaining in popularity as means of disseminating information are the public meeting and, wherever equipment is available, moving pictures.

Government Activities

The control and dissemination of information and propaganda is handled within the government by the Ministry (sometimes designated the Directorate) of Information. It has never been, in the short span of Laotian independence, a separate portfolio, having been more often than not under the personal control of the prime minister. Apparently it is scantly staffed by persons poorly trained and insufficiently aware of their opportunities or responsibilities. Branches of the central office are reportedly maintained in most provinces but salaries have gone unpaid for considerable periods of time.

When it became apparent in 1955 that the Pathet Lao would not cooperate in the holding of national elections, the Special Service for Political Propaganda (SSPP) was created and attached directly to the office of the prime minister. Practically nothing is known of its strength or organization or of its connections with the regular information service. Although its current activities, if any, are unknown, its initial purposes appear to have been to disseminate — through employment of agents and word-of-mouth communication — the idea of the unity of Laos under the king, to educate the people in the procedures of a national election, and to counter Pathet Lao propaganda aimed at boycotting the elections.

The Laotian army also has an information and propaganda service, Service de la Information de la Forces Armées (SIFA), organized along military lines — from a central office at army headquarters in Vientiane down to a small propaganda unit in each battalion headquarters. The SIFA does not confine its sphere of action solely to the army but attempts to influence the general public in the vicinity of military units. Given the geographical distribution of army units, SIFA's opportunities for contacts with the population are more widespread, and its efforts probably more effective, than those of the regular information service, which hardly extend beyond the immediate vicinity of provincial capitals.

There apparently are no outlets or media specifically reserved for or devoted to propaganda or political indoctrination. Given the conditions that restrict the effectiveness of conventional media — the high rate of illiteracy and the scarcity of radio receivers and motion-picture equipment — government agencies have had to make use of picture pamphlets and leaflets. For example, photographs of the king and paper flags are distributed to familiarize the people with their sovereign and their national symbol, and poster-style leaflets have been used to attack Pathet Lao ideas and methods and to denounce control of rebel activities by the North Vietnamese (Vietminh). This reference to the Vietminh is believed to be a particularly potent propaganda weapon as it plays on the general Laotian distaste for all things Vietnamese.

Little can be said of the effectiveness of government propaganda. The fact that more persons than ever before voted in the last full national elections may be due in part to the propaganda effort. Many areas, however, generally those inhabited by the non-Lao minorities, are never reached by government propaganda.

The only propaganda directed abroad is the small-scale radio war that goes on at intervals between Radio Vientiane and the Vietminh's Radio Hanoi. In this running feud Laos usually assumes the defensive, though sometimes sharply.

The Press

There are in Laos a few printed newspapers and a number of small-circulation papers produced by mimeograph or other duplicating machine processes. The government paper, *Lao Presse* or *Khao Kom Khosanake*, is published at Vientiane by the Ministry of Information and has a daily circulation — mostly in Vientiane — of 1,600 in French and 2,000 in Lao. Most news in the usual seven or eight mimeographed pages of *Lao Presse* comes from Agence France-Presse in Saigon, but there will be in addition local news and the occasional releases of the United States and other embassies in Vientiane. Also published in connection with government operations are the army weekly, *Midthaharn*, and the police weekly, *Tamruaj Samphan*, with estimated circulations of 3,000 and 10,000 respectively.

The majority of newspapers in Laos are private, often the personal publications of those persons around whom the present loosely organized and rudimentary political parties revolve. Of these papers, which by their nature are subject to formation and abandonment according to political conditions, the most important in the Lao language at the present are probably *Le Maha Sohn* (Voice of the People), a newspaper of the former prime minister Phoui Sananikone; the *Ana Chak Lao* (Kingdom of Laos), a CDIN paper; and *Lao Mai* (New Laos), the publication of Bong Souvannavong. Influential publications in French include *l'Independant* of Phoui Sananikone; *La Voix du Peuple*, which since the death of Katay Don Sasorith has been campaigning for Prince Souvanna Phouma; and the *Lao Haksa Sat*, the CDIN organ. For a list of these and other newspapers see Table 7.

Radio

The only broadcasting station in Laos is the 1 *kw.* station — Radio Vientiane — in the Laotian capital. This station, which is owned and operated by the Directorate of Information, has fairly complete and modern equipment and was in 1957 broadcasting six and a half hours daily — early morning, noon, and evening — on the short-wave band at 7145 and 6130 kilocycles.

Programming on Radio Vientiane is primarily informational. The news is broadcast daily in Lao, French, and Thai — the Lao newscast at dictation speed — and one hour a day is given over to the "Voice of France," a release of the French Information Service. Most other programs are in Lao but there will be an occasional feature or talk in French and the growing interest in English has resulted in a short daily English lesson.

Although reception of Radio Vientiane is reportedly good throughout southern Laos and the adjacent area of northeast Thailand, reception becomes poor beyond Luang Prabang and Xiengkhouang to the north and everywhere in Laos is inferior to reception of the Vietminh's more powerful Radio Hanoi.

Estimates of the number of receiving sets in Laos vary widely but a figure of around five thousand is most generally accepted. The cost of a short-wave radio is prohibitive and in a country where only six towns have municipal power plants, batteries are an additional, expensive, and almost unprocurable necessity. It is not surprising then that most sets, besides those of the Laotian army, belong to government officials in the principal towns, to the more prosperous Chinese shopkeepers, or to a few wealthier village headmen. It is said that even some provincial governors are without sets.

Foreign Activities

The United States, France, and Great Britain each maintain information services in Laos, including information centers and libraries for public use. French information activities, though considerably decreased since 1954, retain a special importance because of the continued presence of French advisers in various departments of government.

Much of the program of the United States Information Service (USIS) is devoted to publicizing the accomplishments of the United States Operations Mission (USOM) in Laos. In addition the USIS assists the Directorate of Information in informing the people of Laos about their own country and government. Publications, many in Lao, and films, some with Lao or French soundtracks, are the principal media used. Films are especially welcomed in the

140

villages, having on occasion been requested by headmen to augment the carnival atmosphere of local celebrations and festivals.

Practically all overt foreign propaganda activities directed at Laos emanate from the Vietminh in the Democratic Republic of Vietnam (DRV). The USSR and Communist China appear to pay the country little attention, although the latter sometimes supports the DRV line. In typical Communist fashion the propaganda effort is highly organized and in this sense has a considerably higher potential than the government's efforts, although the Communists too are faced with the high rate of illiteracy and other obstacles to mass communication.

The propaganda line of the DRV, and the Pathet Lao before the 1957 integration, was nationalist rather than Communist as such. Since the Geneva agreements of 1954 France has been treated as discredited – defeated, in effect, by the Vietminh. All forms of evil are ascribed to the United States. Following the formal reintegration of the Pathet Lao provinces in December 1957, the DRV dropped its separatist line, but appeared to be holding in reserve the propaganda potential of its own "Tai-Meo autonomous area" closely adjacent to the disputed provinces.

FOREIGN RELATIONS

FOR A COUNTRY WHICH HAS ENTERED the world arena so recently, Laos has shown a commendable quality of realism in its approach to foreign policy problems. Until the recent cold war events produced a change in strategy, Lao leaders consistently shied away from abstract statements involving concepts such as the "free world," the "camp of democracy," or the "Afro-Asian bloc," using them, if at all, only in statements addressed to non-Laotians or destined to arouse sympathy abroad.

As the record of Laos' relations with foreign countries and international organizations shows, the Laotian negotiators have characteristically sought to reduce the various problems involved to a series of smaller issues which can be attacked — and solved, if possible — piecemeal. When the French spoke of full independence, the Laotians patiently negotiated a judiciary agreement with the French. When Chou En-lai extolled at Bandung the virtues of peaceful coexistence (in the abstract, of course) the Laotians promptly requested a concrete statement which specifically left Laos the right to retain foreign bases on its soil.

Although their nation once extended beyond its present limits, the Laotians cannot look back to a past in which they were a major Southeast Asian power. A rather long experience of invasions by their more powerful neighboring states has left Laotians with a keen appreciation of their own helplessness. The recent Indochina war (1946–54) against the North Vietnamese Communists showed every villager how weak and indefensible his country is. This lesson was paid for dearly in refugee treks, burned villages, pilfered crops, and a decline of the already low standards of public services. The 1959 rebellion, which saw a rebel force of no more than 1,200 Pathet Lao and mountaineers play havoc with the whole 25,000-man Laotian army, once more drove home the point of Laos' defenselessness.

142

Thus the foreign policy statement made by Tiao Somsanith on June 3, 1960 as he presented his new cabinet for approval to the National Assembly reflected not a political tendency of his own grouping but an inescapable reality. In the official release of his statement it was noted that the new administration would follow:

> abroad as well as at home — a realistic policy . . . the policy of neutrality *which was willingly* accepted by the Lao people. It [the government] will adhere to the principles of peaceful coexistence and good neighborliness. *Laos has no alternative, placed as it is between the antagonistic forces of two worlds.* The government will respect the principles of the United Nations Charter and the obligations entered into by the Royal Lao Government, *including the Geneva agreements.* [Emphasis supplied.]

There is, perhaps, no other tenet of Laotian government policy which will find more understanding among Laotians throughout the country, for, strange as it may seem compared with Western experience where the reverse prevails, the average Laotian may have no valid contact whatever with his government on the internal plane (i.e., voting, schools, public services) but, by the force of things, he is acquainted with the fact that his country does things which may or may not please its neighbors. This instills a hardheaded approach to foreign relations which — because it clashes with the Western image of the "fun-loving Laotian" — is often ignored and thus leads straight to the recurring misunderstandings which at times befog Laotian relations with Western countries.

Laos' foreign relations in modern times can be conveniently grouped in the following categories: (1) relations with the ex-colonial power, France; (2) relations with the Asian area, both Communist and non-Communist; (3) relations with non-Asian states, notably the United States; and (4) activities in international organizations. All four areas of Laotian foreign policy have had varying degrees of importance at various times. Thus, relations with France, after a period of relaxation between 1955 and 1958, are again becoming closer as an aftermath of the 1959 rebellion; relations with Asian Communist nations have reached the zero-point, for the same reason; Thailand now looms large since it provides the country with its best overland connections and is the logical avenue of military help should it be required; while India —

13. Relations with France

which loomed large in Lao foreign policy in 1955–57 – has lost some of its luster in view of its own obvious helplessness in the face of Red Chinese aggression. The United States is, of course, a vital economic factor for Laos. But the 1959 rebellion seems to have proved to the Laotians that salvation does not lie in military support (which failed to come forth anyway) and thus, the United Nations – present in Laos through technical advisers and observers – is assuming an increasingly vital role in Laotian affairs.

Relations with France

Contrary to the chaotic turn of events in neighboring Vietnam, where the struggle for national independence eventually expanded into a full-fledged war, Laos' progress toward independence proved more leisurely but equally successful. A *modus vivendi* signed by Laos and France on August 27, 1946 reaffirmed Laotian unity under King Sisavang Vong and granted Laos a certain measure of internal autonomy. A Constitutional Assembly was elected in December 1946 and a Laotian constitution promulgated on May 11, 1947.

Lao relations with outside powers were still restricted to negotiations with France, now represented in Laos by a Commissioner of the Republic. An exchange of letters in November 1947 and January 1948 between the King of Laos and the President of France (equivalent in French constitutional practice to an Executive Agreement in the United States) merely reaffirmed Laos' status as an Associated State of the French Union. Laos, however, with the kind of "gentle firmness" that was to become the hallmark of Laotian diplomacy, proceeded to whittle down French encroachments upon its emerging national sovereignty. For example, the French sought to assure the position of Prince Boun Oum of Champassak by a secret treaty with the King of Laos. Sisavang Vong rejected the idea of a secret treaty but expressed his willingness to submit such a treaty project to open debate in the Laotian legislature. Needless to say, the French desisted.

Events in neighboring Cambodia and Vietnam were also reflected in the relations between Laos and France. The Elysée Agreements of March 1949 between Vietnam and France, which granted Vietnam a limited amount of self-government under Chief of State Bao-Dai, were followed by a General Convention signed in Paris on July 19, 1949 by King Sisavang Vong and the President of France.

The General Convention and its Annexes provided for the membership of Laos in the various bodies of the French Union, the joint defense of Laos, direct Laotian diplomatic representation, equality of opportunity for Laotian citizens in France and vice versa. In addition, certain services in the field of economic planning, foreign commerce, customs, currency, and communications were to be operated on a joint basis by Cambodia, France, Laos, and Vietnam. A convention on the judiciary gave French citizens a special status in case of litigation or criminal suits.

The organization of the four-power boards was discussed at a conference among the four countries held at Pau in France in the spring of 1950. Instead of lasting a few days only, as at first expected, it dragged on for months because of clashes of interest among the three Indochinese states and their distrust of the French who were repeatedly — and with some justification — accused of attempting to retain too much power for themselves. The head of the Laotian delegation, Outong Souvannavong, expressed this feeling in his final speech at the last session of the Pau Conference, on November 27, 1950: "There could be no question, for us, of leaving the palisades of the former Protectorate . . . if it were to enter into the enclosure of another surveillance whose regime would be even less bearable than that which we have known before. . . ."

From then onward, Laos began to progress more rapidly toward a greater measure of national independence. Britain and the United States recognized the three Indochinese states in February 1950, followed by most West European and Latin American nations. In Asia only Thailand, in view of its strong anti-Communist stand and close traditional relations with Indochina, extended almost immediate recognition to the three countries and exchanged ambassadors with them. A Laotian representative was accredited to France, yet at least for the duration of the hostilities it was obvious that France's influence over the destinies of Laos would remain preponderant, even if this influence was now clad in the concepts of *quadripartisme* and "independence and association."

One such quadripartite venture into diplomacy was the negotiation for military and economic aid from the United States, where a clear distinction was made between aid granted to the French Union forces fighting in Indochina and the aid separately granted to the three Indochinese states. Until January 1955 France controlled the apportioning of aid funds since the dollar portion of such aid went into the joint hard currency reserve of the new

Banque d'Émission des États Associés which had taken the place
of the old Banque de l'Indochine as the bank of issue.

On the whole, however, the cumbersome quadripartite machinery either failed altogether or did not operate efficiently in most
other cases. In the political sphere, nationalist drives for full political independence in Vietnam and Cambodia at times nearly
resulted in a breakdown of relations between those two states and
France. In Cambodia, King Sihanouk for a time went into voluntary
exile to mark his displeasure with French gradualist methods. In
Vietnam a congress of various nationalist groups refused to support
Bao-Dai in his program of negotiations with France.

The Laotians, unlike their two Indochinese neighbors, abstained from raising abstract principles in their negotiations with
the French, proceeding instead to discuss precise points of transfer
of power. On the basis of the July 3, 1953 Declaration of French
Premier Joseph Laniel, promising to "perfect the independence of
the Associated States," the Laotian government promptly sent a
note to France on August 24, asking for the transfer of all residual
French controls in Laos, with the exception of the judiciary which
the Laotians were willing to discuss separately. These negotiations,
begun on October 15, ended on October 23, 1953 with the signature
of two separate documents: a Treaty of Amity and Association in
which France recognized Laos as a "fully independent and sovereign
State" and in which Laos "freely reaffirms its membership in the
French Union, an association of sovereign and independent peoples,
free and equal in their rights and duties"; and a brief series of Lao-
French Establishment Conventions which, in substance, reaffirm
the equality of Laotian and French citizens on a reciprocal basis.

Neither document materially changed Franco-Laotian relations. Prince Souvanna Phouma, the Laotian prime minister who
signed the Conventions — the Treaty was signed by the King
himself — was acutely aware of the problems facing his country,
particularly since Communist forces from North Vietnam had
invaded Laos early in 1953 and had set up a puppet "Lao State"
(Pathet Lao) under the leadership of Prince Souphanouvong.
In his closing speech at the Conference Prince Souvanna stated:
"These accords which return to Laos all the attributes of its internal
and external sovereignty shall permit us henceforth to affirm its
[Laos'] international personality. But beyond this stage, we shall
still need France's help. . . ."

This Laotian appeal for help was soon to become one of the
major issues in the Indochinese tragedy. As the Communist forces

of the Democratic Republic of Vietnam (DRV) began their 1953 autumn offensive, the French high command faced an acute dilemma: either to concentrate its forces in the easily defensible flatland areas of Indochina (which was the militarily sound solution) and abandon most of Laos in spite of all pledges to defend it, or attempt to defend Laos by offering the enemy an attractive bait. The latter course was finally chosen by the French commander, General Henri Navarre. According to his recently published memoirs — which, on this point, are well corroborated by other sources — French political circles in France felt that to abandon Laos, after it had voluntarily joined the French Union and linked its destiny to France's, would doom outright the whole fragile edifice of the French Union. Navarre was given instructions to defend Laos. He chose the valley of Dien Bien Phu to make his stand.

Laos had its first "coming out" in international politics, when, as the smallest (in terms of population) interested party, it participated in the cease-fire conference at Geneva, from April 27 to July 21, 1954. There its contribution was far from negligible. The Laotian delegation adamantly refused to allow the seating of rival Pathet Lao delegations, and the Communist powers yielded on that point. Undeterred by the sometimes hesitant stand taken by many other powers, Phoui Sananikone, head of the royal Laotian delegation, presented Laos' case to the assembly in these terms:

> . . . First Point. Laos is independent. On October 23, 1953, it signed with France a treaty of independence and association of which Mr. Molotov and Mr. Dong [head of the DRV delegation] appear to be ignorant. . . . We do not think that countries which pride themselves on achieving federal unity amidst a variety of nationalities can fail to recognize that our membership in the French Union merely safeguards and strengthens our independence in a world where absolute autonomy can only lead immediately to the worst forms of enslavement.
>
> Second Point. We maintain that in Laos national sentiment, centered in His Majesty Sisavang Vong, is unanimous to a degree which many countries might envy us. . . .
>
> Third Point. We have said, and we repeat, that the military operations in Laos are the work of Vietminh troops, that is to say of troops foreign to the country by race, tradition, and ideology. We maintain that the so-called "free government," which by a gross abuse of language they misterm "the Laos Resistance Government," has been fabricated lock, stock, and barrel by the foreign invaders.

13. Relations with France

Both Laos and Cambodia were likewise adamant in their refusal to allow foreign enemy forces (Vietnamese Communists) to be permanently regrouped on their soil. While Cambodia was entirely successful, Laos had to pay the price of the deteriorated military situation prevailing at the time of the cease-fire: the two northernmost provinces of Phongsaly and Samneua and a connecting corridor between them remained under Pathet Lao control until a final settlement was reached by the two parties on November 18, 1957.

Laos still fared considerably better than Vietnam with regard to its political and military situation. While the cease-fire agreement for Vietnam specifically prohibits the introduction of certain types of armament (jet aircraft, etc.) and the maintenance of foreign bases, Laos was authorized to retain a 1,500-man French training mission along with two French air and land bases and 3,500 French troops. One of the bases, Seno in southern Laos, is a modern all-weather bomber base which has been expanded since the cease-fire and reinforced by French armor withdrawn from Vietnam in April 1956. Other articles of the Laotian cease-fire agreement also include convenient escape clauses. Article 9, for example, prohibits the introduction of "armaments . . . of all kinds" into Laos but exempts from this prohibition a "specified quantity of armament" (not specified elsewhere) "deemed necessary for the defense of Laos." Likewise, the promise made by Laos and Cambodia in the Final Declaration of the conference not to join military alliances is conveniently qualified by the proviso "so long as their security is not threatened." An International Commission for Supervision and Control (better known as ICC) composed of Polish, Canadian, and Indian members and chaired by the Indians was to supervise the execution of the cease-fire provisions.

The dissolution of remaining quadripartite economic organizations as of January 1955 had brought about a change in Lao-French relations not provided for in the October 1953 treaty. The new negotiations began on October 22 and ended on November 16, 1956 with the signature of five new agreements on monetary relations, economic relations, tax problems, the status of French personnel on duty with the Laotian administration, and relations between the French and Laotian judiciaries.

The 1959 rebellion brought about certain Franco-Laotian tensions. The French government refused to accept without further investigation the erstwhile Laotian thesis that a full-scale invasion was taking place, with Lao rebels being actually supported by

148

Communist North Vietnamese regular troops; the Lao government also attributed the poor showing made by Laotian troops to defective French training methods, with the result that large numbers of American training personnel were hurriedly transferred to Laos.

With the arrival of the United Nations "presence" and the ensuing cessation of open hostilities, Lao-French relations returned to normal. French technical aid to Laos is extensive and in general well-administered, the bulk going into capital construction and education. The effort in the cultural field is considerable and appreciated. As a French delegate to the 21st Conference on Public Education, held in Geneva in July 1958, stated:

> The French government is grateful to Laos which, alone [of all the countries which receive educational aid from France], mentioned in its report the fact that it received such aid from France.

Laos no longer belongs to the now-defunct French Union; neither does it belong to General de Gaulle's Community. As a SEATO member and the only Western power authorized to have troops in Laos, France is in the delicate position of being in effect the "tripwire" should a Communist invasion really occur. This position, for the time being, makes close relations between Paris and Vientiane useful from the Laotian viewpoint.

Relations in the Asian Area

In its landlocked position on the rim of the Sino-North Vietnamese Communist bloc, Laos is a great deal more exposed to pressure and dependent upon the good will of its neighbors than any other country of the area except, perhaps, Nepal. Thus, its independence won, Laos went about with great determination to win acceptance among its Asian neighbors. Though it had gained their diplomatic recognition soon after the Geneva cease-fire conference, actual contacts with them had remained scanty. The Asian-African Conference of Bandung, from April 18 to April 24, 1955, opened a new door for direct diplomatic contacts. At Bandung the Lao expressed willingness to steer an "independent and neutral" course providing that "more powerful nations" (i.e., Communist China) were willing "to give proofs and guarantees to smaller nations." Here again, without raising philosophical and moral issues, the Laotian diplomats concentrated on getting their opponents down to cases. Having roundly denounced DRV illegal activities in Laos in a White

Book whose publication was timed for the eve of the Bandung Conference (which no doubt embarrassed the Red Chinese and DRV delegations) they were now in an excellent position to exact noninterference pledges from Chou En-lai and the prime minister of the DRV, Pham Van Dong.

The Bandung Conference also brought about closer contacts between Laos and its fellow Buddhist neighbors Thailand, Burma, and Cambodia. The possibility of forming a pro-Western "Buddhist bloc" in Southeast Asia with Thailand as its hub had attracted certain American policy planners since 1953, when it became clear that a second line of defense might become desirable should a French military defeat occur in Vietnam. However, here again Laos drew a clear line between what could reasonably be achieved by such a pact and what could be achieved through direct negotiations. Thus a Thai move in July 1955 to bring the Pathet Lao threat to the attention of a meeting of the SEATO Council caused resentment among Laotian officials, who considered the matter a domestic affair and expected to settle it through the truce machinery of the Geneva accords. Thus far, in spite of good relations with Thailand, the concept of a political Buddhist bloc has not made much headway, although Thai economic influence upon landlocked Laos is steadily growing. Recollections of past Thai incursions upon Laotian soil are, however, still alive in Laos. The 1959 events further emphasized the importance of Thailand to Laos, but also that of Laos to Thailand as a buffer in case of a serious crisis with Red China. Although there was some talk in October 1959 about a Thai expeditionary force of 20,000 men to come to the help of Laos, the idea was quietly shelved, much to the relief of the Lao, who live in real fear that any such Thai "help" would first of all result in a Thai re-annexation of the Laotian provinces situated on the west bank of the Mekong.

Relations with India have been cordial since the Geneva cease-fire and Prime Minister Nehru's subsequent visit to the Kingdom. Laos returned the courtesy in September 1955 with a visit of the then Crown Prince Savang Vatthana and Prime Minister Katay to India. The Laotian delegation made full use of the opportunity to stress the bonds of common spiritual origin as well as unity of views with India in seeking peaceful solutions to oustanding political problems, but Katay, speaking before an Indian audience, also used the occasion to express strong views concerning Laos' own Communist rebels: ". . . Laotian public opinion is vigilant. The Laotian people shall never permit foreign intervention. In the forthcoming elections [of December 1955], its verdict shall ban from the Nation those who have failed to join the Laotian community and have remained agents of the Vietminh." It was again certainly no coincidence that Laos, as it had done on the eve of Bandung, issued a new supplement to the Laotian White Book on cease-fire violations on the eve of the delegation's departure for India.

With solid assurances of Indian cooperation and Chinese and DRV promises of noninterference, the Laotian government was now in a favorable position to reopen negotiations with the Pathet Lao rebels who had been stalling for better terms in spite of their repeated assurances that they were ready to "consolidate peace and unify the Kingdom of Laos."

Upon his return from India, Katay met the rebel leader Souphanouvong in Rangoon, Burma, and signed a joint declaration on October 11, 1955. This document, like previous Laotian diplomatic endeavors, dealt with the practical problem at hand — the avoidance of further clashes between the two parties. A buffer zone was agreed upon, and a joint commission to deal with other outstanding problems was to be appointed. Last-minute hedging on the part of the Pathet Lao again prevented a final settlement of the problem. A new round of negotiations began in 1956 and culminated in August with the arrival of Prince Souphanouvong in Vientiane for the signature of a "final" agreement to integrate his forces with those of the royal government.

The Joint Communiqué issued on August 10, 1956 differed little from previous such agreements, except that it contained some face-saving provisions for the Pathet Lao. Thus, the royal government promised to abolish "levies practiced during the colonial regime" (which had been abolished anyway) and gave all citizens "the right to work to ensure livelihood" (which no one had denied them). In terms of concrete concessions, the Laotian government had to agree to let Pathet Lao organizations operate legally throughout Laos. In addition, supplementary elections were to be organized in the border areas and a "government of national unity" was to be formed with participation of Pathet Lao members.

The royal government, already familiar with the somewhat uncertain pattern of negotiations of the Pathet Lao, sagely decided to attack the whole problem at the root — by talks with the Communist authorities in Peking and Hanoi. Within a week after the Vientiane communiqués, Prince Souvanna was in Peking, and shortly thereafter in Hanoi. The Laotian delegation was given the usual red-carpet treatment but — despite American fears that Laos would "turn east to neutralism" — yielded in fact nothing. However, it received in both capitals informal pledges of approval of the Vientiane communiqués and thus could hope that their provisions would be observed this time by the Pathet Lao. Integration of the Pathet Lao elements was accomplished in November 1957 and in the May 1958 supplementary elections for 21 seats, the political party of the Pathet Lao, the Neo Lao Hak Sat, gained a total of 9 seats in the 59-member Laotian National Assembly.

In fear, however, that the voyage might be misinterpreted in the West, the Laotian Prime Minister immediately visited strongly pro-American South Vietnam, where he was cordially received by President Ngo Dinh Diem, and then continued on to Paris, while Crown Prince Savang Vatthana (presently king) paid an unofficial courtesy visit to the United States, in the course of which he was received by President Eisenhower.

The decline of French military and political power in the Far East was followed by the creation of SEATO, sponsored by the United States, to offset the losses of Western prestige and power in the area. By assuring smaller Asian nations of the support of the United States, Britain, France, Australia, and New Zealand in the case of a Communist attack, SEATO now became the corner-stone of a new defensive system which, through the so-called "protective umbrella" clause in its Protocol, also covered the three states of Indochina (which were prohibited from joining such an organization by the terms of the Geneva cease-fire).

Laotian statements with regard to SEATO vary somewhat according to the interlocutor. For example, Prime Minister Katay stated in March 1956, when relations with the Pathet Lao rebels had reached a new low:

> Laos has common borders with Red China and North Vietnam and, therefore is much exposed to Communist menaces. . . . Though Laos is not a signatory of the Manila Pact, it lies within the protective orbit of the Treaty. It is satisfying to receive the promises of the United States [with regard to] their will to defend the principles of security and mutual aid in this part of the world. . . .

However, six months later, after the succeeding prime minister, Prince Souvanna, had received Red Chinese and DRV assurances of nonintervention in Laotian affairs, he declared in an interview with Viet-Nam Presse in Saigon, on September 9, 1956:

152

The Geneva Accords forbid Laos from participating in any military alliance. Not being a member of SEATO, Laos has, therefore, no relations with this organization.

In actual fact, Laos does benefit from the "protective umbrella" of the SEATO alliance in two ways: firstly, through the SEATO Protocol; and, secondly, through its French Union Treaty of 1953, under which France guarantees Laos assistance in case of attack. France, a SEATO member, maintains one military base in Laos with the full assent of both Peking and Hanoi, a fact which Prince Souvanna did not fail to point out during the same interview.

The 1959 crisis was a test of strength of sorts for SEATO. It soon became obvious, however, that the difficult terrain and the special character of guerrilla warfare prevailing in Laos would make a SEATO intervention hazardous militarily — as well as politically awkward in that it would bring American and other Western forces into direct contact with Red China, a situation which had been scrupulously avoided since the Korean War. Thus, the arrival of a UN "presence" saved everyone concerned from a delicate situation.

Relations with Communist Neighbors

Laos established diplomatic relations with Nationalist China early in 1959. This step, taken by a small country, outflanked as it is by Communist states along six hundred miles of its border, was a bold departure from the previous Lao attitude of caution and may, in the opinion of informed observers, have had a great deal to do with the outbreak of the 1959 hostilities. A previous Laotian government under Prince Souvanna Phouma had succeeded in signing a friendship agreement with Peking on August 25, 1956, which clearly was a success for Laos because it recognized the right of the Kingdom to retain its French bases if it so desired. What is more, Laos obtained this written agreement without having to go so far as to recognize the Peking regime. Since the recognition of the Chinese Nationalist government on Taiwan by Vientiane, however, it is obvious that Laos is beyond the pale as far as its neighbor to the north is concerned.

With regard to Laos' relations with the Democratic Republic of Vietnam, the situation is even more difficult. After a series of border incidents in 1958, which Laos finally submitted to the United Nations on January 18, 1959, the situation suddenly degenerated into almost outright hostility as the CDIN administration headed by Sananikone veered off on a pro-Western course, attempted to enforce the integration of the Pathet Lao battalions, and arrested the Neo Lao Hak Sat leaders. Ever since, North Vietnam (which, in the Security Council Report of November 5, 1959, was found to have, at the least, given the Laotian rebels support "consisting mainly of equipment, arms, ammunition, supplies, and the help of political cadres") has been exerting a steady amount of pressure on the Vientiane government to return to a path of "true neutrality," including the revival of the International Control Commission (ICC). In a note addressed by DRV Premier Pham Van Dong to the Soviet and British foreign ministers — as former chairmen of the Geneva cease-fire conference of 1954 — on March 3, 1960, the DRV requested the two ministers

> to take appropriate and timely measures to check the penetration of the US imperialists in Laos and ensure respect for and strict implementation of the Geneva [cease-fire] and Vientiane [Pathet Lao] agreements.
>
> The DRV Foreign Minister urges reactivization [*sic*] of the International Commission in Laos and release of Prince Souphanouvong and the other detained leaders of the Neo Lao Hak Sat. . . .

This request was not acted upon, and the DRV now continues to build up further pressure upon the Vientiane government to return to the *status quo ante* of the 1957–58 period. The fact that Tiao Somsanith in his program speech of June 3, 1960 specifically mentioned that his government would respect the various international obligations "entered into by the Royal Lao government, including the Geneva agreements," appeared to be a Laotian attempt at reaching again at least an informal *modus vivendi* with Hanoi. The escape of the rebel leaders from prison on May 22, 1960 conveniently solved the other outstanding issue.

Relations with the United States

Laos is one of the most isolated and exposed recipients of United States aid. Its strategic importance is such that a failure of American policies in Laos, whether such a failure were imputable to the policies themselves or not, could have severe repercussions in other small countries living in the shadow of the Communist bloc.

Averaging more than $40 million a year (two-thirds of which are spent for the 25,000-man Laotian army and other internal-security projects), American aid to Laos is higher, on a per capita basis, than that granted by the United States to any other country. Some of the aid projects in the fields of public health and transportation have found widespread and grateful acceptance. However, prior to the monetary reforms of late 1958, they had not been able to stave off a serious inflationary trend or to solve the problem of providing capital equipment which the Laotians consider essential if their country is to become more nearly self-sufficient in the future.

To Laotian objections that too much of the aid is concentrated upon consumer goods (ranging from toothpaste to high-powered automobiles) American aid experts reply that a good many such consumer goods are needed to absorb the large amounts of purchasing power generated by payments for public works and by the military establishment which itself represents nearly ten percent of the total labor force and is the largest single wage-earner in the country. They also point out that certain Laotian demands for industrial equipment are unrealistic in the face of world market conditions and local transportation difficulties, which would prevent Laotian producers from competing effectively in price and quality.

Together with the far larger Vietnamese program, the US aid program to Laos has become one of the most studied and surveyed programs in the world. Several Congressional committees as well as private social scientists have studied the effect of massive aid on so primitive an economy and the programs have been the subject of much criticism.

Aid officials counter such criticisms by pointing out that the very extent of the underdevelopment of the country does not allow for the kind of rational and efficient planning which could be applied under other circumstances. Also, the frequent emergencies of a political, military, or economic nature which seem to have dogged the Laotian scene almost constantly since 1956 have to be met by "crash-programs" which are always expensive and often wasteful.

A variety of private programs operate in Laos with varying degrees of success. Perhaps one of the most successful in terms of direct usefulness and permanent good will is Operation Brotherhood. Founded by the U.S. Junior Chamber of Commerce, Operation Brotherhood now receives funds from J. C.'s in many parts of the world and operates three hospitals (Vientiane, Xiengkhouang, Samneua) in Laos, entirely staffed with Filipino personnel.

There is also a great deal of respect for United States proficiency in the technical field among many Laotian military officers who go on training missions to American overseas bases or to United States military schools.

The 1959 crisis has left a profound mark on Lao-American relations, for many of the young Laotians of the CDIN feel that their extreme pro-Western stand of the spring of 1959 was at least tacitly encouraged by the United States, with the understanding (on the part of the Laotians) that serious repercussions for Laos would bring immediate massive support of the Laotian position by this country. The fact that this proved neither feasible nor desirable in October 1959 in large part determined the apparent return of Laotian foreign policy to its present more balanced position.

With the United Nations now bearing a part of the political burden, American aid programs in Laos may perhaps turn to the type of long-range planning which provides for maximum beneficial effect.

In recent years also, Laos has experienced an increasing amount of contacts with some British Commonwealth countries which participate in the Colombo Plan or other aid schemes: Australia, New Zealand, and Canada particularly. There are little contacts with other European countries outside France and Britain except perhaps an occasional West German economic mission, whose effect, for the time being, does not go beyond expressions of good will.

Laos in International Organizations

Laos' experience with international organizations is limited to a few in which it has special interests: the United Nations, its Economic Commission for Asia and the Far East (ECAFE), UNESCO (from which it receives several experts), and the Mekong Commission. Laos is, of course, a member of many other international organizations and United Nations specialized agencies, but their effect upon Laotian foreign affairs is rather remote.

Within the United Nations, where Laos has been a member since December 1955, the Laotian delegation has adopted an attitude distinctly different from the bloc votes which the other "Bandung nations" deliver on many issues. Its over-all voting record in the UN is consistently more pro-Western than that of the average Afro-Asian bloc member.

The United Nations has now assumed a major role in Laos as the sole effective buffer between the small nation and its powerful Communist neighbors — replacing in effect the Western "tripwire" by another which, under the circumstances, may be considered as more adapted to the local situation. The form under which this United Nations protection takes place in Laos is that of a personal representative of the Secretary-General, thus avoiding approval of the mission under conditions which could give rise to a Soviet veto.

This United Nations "presence" has brought in its wake a fairly substantial UN commitment to Laotian economic and cultural development and has been the subject of severe attacks by the Communist bloc as an "unwarranted interference of the UN in Laotian internal affairs."

The ICC in Laos also has had its share of troubles. Both India and Canada felt that the Commission had fulfilled its duties in Laos after reunification of the country and the holding of free elections in May 1958, where the pro-Communist minority had seen all its rights fully respected. The third ICC member, Poland, nevertheless felt that the ICC should continue its stay in Laos. The Indian Chairman, Dr. Ansari adjourned the meetings of the Laos ICC *sine die* on July 20, 1958 — exactly four years after the Geneva cease-fire. Further British-Soviet conversations on the subject reached a deadlock in August 1958. It seems likely, however, that the ICC will not be resurrected in its old form.

Thus, in spite of repeated pressure from both East and West to pursue a policy aligned upon one of the two power blocs, the small Kingdom of Laos has in fact succeeded in pursuing its own foreign policy of "practicality" and "realism." One definition of diplomacy is that it constitutes the "art of the possible." The Laotian policymakers — save for a few minor errors for which they are largely not to blame — have on the whole shown that they have mastered this difficult art a great deal better than could have been expected.

CHARACTER OF THE ECONOMY

ALTHOUGH POSSESSING EXTENSIVE and valuable natural resources, with great potential for commercial use, Laos has the least developed economy of the three former Indochina states. Very little of the known resources in Laos have been exploited and only recently have the beginnings of a systematic geological survey been undertaken.

That its economic development is markedly lower than either Vietnam's or Cambodia's is often attributed to the role assigned Laos by the French: it was seen as a buffer against the eastern expansion of the Thai and against the British in Burma. French developmental efforts were devoted primarily to the construction of a road network to facilitate political and military administration of the area. The strain on the economic stability of France itself from two world wars and a world depression precluded going much further. Laos, in effect, remained a reserve pool of incompletely explored and almost entirely unexploited resources. There was some investment of private French capital — in tin and coffee, for example, both for export — but the effect of these enterprises on the economy was slight.

Under the development programs of the French administration, Laos became part of the Indochina economic complex and little practical importance was attached to the creation of a viable Laotian economy, now the goal of a politically independent Laos. Expenditures always exceeded revenue yielded by the local economy and international payments were always greater than foreign earnings. Deficits in both instances were met out of the surpluses derived from Cambodia and Vietnam. Today these budgetary deficits are largely made up through the operations of the American and French aid programs.

But although the low level of economic development in Laos is partly attributable to the official French design for Indochina, nature itself poses huge obstacles. Laos is a landlocked country, without easy access to the sea through either Vietnam or Cambodia, and its terrain is difficult. The colonial government took some steps to improve the "physical climate of investment," but exploitation of natural resources was left to private capital, with few inducements.

Further, certain characteristics of the Lao themselves posed labor problems for those companies that chose to invest in the country's economic possibilities. The Lao, practitioners of a subsistence agriculture eminently satisfactory to them, saw no advantage in employment for hire. The French accordingly imported Vietnamese, already trained in clerical and other skills and accustomed to working with French administrators. Hence the Laotian labor force under the French remained almost entirely agricultural and lacked even semiskilled labor.

That Laotian workers are not unsuited to modern production techniques was proved during the hostilities that followed World War II, when they were successfully trained to operate and repair military equipment. There is a certain parallel, however, between the French colonial experience and the staffing problems initially faced by United States technical aid directors, who found it necessary to import Thai, Vietnamese, Filipinos, and Chinese from Hong Kong for most clerical and specialized jobs.

The arrival of large supplies of automotive equipment and other evidences of Western technological progress in connection with technical aid programs has already had some effect on Laotian values, providing new incentives for some sectors of the population. Meanwhile the full import of the economic challenge posed by political independence is understood by only a handful of the Western-educated elite. The majority of the people continue to work for the satisfaction of traditional needs, which remain minimal by Western standards.

Lack of transportation and communication remains the major obstacle to economic development. There are, for example, less than a thousand telephones in all of Laos. Divisive barriers mark the Laotian terrain, cut into the body politic, separate urban from rural groups, and delineate economic systems based on ethnic as well as geographic factors. Industry is in its infancy and there is little or no familiarity with any type of power-driven equipment. What marketing takes place — a proportionately small amount of the value of the country's total production of goods and services — is often on a barter basis. Legal tender coinage is negligible, and paper currency is only gradually gaining acceptance throughout the country.

Village self-sufficiency at present leaves the urban centers greatly dependent on imports of rice and other foods from foreign sources and, given the transportation problem, leaves the villages themselves in serious straits if their own crops are poor. This was the situation in 1955 when rice had to be airlifted into several such areas to avert famine.

Domestic marketing of handicrafts and of produce other than rice is handled for the most part by the producers themselves. As for imported merchandise, the dealer has until recently been a composite of importer, wholesaler, and retailer. The country's banks have thus far played a negligible role in the extension of rural credit or the granting of long- and medium-term loans of the sort needed for development of the production base of the economy.

Laos nationals are beginning to enter foreign and domestic trade — until recently dominated by Chinese businessmen. Prior to 1958, the United States commodity import program, coupled with a patronage-ridden import licensing system and an unrealistic exchange rate vastly increased the number of importers and the quantity of imports into Laos. As a result Lao traders emerged in sufficient numbers and strength to pose at least a minimum challenge to the traditional position of the foreign businessman.

The import trade, which has since stabilized with the monetary reforms of late 1958, has in addition accelerated the formation of Lao-financed commercial enterprises by attracting some foreign capital into Laos. Thai as well as Chinese are known to have combined with Lao investors to capitalize on the new trade opportunities.

These shifts in commercial patterns, while promising, do not satisfy the great need for investment in the production of raw materials and consumer manufactures. It may be, however, that the considerable profits earned from trade will provide capital for the kind of investment Laos needs most of all. The fact that most business in Laos has been in Chinese hands has in the past automatically earmarked a large percentage of such profits either for expansion of those trading enterprises or for remittance abroad. There is little evidence that private Lao enterprise is likely soon to be more farseeing with respect to its country's economic requirements, which appear so far to be recognized realistically only by government officials. It may be that government itself will have to finance and operate, at least initially, enterprises which in the West are usually undertaken by private investment. The government is making some effort to encourage private capital, but the lack of adequate transport, of managerial, technical, and mechanical skills, and of information on natural resources; the hesitancy to take long-term as against short-term investment risks; and the limitations of the domestic market all combine to retard investment of both foreign capital and the relatively small amount of domestic capital.

The government is faced with the formidable problem of how to bring about the reversal of an economic condition that manifests itself in low consumption, high-price and interest-rate barriers, and perennially serious deficits in the internal budget and in international transactions. Any corrective measures must contend additionally with the political uncertainties of a newly independent country, impediments of physical geography, and generally unenthusiastic popular attitudes toward change and toward rising living standards.

In the long run, however, continued foreign economic aid and technical assistance will undoubtedly improve the productive base of the economy and the means of exploiting it. There are increasing signs of achievement both in the rural areas and in the administrative offices that must carry on the development programs beyond the duration of any external assistance program. Reconstruction and expansion of the internal transport system, use of the time- and cost-saving trade channel between Vientiane and Bangkok, and expansion of the processing plant for raw materials have already noticeably increased exports of raw materials. Recent monetary reforms have stopped a speculative import boom. With the rise in exports and the curtailment of imports, there are signs that Laos' large foreign trade deficit will continue to shrink.

A five-year general plan for the development of Laos was drawn up initially in 1952 with a projected expenditure of 900 million Indochinese piasters. The involvement of France in the Indochina war and subsequent internal difficulties and crises within Laos prevented its execution, however, and little was accomplished beyond the setting up of a National Planning and Foreign Aid Council in June 1956. In April 1959, however, the Phoui Sananikone government promulgated a Five Year Plan for the Economic and Social Development of Laos. To take effect in July 1959, the plan called for total expenditures of some four billion *kip* over the five-year period. Included in the plan were provisions for promotion and development of industries for which raw materials are available locally, increased exports, improved communications, expansion of educational and health facilities, and surveys of natural resources. While the Lao government has stated its intention of fostering private investment through such measures as loans to business and incentive legislation, it is clear that the major share of the financial burden will have to come from foreign aid sources. At present the plan remains more a "working paper" than a final blueprint.

If present government plans are to bear fruit, Laos needs most of all a sufficient, dependable, and well-managed foreign aid program together with the assurance of domestic and regional tranquility that will enable it to explore and exploit its own potential, to participate in regional programs, such as the Mekong River Project, for the development of new sources of power and a better transportation system, and to train the people necessary to run a gradually industrializing national economy.

LABOR

THE ATTAINMENT OF ECONOMIC SELF-SUFFICIENCY for Laos is dependent on the development of an industrial base, but whereas the government planners have been able to map a course for such development the lack of a skilled labor force presents an immediate practical obstacle. For centuries Laos has been an almost exclusively agricultural country — an estimated 95 percent of the population today continues to follow the traditional pattern of subsistence farming on a family scale.

High government leaders are convinced, however, that the people, despite their lack of technical experience, can be trained — slowly at first in the simpler mechanical skills and only later in complex technical projects. The reasoned gradualness of their approach seems to offer some chance for national development in the field of labor skills and may be the only workable method of preparing the country for any significant measure of industrialization.

Industrial Labor

The almost complete absence of a native industrial labor force in Laos can be explained historically in terms of both the minimal industrial development of the country and the ready availability of the more energetic Vietnamese and other foreign nationals. The industrial development that has characterized the years since independence is still limited largely to small-scale enterprises such as garages, brick works and carpenter shops in the vicinity of the few urban centers, in particular Vientiane. Sawmills, ricemills, a tobacco factory outside Vientiane, the Nam Patene tin mine, and the construction projects incident to foreign aid programs constitute the major employers of industrial labor. The country's limited, but growing, transportation and commercial facilities employ some additional labor.

Prior to 1920 operations at the tin mine of the Nam Patene basin in Khammouane province were conducted on a small scale by native workers using primitive methods. In 1923 a French company took over, introducing modern methods and at the same time importing over six thousand Annamese from what is now Vietnam. Operations were interrupted by World War II and the Vietminh invasion of 1953, the latter causing much damage to the mining equipment, but tin is again being mined there although by a reduced force which in 1957 numbered about seven hundred laborers, principally Vietnamese. The recent installation of modern plant equipment and the resultant increase in production will undoubtedly result in the employment of a larger labor force.

The composition and size of the labor force employed at the sawmills, which are often in geographically remote areas, are more difficult to ascertain. The seasonal nature of most operations, carried out in the dry season following the harvest, makes likely the employment of local inhabitants, and indentured Kha are known to be used at some sawmills.

Only at Vientiane and Luang Prabang is urban construction sufficiently continuous or intensive to permit the regular employment of building trades workers, but as no statistics are kept on these workers knowledge of the composition or size of the construction force is limited to the reports of observers. Few Laotians are employed in the industry, and much of the heavy work is left to Kha villagers and coolie labor from northeast Thailand. These coolies, in some cases women, can be seen carrying bricks to the masons, mixing concrete, making excavations, and doing most other heavy tasks. Local contracting firms are largely in Thai hands whereas the foremen and skilled workers on these jobs are in many cases Vietnamese.

In a country where human strength and hand tools remain the major means for moving earth or for building and maintaining roads there is continuing demand for coolie labor. The recent arrival of bulldozers, tractors, power shovels, and other modern mechanical equipment from the United States may well produce rapid changes in this field but it is too soon to predict the effect on labor conditions that foreign technical assistance will cause. Foreign aid teams have found their problems many. Laotians happily and quickly learned to operate the first bulldozers, for instance, but being without mechanical knowledge proceeded almost as quickly to run the new equipment into disrepair for lack of lubrication. Their training in the operation and maintenance of machinery is proceeding under technical assistance programs.

This general labor pattern can also be observed in the country's commercial and transportation activities where loading, unloading, lifting, and moving — all done by hand — are coolie functions. A few drivers and mechanics are the only skilled workers employed by the trucking companies. The airlines, on the other hand, are providing more and more opportunities for mechanics, pilots, and other technical and skilled personnel and there is good reason to expect a rapid increase in the number of skilled workers in Laos as modernization proceeds.

Migratory labor is practically nonexistent and at present there seems to be no significant drift toward urban employment. Very little is known about the social or geographic source of such urban labor force as exists. There was in Vientiane in 1958, however, a colony of perhaps three thousand Black Tai, refugees from Communist rule in North Vietnam and the border regions, who at that time furnished most of the labor in the brickyards that were supplying building activities.

Handicraft Workers

Throughout Laos handicrafting forms an integral part of the generally self-sufficient village economy and occupies large numbers of people. Although handicraft products are fashioned by villagers primarily for home consumption, more intricate items requiring a higher degree of artistry and skill will sometimes be produced by a few village artisans and in certain cases become the specialty of a particular village or locale. Lacquering, goldsmithing, and silversmithing, for example, are practiced in a few areas, mainly in and around Luang Prabang, where royal patronage is assured.

In the larger Lao villages there may be found blacksmiths and forgers. Brick and pottery making, distilling, and ironworking are widespread as specialties of individual villages, although the fashioning of simple iron plow points is done by Lao villagers everywhere.

In certain areas along the rivers women specialize in weaving silk fabrics of intricate design for use in making traditional skirts, *sampots*, scarves, and other wearing apparel. Lao village women have always been skilled in spinning and weaving fabrics for the family wardrobe. In some areas, particularly around Vientiane, this skill is today beginning to disappear. Cotton is cleaned and prepared for spinning, sometimes with the help of the children, and in localities where silk is more plentiful than cotton women learn to tend the silkworms and unwind the cocoons as they are ready.

Qualitative Factors and Productivity

Regarding the question which has been raised about the quality and efficiency of labor in Laos and the capacity of the Laotian to absorb instruction in labor skills, it must be remembered that effective French control in Laos lasted only about half as long as it did in most of Vietnam and Cambodia, and that the country was in general run with a much lighter hand. Further, for one reason and another, the French made no serious effort to make Laos productive of goods or income; they did little to raise the standard of living — already satisfactory to the Laotian — and created few demands which would cause the Lao to enter the labor force in order to earn money to satisfy such demands. Also, the French had at hand a superfluity of Vietnamese, skilled or partially so. This removed much of the necessity of training Laotians to perform such labor as seemed needed. It thus appears entirely possible, on the evidence, that the Laotian's reputation for indolence and inability — or lack of desire — to learn is traceable principally to sheer lack of opportunity.

This situation changed with the creation in 1949 of the three Associated States and with the build-up of the Royal Laotian (as distinct from French Colonial) Army. The French then began with some success to train Lao soldiers as technicians of various kinds. The experience of one group of Americans (related in a 1956 issue of the *Christian Science Monitor*) testifies in some degree to this success and to the transferability to industrial fields of the skills taught the Lao soldier. Said one member:

> You ought to visit a [military] machinery repair shop. There the workers are all Laotians. They were trained by the French. They do not use our methods but I can tell you it is a good operation. You know what a military machine is like? I can show you Laotian boys who are really expert in handling one. If you can handle a military machine you can handle most anything.

Civilian workers with the French army have been trained successfully to do many kinds of jobs, some of them quite intricate and calling for a high degree of skill, through a form of apprenticeship in which skilled French workers worked next to Laotians on modern machine tools over considerable periods. There are native Lao now operating metalworking lathes, boring machines, planers, and other equipment. In addition the French have provided training, much of it in France, in various skills connected with military operations, such as that of pilot, meteorologist, and radio operator.

On balance, it seems unlikely that the inhabitants of Laos, unhabituated though they are to an economy based on mechanized industry, present any more obstacles to technical training, when need appears, than do the people of any other underdeveloped country; in fact, they may be more adaptable than some.

Wages and Benefits

Although foreign aid programs are creating some new job opportunities, the number of full-time wage earners in Laos remains relatively small and wage rates and worker benefits are of little interest to the people at large. Part-time agricultural wage workers are often paid in kind or possibly silver but generally tend to avoid payment in paper *kip* (the basic currency unit of Laos). As the number of wage earners increases this situation will change, as in Vientiane and other urban centers where the payment of wages in paper *kip* by the government and other employers has long been the rule.

Common laborers doing such work as road building and maintenance, ditch digging, or the heavy lifting and carrying jobs on building construction averaged 35 *kip* a day in 1956 (one dollar at the official rate at that time of 35 *kip* to $1.00). The average wages of skilled, semiskilled, and unskilled workers as paid by the Ministry of Public Works and private contractors in 1956 are given in detail in Table 8.

To almost all wages and salaries in Laos is added the so-called family allowance. An official order issued by the High Commissioner for Indochina on September 26, 1947 authorized Laos and the other Indochina states to set up a scale of family allowances to be paid by privately owned businesses to their employees over and above their wages or salaries. This provision for differential wages on the basis of family size seems to have been revived by independent Laos and to be generally enforced both in private industry

and within the government itself. Government employees currently receive allowances ranging from 800 to 950 *kip* per month for a
wife (80 *kip*=$1.00) and from 400 to 500 *kip* for each child.

The great majority of white-collar workers in Laos are government employees, divisible into clerks and officials or teachers.
Within the four major categories of the civil service may be found
nearly all government staff, from beginning clerks and technicians
to provincial governors and ambassadors; government salaries
therefore vary widely (see Table 9 for the salaries paid in 1959 to
government personnel in Luang Prabang).

Meo and Thai women are frequently to be observed among
the coolies working on construction projects in the vicinity of
urban centers. From time to time young women will be found working for shopkeepers and there are growing numbers of young Lao
women seeking clerical and secretarial work in government offices.
Although women are being increasingly employed in commerce
and industry their wages, somewhat less than male wages, are
still a relatively unimportant factor in the wage-labor picture.

Employer and Employee

Virtually all of the relatively few industrial and commercial entre-
preneurs are of foreign extraction although Lao businessmen are
increasingly in a position to lend money to such enterprises and
in some cases have a voice in their management. As mentioned,
the tin mines are owned and operated by a French company; most
of the shopkeepers in the cities are Vietnamese and Chinese; many
small service and hand manufacture operations are conducted by
Vietnamese, Indians, and Pakistani; construction firms are most often in Thai hands. By far the greatest number of the individual
enterprises employ but one or a few workers, and employment,
working conditions, grievances, and discharge are evidently matters
of direct negotiation and thoroughly under the control of the employer. Laxness in application of the Labor Code (see below) permits private employers in most instances to make the wage determination, offering no incentives and paying no more than they are
obliged to in order to attract the workers they need.

Where labor recruiting is necessary workers customarily are
hired through a labor contractor, or *cai*, who makes it his business
to know where he can hire individuals and groups of workers. The
cai, who sometimes also acts as gang foreman, is given a lump sum
by the employer from which he pays the workers after deducting

his fee from each man's wages. Abuses are common; the *cai* usually holds out as much as he can for himself.

Another hiring method, most often found in the provinces, uses provincial chiefs, who keep registers of workers who apply to them and try as well to keep posted on where laborers are needed. When an employer needs workers, he notifies the chief.

Workers are discharged at the completion of the job or at the will of the employer at any time. Customs regarding "notice" and severance pay are apparently unknown.

Lao workers generally are deferential toward employers and supervisors. Girls who work in shops are reported to be very respectful of their employers, and this trait is even more pronounced in the coolies who do heavy labor on the roads and public works. In the countryside deference to the point of obsequiousness is commonly exhibited toward persons of authority, most of whom, outside of government, are foreigners.

In the cities, on the other hand, employer-employee relations are noticeably more relaxed and there is greater awareness among workers of their rights. The only formal organization of workers of any kind in the country at present is the Government Employees Association in Vientiane, to which apparently most white-collar workers of the civil service belong. The protection of members' interests through such means as grievance committees is one of the purposes of this organization.

The Labor Code

Unlike Vietnam, Laos has not made changes in its labor legislation since the withdrawal of the French colonial administration: the Labor Code of 1937 as promulgated by the French for Indochina is still the basis of Laotian labor law. A more recent labor code, which would have brought Indochinese labor legislation more into line with the labor laws of Metropolitan France, was proposed at the Dalat Economic Conference in November 1947 but has never been put into effect.

A General Inspectorate of Labor and Social Welfare was established under the governor general of Indochina by a decree dated November 22, 1937. The decree also provided that labor administration in each Associated State be handled locally, with national administration only for larger operations such as mines and railways. Laos already had (by a French ordinance of 1927) part-time "labor controllers" whose responsibility was the enforcement of existing labor laws.

The Labor Code is in fact all but inoperative at present. Only a substantial development of industry seems likely to change that fact.

The Code provides for conciliation and arbitration of labor disputes; in cases that go to arbitration, the decisions of the boards of settlement are final. It is doubtful, however, that arbitration is frequently employed, for disputes are few and usually settled by the parties involved.

Certain provisions of the Code are for the protection of contract labor. Contracts must specify the period during which work is guaranteed. Free transportation to the place of work and reparation after conclusion of the contract are called for. The Code stipulates that minimum daily wages, which do not include food and lodging, shall be established.

Women may not work underground or do any night work in factories, quarries, yards, and workshops. Children under twelve years of age are not permitted to work in industrial or commercial enterprises. Boys under eighteen and all women are prohibited from working between the hours of 11 P.M. and 5 A.M., except in agriculture.

A French decree of October 25, 1927 prohibits work by contract laborers in excess of ten hours a day unless paid at the rate of one and a half times the normal, provides penalties for contract workers in agriculture who leave their work without justification, authorizes the imposition of fines or imprisonment, or both, on striking noncontract workers. Another decree provides that compulsory minimum wages shall be fixed in all industrial and commercial occupations, and that wages must be paid at least once monthly and within ten days of the date they are due. Base-pay standards plus a bonus linked with the cost-of-living index by an escalator clause were set in December 1945. Vacations with pay for all industrial and commercial workers are also provided for. Apprentices may be employed in a proportion of one for each ten skilled workers but there is nothing in the Labor Code to indicate how much apprentices shall be paid.

In a country where government officials have been known to accept favors for permitting breaches of the law, the nuisance value of the Labor Code could be used to put pressure on the larger employers of labor. Foreign-owned enterprises could become the natural target — being forced to deal generously with officials as an alternative to finding themselves unreasonably harried about compliance with the provisions of the Code — and there is reportedly some evidence of a tendency in this direction.

Requisitioned and Indentured Labor

Forced labor was abolished by the French and is not legally sanctioned in Laos at present although a form of corvée is permitted in the north in the Kha territory.

The people of Laos have, however, known forced labor, even slavery, in the relatively recent past and it is recalled with aversion. The historian, Le Boulanger, discussing the period between 1300 and 1700, states that slaves could be captured in war, acquired for debt, and bought and sold. In addition certain Kha tribes were regularly pressed into serfdom by the king, princes, and powerful nobles. A French order of 1914, reminiscent of the corvée, called for an assessment of taxes in the form of labor on natives of Laos and other assimilated Asiatics. Although very unpopular the order remained in force until 1941.

In reply to a questionnaire from the International Labor Organization, the Kingdom of Laos answered that, under specific regulations, workers for porterage may be requisitioned. These workers are pressed into service to overcome serious transport difficulties in certain mountainous regions and must be paid in accordance with wage scales established by royal decree. The government added that "such requisitions have been diminishing and will soon be unnecessary in view of the progress achieved in road, inland waterway, and air transport." In view of the still serious condition of much of the road system, it is doubtful however if porterage service, at least in the hinterland, can be reduced for some time to come.

There are in Laos a considerable number of indentured laborers who over the years have fallen into a sort of debt peonage forced upon them through inability to support themselves. For many years members of the Kha tribes and occasionally the tribal Tai have worked as indentured labor. In years of rice crop failure it is not uncommon for Kha tribesmen to offer themselves for work in Lao rice fields or lumber camps.

Tribal women may also offer themselves for work, often as domestics in the homes of Lao families. The pay is perhaps a few *kip* a year. If they bring along a child who must be fed and housed as well, even this much may not be offered.

A few indentured Kha live in small camps while working at the Lao sawmills and in the rice fields. Their treatment under these conditions does not appear to be very good and is reportedly deeply resented. In theory, the indentured Kha can leave their work; economically and traditionally this is hardly possible.

PUBLIC HEALTH AND WELFARE

THE LAO HAVE RETAINED MANY OF THEIR traditional ideas and practices relating to illness and disease while at the same time accepting some of the methods and ideas of the West. The degree of acceptance of Western medical techniques varies among different classes and areas, but even the most educated Lao may call both a Buddhist monk to perform traditional practices and a Western-trained doctor to prescribe Western-type medication.

Long accustomed to the use of medicines made by herb-doctors, the Lao will usually accept equivalent Western medicines when these can be shown to be superior. They still, however, tend to reject the notion that many of their common ailments — such as malaria, parasites and dysentery — do not result from the activities of evil spirits but from preventable natural causes.

Given the cohesive village communities typical of Laos, it is easy to see why no concept of government responsibility for group welfare developed. The thousands of villages, each usually with its own pagoda, were and to a large degree still are self-contained social units. Village self-sufficiency in matters of public health and welfare was complete, so far as the problems were recognized. Unemployment in the Western sense does not, in fact, exist in a subsistence- farming community, and the aged and otherwise handicapped are supported within the family as a matter of course. Among the mountain peoples isolation and self-dependence is, if anything, more pronounced.

In the past, government centers intermediate between village and ruler — such as the *muong* or district — were concerned solely with general administration and tax-collecting. The royal court found little reason to concern itself about things that normally took care of themselves. Government, then, had neither cause nor inclination to intervene in matters of public welfare.

16. Public Health and Welfare

As for Buddhism, even in areas where it is quite thoroughly institutionalized, it remains a religion which emphasizes the individual's responsibility in determining his own destiny. The bonze is in no sense the pastor of a flock. The pagoda assumes no responsibility for the general welfare of the village; it is itself dependent on the village for material benefits. The net result of these social attitudes is that first the family, then the village, look after their own and expect no aid, even from other villages. If disaster strikes a person, his family and neighbors will help him. Villages will cooperate when floods or typhoons bring destruction to the rice fields and dwellings, but no aid is expected from the government or from the local aristocracy. There is, however, a tradition of public service or private charity by high-ranking officials operating within the framework of the established social structure.

French efforts were largely concentrated on establishing public health facilities and these services accustomed hundreds of thousands of Laotians to receiving direct aid from the state at the provincial level. The French also introduced the first sanitary regulations and the first legislation (labor regulations protecting plantation and mine workers) bearing in any way on the subject of social welfare. In cases of large-scale natural disasters, government aid was provided. Some other welfare activities were initiated by Christian missionary organizations, which founded and operated, for example, orphanages and leper colonies.

When an independent Laos undertook to govern itself it created a national Ministry of Health out of the former French health services and in 1948 formed the Ministry of Social Affairs (Prévoyance Sociale). While the Ministry of Health was concerned with the care of persons already ailing, the new ministry assumed responsibility for preventive protection of the population in matters of health, sanitation, living conditions, and labor.

The first efforts of the Ministry of Social Affairs were directed toward providing nutritional, prenatal, and other social services. Today its functions have been considerably expanded. One of the most notable efforts is that of the Ministry's Commission of Rural Affairs, whose special concern is village development, in particular the building of roads, wells, rest houses, and schools. In addition, the Ministry of Education has with the help of UNESCO been pursuing a program of "fundamental education" using Lao teachers trained at centers in Thailand.

Nongovernmental organizations are also playing an important role today. These include the Lao Red Cross which provides emergency aid in case of disaster, and the Lao Women's Association which, in addition to aid in emergencies has also been interested in rural extension work. The Filipino medical organization, Operation Brotherhood, also includes social workers on its staffs scattered in rural areas throughout the country, and the American International Voluntary Service group, too, has done work in the field of social welfare.

The large number of refugees from both North Vietnam and China have placed a major strain on the limited resources of the Lao government as well as on the voluntary organizations, but attempts have been made to cope with the problem in terms of providing food and clothing and also attempting to effect permanent resettlement. Significant aid in the implementation of these programs has been received from the American aid mission.

Standard of Living

Although low by Western criteria, living standards are high in Laos as compared with those of some other Asian countries. By Lao standards the majority of the people are adequately fed, housed, and clothed. But hunger is sometimes known before harvest time, and many people, particularly in the mountain regions, shiver through the night during the cold winter months. Class differences exist, but the Western-educated and Western-oriented aristocracy is small, and though its accumulation of wealth permits it much greater ostentation in the display of material possessions, traditionally its basic tastes in the matter of diet and dress are not far removed from the general standards. The gap appears to be widening, and the manner of living of the elite occasions increasing resentment which is exploited by the Pathet Lao. Among the majority of the population living standards vary within a relatively narrow range. There is no concentration of land resources by a few, no notable land scarcity, and no grinding poverty, although many of the Kha peoples are impoverished compared to the valley Lao.

Once having acquired the necessities of life, rural Lao generally show little further concern for acquisition except for articles that play a part in their religious festivals and family ceremonies. The hoarding or hiding of wealth is not customary among the Lao. When there is surplus, the adornment of the women of the household appears to be somewhat more significant than improvement in either housing or food, for such adornment affects family ranking in the community. In villages nearer the towns, manufactured items such as bicycles, clothing, and cigarettes have become increasingly important.

As important to the Lao family as its own living requirements — and sometimes more important — are its contribution to the pagoda, the bonzes, and the frequent festivals that revolve around the pagoda. Every family contributes according to its abilities. The usual daily food contribution of a family to the bonzes is about two bowls of rice and corresponding quantities of other available food. Additional gifts of poultry, fish, or other items are made on special occasions. Preparation for festivals at the pagoda may be both costly and time-consuming, occupying the whole village population for days in advance. Work for the festival brings religious merit and also gives pleasure — two high-ranking values in Lao culture.

The villager cultivates as much as he wants to eat — and very little more. A single rice crop is often raised where two could be grown. The attitude regarding food production was well expressed by the response of some village chiefs to a French governor who was demonstrating means by which rice production could be doubled. The village leaders were delighted because the new method would enable the villagers to work only half as hard to grow their accustomed crop. There is evidence that this attitude has begun to change, at least in the areas of the major towns where there is an increasing demand for agricultural products. For example, Vientiane now imports less food from Thailand than was the case five years ago.

Even in times of rice crop failure acute hunger is unusual in the lowland regions, for there are a number of secondary and dry crops to fall back on, some of which are planted as a safety measure as well as a dietary supplement. There are also many roots and fruits available in the forests along the rivers, near the main populated areas. For the mountain tribes, who lack the resources of the lowland dwellers, crop failures may be more serious, but they can rely on hunting to a great extent.

The Lao is a moderate eater. The mainstays of his diet are glutinous rice, vegetables, fish or fish sauce, meat, eggs, and fruit. He eats three meals daily, a typical meal consisting of rice flavored with hot peppers, fish paste, or sometimes a curry of vegetables. Meat is eaten on rare occasions, fish and eggs somewhat more often. A variety of fruit is eaten in season. Many meals consist of little more than rice and pimentos, and perhaps some *padek,* the universal fish paste or sauce made of salted fermented fish.

This sauce retains many of the proteins, minerals, and vitamins of fresh fish but is inadequate as a complete substitute. Insects, frogs, and small fish provide important supplements to the Lao diet. It would not be difficult to grow more beans to fill the protein requirements, but this is rarely done. One Western health official has estimated that an average adult consumes about one pound of rice daily.

The average family garden provides Chinese cabbage, green peppers, pimentos, beans, and onions. Yams, pumpkins, gourds, and melons are also grown. Pineapples, bananas, mangoes, papayas, coconuts, and other fruits are produced on the family plots for local consumption, while sugar is obtained from sugar palms, wild honey, or more recently, from sugar cane. Yet despite this potential or actual variety, the diet is often deficient because not enough of these products are grown or eaten.

Nearly all families raise a few pigs and poultry, and some own water buffalo for field labor. Some households have a few head of cattle as well. The buffalo are generally eaten only on very special festival occasions, although they may be used for food when they are old or have been killed accidentally. Beef is costly and is eaten only rarely.

There is little the Lao will not use for food in the infrequent times of crop failure, but he does not consume milk, cheese, butter, or other milk products. (Many people are, however, acquiring a taste for canned milk and discussions are under way to introduce dairy cattle in some of the plateau areas.) An overdependence on milled rice is a contributory factor to malnutrition although here the Lao may fare better than villagers in Thailand since his foot-operated mills leave part of the hull protein intact.

Cheap Western clothing, particularly for working dress, is rapidly making inroads on the colorful and often costly traditional costumes of the various ethnic groups of Laos. Throughout much of the country, clothing for work consists of odd, nondescript pieces: for men, Western shorts and perhaps a shirt; for women, a wrap-around skirt and a cotton blouse or halter.

On festive occasions, however, traditional hand-woven attire still predominates. Even the most Westernized males retain the *sampot* (the iridescent silk knee-length trousers formed by drawing the ends of a sarong-type skirt between the legs) below a white formal jacket, worn on all important ceremonial occasions. All Lao women wear the traditional silk skirt with its wide band of intricately woven silver or gold trim around the hem. Under the silk scarf that once served alone as an upper drape to the costume, women now add a blouse, especially for daytime wear.

The Lao skirt is a special source of pride and a woman will usually own several of these costly hand-loomed silk garments. All Lao women, no matter how Westernized, retain this skirt even when traveling abroad. Expensive clothing and jewelry when worn by a woman are important symbols of her family's prestige and wealth, although these items are, of course, more modest and limited in the rural areas. Women's jewelry is in effect a Lao family's "bank account," much surplus family wealth being invested in this manner. Many of the ethnic minority groups find similar use for jewelry. The extensive use of silver jewelry by Meo men as well as women is a reflection of the profits derived from raising opium.

Only a small minority of the urban elite have adopted French-style houses built of brick, wood, stone, or more recently, stucco and poured concrete. For most people housing is a relatively simple matter. Materials are supplied by the neighboring forest and the labor by the householder, his family, and possibly his neighbors. The typical house is rectangular with a covered veranda along one side, and faces the stream near which the Lao builds whenever he can. Supported on wooden piles, the house is constructed at a level of six to eight feet above the ground. Split bamboo floors, woven bamboo walls, and thatched roofs are traditional. Plank floors, wooden walls, and galvanized tin roofs are generally regarded as signs of prosperity and prestige, particularly in rural areas.

The open construction facilitates ventilation in the subtropical climate, despite the small number of window openings. The house interior is lighted at night by candles when necessary, or more rarely by kerosene lamps. Electricity is available only in the few larger urban areas, and even there the supply is uncertain and restricted. Furnishings are simple — mattresses or sleeping mats, low wicker stools, blankets, chests or suitcases for storing clothes, floor mats, and cooking utensils nearly complete the inventory. Chairs and tables are a recent innovation in rural areas and are limited to the more prosperous homes.

The area beneath the house serves as a stable for farm animals and here, too, may be the loom and other household tools and equipment. The harvest is usually placed in a separate storehouse. Cooking may be done in a separate small building or in a sand pit at one end of the veranda, but sometimes the kitchen is combined with the storehouse. Near the house will be found the

178

foot-operated mill in which rice is husked daily. While Lao-style houses are light in construction, they are cool and comfortable and usually provide adequate protection from storms. The more prosperous homes with plank or wattle-and-daub walls are much less effectively ventilated.

Household garbage is fed to the chickens and pigs with the result that flies are abundant but the Laotians, who are generally unaware that there are fly-borne diseases, do not seem to be bothered.

Each rural family supplies much of its own food and clothing needs, although the household is dependent upon outsiders for salt, iron, and a few other essential items, and may buy locally-made soap, jewelry, and the rice wine used for ceremonies. Extensive trade takes place between the lowland Lao and the mountain peoples, each supplementing the products and manufactures of the other.

Sanitation

The valley Lao, by preference a clean people, bathe frequently, although in contaminated water which may contain disease parasites. Poor sanitation, particularly among the hill people, and especially among the Kha, ranks high among the major health problems of Laos. Only a few major towns and villages have a sanitary water supply, and still fewer have running water. Most of the villages draw water for all purposes from the rivers and streams in the rainy season and from unsanitary open wells in the dry season. Until sanitary wells can be introduced for year-round use, control of water-borne infections will be difficult.

The disposal of human waste presents another very serious sanitation problem. It represents an important cause of water pollution and parasitic infection, although it is not generally used as fertilizer as it is in China and Vietnam. The river or a nearby stream may be used, or surface defecation may be practiced. A more common method is the "cat-hole" system, where a person digs a small hole and then covers the waste with a thin layer of dirt. "Cat-hole" disposal is a greater breeder of parasites than surface disposal. Hookworm eggs thrive in the moist earth, and worm parasites have been known to work their way up through as much as 30 inches of loose soil.

Prevailing food-handling techniques and eating habits are a source of many infections. No protection is provided against the ever-present flies and other insects, no refrigeration is available, and no system of food preservation is practiced other than pickling, drying, or smoking. The habit of eating raw pork and raw fish causes many parasitic infections.

Meals are customarily served in a common bowl set on the floor mat, around which the entire family sits; all dip their hands into the bowl. Hands are usually washed before and after eating, but the water used is often not sanitary. Chopsticks are used by many mountain Tai tribes and by some other hill people of relatively recent migration from China.

Lao and foreign health officials are attempting to improve both urban and rural sanitation, but there is much apathy and ignorance to be overcome. It is difficult, for example, to convince a villager that an age-old preference for taking water from a running stream may be the cause of his illness.

Disease

The greatest single problem in Laos is malaria, despite the extensive house spraying and other anti-malaria work that has been under way for years. It is of incalculable cost to the country in suffering, loss of life, and working energy. With American aid, extensive spraying is now going on and a real attempt is being made to eradicate malaria in Laos.

Malaria is found in all parts of the country but the incidence and type varies with latitude and altitude. Of the three types found, two of them, *plasmodium falciparum* and *plasmodium vivax*, account for 94 percent of the cases. Double infections are common, although the latter type is most often found in the northern section and in the higher altitudes while the former is most prevalent in the lowlands and the south. The incidence of malaria among children tested in the more seriously infected regions runs to above 70 percent.

Acute upper respiratory infections, including pneumonias and influenzas, cause much sickness and death throughout the country, particularly in the cooler northern regions. Among many of the mountain peoples their incidence is aggravated by a lack of adequate clothing.

Bacterial and protozoal diarrhea and dysentery, including the amoebic type, are very prevalent and very costly in lives and labor.

Perhaps even more widespread are the parasites. In surveys of

school-age children, over 70 percent were found to be infected
with one or more types of parasite. Roundworm, tapeworm, hookworm, and strongyloides are common, along with other types.
Owing to the habit of eating uncooked freshwater fish and snails,
oriental liver flukes are also frequently found. Even if the patient
is cured of his parasites, reinfection will be almost certain until
age-old habits of preparing and eating food and of disposal of
human waste are changed.

Yaws remains a serious problem, especially in southern Laos.
The work done in yaws control with penicillin injections by the
Laotian government in collaboration with World Health Organization experts has been successful, although surveys in southern
provinces still show an incidence of serious yaws cases ranging
up to 19 percent. Yaws is a serious drain on the country, invalidat-
ing many for military service and for labor generally.

A large variety of skin ailments, fungal and nonfungal, comprise a significant part of the cases treated in the infirmaries and
clinics throughout Laos. These frequently are made more serious
by the lack of resistance due to the prevalent dietary imbalance,
which permits a slight infection to develop into large persistent
ulcers.

Acute diseases of childhood cost many lives. Although most
children contract mumps, whooping cough, chicken pox, and
measles, and a few also suffer from scarlet fever and diphtheria,
there is no national program of immunization for this group of
diseases.

Tuberculosis ranks tenth in over-all prevalence in Laos and is
receiving considerable attention from health authorities. A disproportionate part of the hospital beds are occupied by advanced
pulmonary tuberculosis cases which come to the hospital too late
for effective treatment. In some provinces 24 percent of hospital
deaths are from this cause. Dietary deficiencies are probably a
factor in the susceptibility to tuberculosis.

Venereal diseases are found throughout the country, but in
varying incidence. They are concentrated mainly in the urban
centers along the Mekong, but military operations have spread
them more widely. Gonorrhea is the most common type. Syphilis
is believed by the Lao to have been introduced by Siamese soldiers
shortly before the French took over. Although prior to World War
II the mountain tribes were not generally affected, subsequent
infection of some Kha villages in areas where Japanese soldiers

were garrisoned has, according to one American doctor, reached as high as 100 percent of all adults. The recent widespread use of penicillin has shown good results, but no organized education and popular information program for venereal diseases exists, and the acceptance of the establishment of brothels near military camps has not helped the situation.

The three hundred registered leprosy cases probably represent a fraction of the total number of those afflicted, which, according to one American observer, in some southern regions may amount to three percent of the population. Only a part of those registered and isolated are receiving adequate treatment. Lepers are social outcasts and their care is left largely to members of Catholic orders with no medical training. Where isolation is attempted, no regular method has been worked out to separate patients from their families, even when there are small children not yet afflicted.

Trachoma is endemic in Laos, though not so seriously as in Vietnam. There are no areas of high concentration. Cases are treated in local medical centers or infirmaries rather than by mobile teams as in Vietnam.

Other diseases found occasionally are rabies, tetanus, typhoid fever, and louse- and tick-form typhus (chiefly in winter months). Typhoid and para-typhoid are endemic in Laos. Provinces along the Chinese border also report some cases of encephalitis and cholera. Rheumatism and arthritis are frequent complaints, and diabetes cases appear, but not on a major scale. Visible goiters are found more among hill-dwellers than in the lowlands.

Caries and other dental problems are widespread, although the painting of teeth and the chewing of betel-nut are alleged to have some protective value. Laotians claim they have better teeth than do Europeans. Prophylactic dental programs are very poorly organized in the urban centers and are nonexistent in rural areas.

Beriberi and pellagra are the most common diet-deficiency diseases, but others are present. Vitamin deficiency also contributes to the severity of the infectious diseases and causes some fatalities.

Before the French came to Laos there were few if any differences in health conditions or outlook between different classes or between urban and rural areas. Today, although there are still very few true urban centers, conditions have changed sufficiently to affect the relative incidence of certain diseases and to change health attitudes.

The limited health facilities and few Western-trained doctors

182

and nurses are concentrated largely in urban areas. The urban population has thus had more chance to learn about Western medical practices, and their accessibility has reduced the incidence of many ailments. Because of improved sanitation and the use of medicines, malaria is now less prevalent. Prenatal and postnatal child care has reduced infant mortality rates. Paved streets, the wearing of shoes, and better disposal of human waste have reduced in recent years the incidence of hookworm in the towns. Many minor ailments such as skin diseases, which might go untreated and become serious in the villages, are now quickly attended to in the provincial capitals.

On the other hand, tuberculosis and venereal diseases are most prevalent in the towns. Dietary deficiency diseases, especially those caused by lack of vitamin B, are most common in the urban areas where fresh vegetables and fruits must be bought and where the habit of eating white polished rice has been acquired, with the consequent loss of the completely milled-off vitamin-bearing bran. Conversely, the people in the country — though their diet is generally better balanced — have poorer sanitation and less knowledge of and access to modern health practices and facilities. They suffer more from malaria, hookworm, yaws, trachoma, diarrhea, parasites, and skin diseases.

Traditional Practices and Attitudes

The Lao ascribes disease to pathological causes, the intervention of malevolent *phi* (spirits), or the departure from the body of one of its thirty-two souls. Treatment for an ailment depends on its cause. One traditional method of determining cause is to examine the contents of a fresh egg broken according to prescribed ritual: the condition of the yolk will determine which of the various types of healers should be summoned to treat the case — an herb-doctor, a shaman, or an elderly bonze. All except the bonze expect remuneration for their services, and this varies with the wealth of the patient. In at least some cases more than one kind of healer is called upon.

The herb-doctor, who handles most cases, combines prayers and ritual formulas and prescribes a variety of herbs, roots, powdered bones and horns, and other materials. His knowledge, drawn from the traditional medical practices of India and China, is handed down orally from generation to generation, usually within one family. Most housewives know at least some of the more common remedies. Western doctors have come to respect many of these traditional medicines; chaulmoogra oil for leprosy is an outstanding example.

The Lao herb-doctor can relieve pain and eliminate or alleviate some fevers, diarrhea, and other symptoms of the more common ailments of Laos. A cure may not always be effected but the patient who has been relieved of his misery does not distinguish between temporary relief and permanent cure; good health is absence of pain and recurrence of the same symptoms tends to be viewed as a new ailment.

Several types of *phi* may cause sickness. The function of the shaman is to decide which spirit is the culprit and what offended it, and then to propitiate or eliminate the *phi* by appropriate ceremonies and offerings. This must be done carefully to avoid offending other *phi*. As protection against evil *phi*, amulets are worn and rites periodically performed.

Many Laotians believe sorcerers can induce illness or death from a distance by causing foreign objects to intrude themselves into the body of a person over whom they cast a spell. If this is suspected a specialist is called to remove the object, which he locates by various rites and "removes" either by sucking or biting or by causing the patient to vomit. The object removed may be a stone, a chicken bone, a piece of leather, or some similar object.

The Lao believe that the body houses thirty-two *khouan,* or souls, one for each bodily function or intellectual faculty. Only when all thirty-two are present and functioning is the body well. Should one wander off for some reason, the corresponding organ ceases to function. In such cases the bonze entices the wandering soul to return; this he does by performing a ritual of calling the soul, or *soukhouan.* (Variations of this ceremony are also performed for other occasions such as weddings.) The amulet used to prevent the escape of any of the *khouan* from the body is a white cotton string, which is blessed and tied around the wrist.

The Lao have come to accept many Western medical techniques as complementing, but not replacing, their traditional practices. Under French control they were introduced to vaccination, quinine, penicillin, and other modern innovations. From the outset French army units provided medical services to the civilian population wherever they operated. An active Indochinese Public Health and Medical Service, founded by the French, built hos-

pitals in the towns (Vientiane, Luang Prabang, Thakhek, Savannakhet, Pakse, and Xiengkhouang) and established infirmaries or dispensaries, several maternity centers, and first-aid stations in many
rural areas. Health officers were appointed for the provinces. The
facilities of the famous Pasteur Institute in Saigon which manufactured drugs and vaccines and studied local health problems, and
those of the Hanoi Medical School and of other French public
health services and schools were available to Laotians as well as to
Vietnamese and Cambodians.

Although public health services were gradually improved
during French rule, lack of sufficient money and personnel restricted most of their benefits to the urban populations. Nevertheless, hundreds of thousands of rural inhabitants received treatment
at one time or another — vaccinations for smallpox or cholera, occasional injections and other medicines, hospital treatment or first
aid. Even outlying hill tribes received medical treatment from
army units that policed these areas. Public health officers or French
army medical personnel, who periodically toured the provinces,
often could do no more than administer first aid or direct serious
cases to an urban hospital. Yet these occasional services over a
period of fifty years, together with the easily proved value of many
Western medicines such as quinine, awakened real respect for
Western-trained doctors.

Present Facilities and Organization

Prior to 1945 the health service of Laos was directed by French
officials headed by a director of health. In each province French
doctors were charged with maintenance of public health, and four
other European doctors directed the government laboratories and
mobile health units. Many of the more routine duties were performed by *médecins indochinois*, working under the supervision of
these European official doctors. Public health services suffered
disruption at the end of World War II but eventually were reor-
ganized under a Ministry of Public Health at Vientiane. The Ministry was actually established in 1948. Later all responsibilities for
public health and sanitation were transferred from French to Lao
officials.

Since then the ministry has established departments and
placed a chief doctor in each province to take charge of health
activities and facilities. An effort has been made to maintain

services in the various hospitals, infirmaries, and dispensaries previously set up by the French. Most provincial medical centers are in fact little more than dispensaries. In 1957 there were 113 health facilities of various kinds in Laos (see Table 10).

It was the intent of the Western-educated, French-guided framers of the new government of Laos to establish a reasonably complete public health system on the French model and to insure as far as possible the benefits of the work the French had already done in that field. Filling the posts thus created and replacing the French incumbents with qualified Lao personnel was impossible, however, and numbers of French doctors and public health administrators were retained as advisors to the new officials, though far from enough to staff even the key posts in hospitals and other installations. The framework and the intent exist: the problem is to produce personnel with the requisite professional competence. Table 11 summarizes the trained medical personnel in Laos in 1958.

Among the qualified doctors now practicing medicine in Laos, only one Lao, a former Minister of Health, has received a Western medical degree (in France). The majority of the *médecins indochinois* obtained licenses to practice by passing a state examination based on training at medical schools in either Hanoi or Pnompenh. Entry to these schools requires the equivalent of a high school education. The course lasts four years, and the final examination may also be taken by persons who have acquired their knowledge by apprenticeship to a practicing doctor. They receive a certificate as "medical assistants" or "public health assistants," but the Laotians accept them as doctors.

Assisting the medical officers are *infirmiers* who receive a six-months course in Vientiane under French supervision. Supplementary training for such personnel is also being established in provincial hospitals with the assistance of the ICA Nurse Consultant. Also more than one hundred Lao health technicians and nurses have recently received training in Thailand under the auspices of the American aid program.

Although they lack full formal training, the *médecins indochinois* often have greater professional competence in treating common diseases than most newly arrived European or American doctors. They tend, however, to deal only with the most obvious symptoms and are weak in diagnosing complicated or unfamiliar cases. Whatever their failings in the eyes of Western doctors, they are highly respected by their countrymen, for whom they tend to replace the traditional herb-doctor where they are available. They are generally willing to learn new ideas and techniques, but they are perhaps understandably very sensitive to unsympathetic criticism.

As Laotians, the local doctors share in varying degrees their countrymen's religious attitudes and beliefs. For this reason they often lack aggressiveness or a sense of urgency in dealing with health problems which Western doctors consider highly dangerous. It is reported, however, that through instruction accompanied by a patient understanding much can be done to improve their practices and knowledge.

Although the shortage of Western-trained medical personnel of all types in Laos is acute, the Lao have shown a reluctance to attend the Hanoi Medical School, one reason apparently being their strong dislike for things Vietnamese. The opening of new medical training facilities in Saigon consequently did little to relieve the shortage of doctors in Laos. The founding more recently, however, of a four-year School of Public Health in Pnompenh appears to have provided a possible solution. The new medical school established early in 1956 in the same city should also further training of Lao doctors. It is perhaps of significance in this context that all the Lao in training at Saigon have voluntarily transferred to the new schools in Pnompenh.

A Royal School of Medicine, to be staffed with local doctors assisted by French personnel is envisaged as part of the National Education Center now under construction in Vientiane.

There are very few fully trained Laotian nurses, pharmacists, laboratory technicians, or midwives with the result that most of the health services are performed by subprofessional personnel. In 1959, sixteen nurses of both sexes were taking a year's training at the Siriraj Hospital in Bangkok under scholarships received through American aid to Laos, with a similar group scheduled for the following year. A partially trained nurse may be the health educator and chief infirmary nurse of an entire province, which also may have only rural midwives with six months of training or less.

Accurate recent statistics are not available, but it can be roughly estimated that there is about one indigenous doctor (partly trained) and one midwife (including six-month trainees) for every 40,000 inhabitants, and one nurse (often only partly trained) for every 10,000 persons.

The doctor ratio compares very unfavorably with the 1:3000 ratio for the Philippines. Further, nearly all of the doctors and most of the midwives and nurses are concentrated in a few urban centers. Only by making long journeys on foot, by pirogue, or occasionally by bus, can a large part of the population expect to receive medical attention, except possibly that provided by a local, substandard infirmary nurse or a still less trained first-aid assistant.

In a few areas Christian missionaries have provided some health education and first-aid facilities.

An American doctor, Thomas A. Dooley, operating as a private citizen under an international health program known as MEDICO, has worked in Vientiane and Nam Tha provinces, setting up two hospitals.

Operation Brotherhood has had combined teams consisting of at least one doctor, one dentist, and several nurses operating in both northern and southern Laos. They are sponsored and supported by the Lao Junior Chamber of Commerce.

The French, while not in direct control as in the past, are still helping Laos in many ways. The French Mission for Economic Aid and Technical Assistance to Laos has been most active in supplying and training specialized personnel in the fields of medicine and public health, but has in addition contributed to the build up of medical facilities in Laos, for example by providing modern surgical and radiological equipment for the hospital at Vientiane.

Social Problems

Laos is relatively free of serious social problems although class antagonisms and rural-urban cleavages, for example, are beginning to emerge. In Vientiane and other centers there is a shortage of Western-style housing and some crowding, but serious slum problems such as are found in other larger Asian cities have not yet developed. Some 3,000 Black Tai from North Vietnam have been located in camps in and around Vientiane, adding to the city's housing problems.

Juvenile delinquency is now found in Vientiane, and the crime rate, while low, is rising. There is some vagabondage and beggars, too, are increasing.

Because of the reluctance of the Lao to work for hire, labor shortage is chronic, a condition which prevents the rise of urban unemployment. In Vientiane large numbers of coolie labor from northeast Thailand have migrated there in search of work, creating some friction and contributing to the emerging social problems in the capital city. In rural areas, where the traditional family and village systems have remained intact, individual hardships such as sickness, temporary unemployment or physical handicap are not regarded as social problems.

Under French control, opium was sold openly by a state monopoly. On achieving independence, Laos formally received responsibility for the enforcement of various international drug-control conventions previously signed by France on its behalf. Laws controlling the production and sale of opium exist today but they are not fully enforced and much opium is traded illegally both within Laos and across its borders with neighboring states.

Despite free use of opium for pain relief, the Lao are rarely addicted to the drug, but some of the minorities — certain hill tribes such as the Man and Meo and some Kha — are important consumers as well as producers. Opium is bought and sold openly on the market at Xiengkhouang but elsewhere is sold only by licensed dealers. The opium-producing Meo area of Xiengkhouang province is set off as an "opium preserve" around which control barriers are placed by the government.

In general the lowland Lao rarely drink alcohol. When they do indulge it is in moderation and usually on ceremonial occasions. Drunkenness is rare. Among the hill tribes, alcohol is consumed in greater quantities, although this varies widely from group to group. The Kha use alcohol chiefly for ritual purposes, but these rites are celebrated frequently and become virtual drinking contests for an entire village and its guests. A visitor to a Kha village is expected to join in the drinking of crude, raw rice alcohol (*shoum*) which is sucked through reed straws out of large pottery jars.

17

FINANCIAL SYSTEM

EVERY YEAR SINCE INDEPENDENCE the civil budget of Laos has shown a deficit, while military expenditures, not included in the civil budget, have risen rapidly until they now stand at an annual amount in excess of the total civil budget. The deficit, primarily the defense cost, must be covered by extraordinary income, which has been supplied by foreign aid mostly from the United States and France. The large amounts of aid have, however, also contributed to a steady inflation in Laos.

Currency

Until 1955 the currency of Laos was the Indochina piaster, issued under responsibility of the French colonial government and linked to the French franc at 10 francs per piaster. As the franc had an official value of 350 to the dollar, the official rate of the piaster was 35 per dollar.

This rate had been in effect since May 11, 1953 when the French authorities devalued the piaster from 17 to 10 francs per piaster, thus reducing it from about 21 to 35 per dollar. The move, coming at a time of strong anti-French feeling and the rampant inflation which accompanied the futile attempt to conquer the Vietminh, raised a furor in nationalistic circles and devaluation, though economically advisable, was blamed for price rises actually caused more by the continuing issue of paper money, the civil war, and variations in crop yields. But the exaggerated fears raised at that time in the area — that devaluation in foreign exchange is bound to cause a corresponding general price rise — still held back needed monetary reforms in the successor states of Laos, Cambodia, and Vietnam.

The present monetary unit of Laos is the *kip*, which came into use January 1, 1955 when the three Indochina states established separate systems. The *kip* retained the official exchange value of the piaster, 35 per dollar, but inflation continued. Prices by 1958 were well over 50 percent above the level at the end of 1954. The *kip* (along with the currencies of Cambodia and Vietnam) became overvalued and promptly went to a large discount in the so-called black market: rates for *kip* at Hong Kong and Bangkok ranged between about 75 and 120 per dollar in 1957–58.

On October 10, 1958 the Lao government, which for a long time had resisted any thought of changing the rate, put into effect a far-reaching program of monetary reform, including adoption of a free market based on a value of 80 *kip* per dollar and elimination of the old system of import licensing and exchange control. The latter system had led to grave abuses: those who had been fortunate enough to be granted dollars at the rate of 35-1 could either import goods and sell them at a price level in harmony with black market rates of 75-1 to 120-1 or transfer the privilege to others for a large premium.

One effect of the overvaluation of the *kip* was that the United States-financed aid program got only 35 *kip* for a dollar when it should have gotten much more. Thus the real value in Laos of the approximately $153 million of American aid in the period from January 1955 to June 30, 1958 was much less than the figure suggests.

Of special difficulty has been the problem of granting millions of dollars of aid in an area that in the French period had a foreign trade measured only in hundreds of thousands of dollars yearly. It has been the reverse of the usual "transfer problem" in that the difficulty was to raise large sums in the currency of the weaker country without provoking serious inflation and other evils. So hard was it to raise *kip* through the complicated system of "procurement authorizations" (PA's), which the International Cooperation Administration uses, that the main reliance has had to be on "cash grants." These meant that instead of generating *kip* by sale of imported goods *kip* were created by the National Bank of Laos for use in the aid program against dollars paid over to it by foreign governments. The resultant inflationary tendency was checked somewhat, however, by the sales of dollars to importers and others by the National Bank — albeit at the rate highly favorable to them of 35-1 — since these sales withdrew currency from the market.

The currency reform of 1958 has been successful. The previous inflow of dollars had given the National Bank large reserves for currency support, and continuing large foreign aid is technically favorable to future success. Creation of a free market at the realistic rate of 80-1 abolished the black market and did away with the abuses of the old system of controls. The reform removes incentives to exchange speculation and promotes a more normal economic situation. Contrary to the fears of many, no serious disturbance to the general price level attended the reform. The change gives the United States aid program reasonable value for dollars converted into *kip,* reducing the cost of aid, and its generally beneficial effects have set an example which, it may be hoped, will influence Cambodia and Vietnam to adopt needed monetary reforms.

The *kip* is a paper currency whose value is pegged by government decree and issued by the National Bank of Laos. Although circulating freely in urban areas, this paper currency is less readily accepted in rural areas, where payment in silver coins (mainly French Indochinese piasters) and silver bars (said to be smuggled into the country from Thailand or China) is more the rule. Silver bars currently sell for 800-1,400 *kip,* depending on the weight and purity of the silver.

The National Bank of Laos

The joint Bank of Issue of the Associated States (Banque d'Émission des États Associés) — a joint venture of Laos, Cambodia, and Vietnam with France — was dissolved at the end of 1954, together with the other instruments of joint action in economic affairs. In Laos its place was taken by the National Bank of Laos (Banque Nationale de Laos), a government institution with semiautonomous status.

Entrusted with responsibility for monetary stability at home and stable relations between the *kip* and foreign currencies, the National Bank carries considerable if not overriding weight in the government's financial decisions. Its wide powers include issuance of currency, fiscal services for the national government, control of credit, supervision and control of the commercial banks, and control of foreign exchange. It is also charged with responsibility for the development of financial institutions to assist agriculture, handicrafts, and machine industry, and with provision for participation in the financing of all institutions of this nature up to 25 percent of their capitalization. It may also grant harvest loans to cooperatives and is authorized to buy private securities on the open market. The bank is required to maintain a monetary reserve, in the form of foreign exchange and gold, totaling at least 30 percent of the combined value of notes in circulation and demand deposits. In practice, reserves have remained well above this minimum owing to the large amounts of foreign exchange received under the American and French aid programs.

As fiscal agent to the government, the bank is authorized to loan money to the national treasury for periods of three months. For the first five years of operation (1955–1960), the maximum total of these advances was set at 50 percent of regular government receipts in the preceding year; after 1960 the limit is to drop to 25 percent. The actual potential limits of these loans were greatly increased by the modification of the National Bank statutes in October 1956 which permitted foreign aid receipts to be included in government receipts for the purpose of calculating the maximum percentage of advances.

The statute setting up the bank provides for a capital of 100 million *kip,* to be subscribed in full by the Laotian government. Actually no such capitalization exists. Since the government did not have the 100 million *kip* to commit permanently for this purpose, it loaned the bank about 67 million *kip* to be reimbursed out of the bank's operating profits. The bank is required by statute to allocate half its net profits to this purpose, the other half to the reserve fund. When reserves reach a level of 60 million *kip,* the total net profit is to be used to repay the government's capitalization loan.

Government obligations to the bank arising out of the liquidation of the old Indochina treasury, and those deriving from Laos' share of the old joint Bank of Issue loans to the Laotian government, have been consolidated into one sum on which the bank though not allowed to claim reimbursement earns interest. There has been no settlement of the complicated affairs of the former Indochina Bank of Issue, involving debts and claims of Laos, Cambodia, and Vietnam, in view of unsatisfactory relations among these new states.

In the control of credit the bank is authorized to discount and rediscount commercial paper and to vary the rediscount rate, to limit the amount and type of loan offered by the commercial banks, and to vary their reserve requirements. Commercial banks are required by law to maintain reserves of at least 15 percent of all demand deposits, and the National Bank may raise this to 50 percent. In order to keep closer control over the operations of the commercial banks, the National Bank may periodically inspect them and examine their accounts.

Control over foreign exchange was a function of the Exchange Department of the National Bank in conjunction with the Lao National Exchange Office until October 1958 when the new monetary program went into effect.

The bank may accept deposits from individuals and engage in regular commercial banking transactions with them, even granting loans on harvests. But although private deposits with the bank in 1956 amounted to 112 million *kip,* commercial banking is the bank's least important function.

The governor and deputy-governor are chosen by the Cabinet and two auditors are appointed by the prime minister on the recommendation of the Finance Ministry. The governing board is called the General Council and consists of the bank's governor as president, its deputy-governor as vice-president, and six other members as follows:

> Representatives of the private sector of the economy:
> > one representative of industrial and commercial interests;
> > one representative of crop agriculture; and
> > one representative of the livestock industry.

> Representatives of government interests:
> > one from the Ministry of Finance;
> > one from the Ministry of Commerce and Industry; and
> > the Inspector General of the Kingdom, as general counsel.

The council members who represent the various economic interests are chosen from a list of nominees selected by the group concerned and serve without compensation, except for travel and per diem allotments when they attend meetings of the council; the government representatives are paid by the departments they represent.

The management and operations of the National Bank have been seriously impeded by the lack of Lao personnel sufficiently experienced in the complexities of modern banking. During the first year of its operation the bank was without a research department. As late as mid-1958 it had not exercised its powers of bank inspection and control of the rediscount rate, nor had it discounted any commercial paper or granted any loans for production or processing. From the beginning the bank has had the services of French banking experts, who have played a useful part in helping it to function. Since December 1957 there has also been an American banking adviser provided by the United States Operations Mission.

Other Banking Institutions

The first commercial bank in Laos was opened in 1953 when the Bank of Indochina (now the Banque Française d'Asie) established a branch in Vientiane. Since then at least four other banks have opened, all located in Vientiane: Banque Lao-Vieng (1956), the Lao-Thai Bank, the Lao Commercial Bank, and a branch of the Bank of Tokyo, Ltd. (1957). The first and second of these are Lao institutions. The Lao-Thai Bank is financed mainly by capital from Thailand, including some Chinese capital, and reflects the more prominent position Thailand has assumed in Laotian trade since 1955. Establishment of a branch of the Bank of Tokyo, successor of the old Yokohama Specie Bank, is part of the combined trade, aid, and developmental effort that Japan has directed toward the former Indochinese states since World War II. One bank, Lao-Vieng, also maintains branches in Pakse and Savannakhet.

The appearance of these new commercial banks is by and large a result of the demand for banking facilities that accompanied the United States commodity import program and the large increase in import transactions. Because the commercial banks showed no interest in long- or medium-term loans of the sort needed for development of the productive base of the economy, the government created, mainly for this purpose, the National Lao Credit for the Development of Agriculture, Commerce, and Industry (Credit National Lao), an agency which has in effect taken over the functions once served by the French-administered Office of Popular Credit. Its capital is subscribed up to 25 percent by the National Bank. Thus far its function has been a minimal one, owing in part to lack of legislation defining the rights and obligations of lenders and borrowers in Laos.

Commercial banks are used primarily by business firms as those individuals who use money, almost exclusively urban dwellers, either store their cash at home or invest in jewelry, gold belts, religious objects, or other portable objects of value.

The individual Laotian more often than not will turn for credit to the uncontrolled moneylender, usually Chinese, sometimes Indian or Vietnamese. Borrowing from moneylenders involves rates of interest that are seldom less than 2.5 percent per month, and may exceed 100 percent per annum. If the moneylender is Chinese, he is most likely also a middleman who buys whatever rice the villager has available for market and sells him supplies. Payments on loans from Chinese moneylenders-middlemen are usually made in rice at harvest time — valued at low prices, to be sold later on the market at higher prices. Thus to the villager the terms of such a loan may seem more attractive than the currency payments called for in loans negotiated with banks or with other moneylenders, who serve no other economic function so far as he is concerned.

To weaken the moneylenders' grip on the economy, as well as to expand the use of credit in general, the government has established facilities for rural credit. But factors perpetuating the moneylender are the ready availability of his loan capital; his auxiliary roles as a purchaser of marketable produce and a source of essential operating supplies; and the familiarity of the Lao farmer with him as a person and with his ways of doing business. Until substitutes are found for these facets of moneylending enterprise, government efforts in the field of rural credit may fall far short of the desired goals.

The Budget

The Vietminh guerrilla warfare which has plagued Laos from independence put first priority in the newly formed state on the organization and equipment of an effective national army. Given the high cost of such an army, however, the Laotian government was unable to provide anything approaching adequate defense for the country and foreign assistance was rushed in on the premise that the elimination of aggressive pressure in Laos was of vital concern to the Western world.

The amount of money entering Laos for army support dwarfs most other income with the result that foreign aid, especially American, is presently by far the biggest factor in Laotian government finance. In the two fiscal years ended June 30, 1959, American aid was $32 million and $25 million respectively. But, as explained earlier, the dollar figures are misleading as to the value obtained in Lao currency due to the very unfavorable conversion rate of 35-1 used until the 80-1 rate took effect in October 1958. Aid from France is equivalent to several million dollars yearly. In consideration of Laos renouncing any claim for war reparations, Japan has granted aid equivalent to almost $3 million available over a two-year period, none of which had been transferred as of the latter part of 1959.

Reliance on foreign aid could be substantially reduced at this point only by effecting drastic cuts in defense expenditures, which absorb about 65 percent of the United States aid, but such a measure is highly unlikely in view of the recurring activity of the Pathet Lao in the northern provinces. In fact for the fiscal year 1959-60 total American aid was allocated at about $40 million, substantially more than in the previous fiscal year.

The next largest use of foreign aid is for public administration and the internal communications system. Both of these are critical for economic development and their curtailment would only retard weaning the economy away from dependence on foreign aid. It is apparent then, that the Laotian government will necessarily continue for some time what for it is a high rate of expenditure and will require external assistance.

The Ministry of Public Works consistently spends more money than any other civil department. That reflects the critical inadequacies of the internal communications system and the priority given to road, ferry, and bridge construction and the improvement of river transport. Other sizable ministerial budgets are those of education, interior, and public health. Most of the expenses here have been for training and paying personnel — i.e. teachers, the civil police, and medical doctors and technicians. Within the last year there has been an effort to raise the salaries of important civil servants in order to reduce graft and corruption and to increase loyalty.

Foreign aid much exceeds the yield of local revenues, which at 80-1 are believed equivalent to less than $10 million. The government's sources of income have been limited by the undeveloped and generally unproductive nature of the economy, by the attitudes of the people toward taxation, and by administrative inexperience in the assessment and collection of taxes. There is little industry to tax and, since the government is trying to stimulate industrial development, it is inclined to make tax concessions. The rural areas tend to resist any form of taxation, particularly direct taxes. There are signs that productivity and taxable resources are gradually rising. But it will be some time before there can be any significant increase in government revenues.

The government has had to rely primarily on indirect taxes and on the proceeds of enterprises which are under its own control. The revenues consist of customs duties, the proceeds of state monopolies, royalties from timber concessions, registration fees on the recording of business transactions, revenues of the postal and telecommunications systems, the government lottery, and direct taxes on land and on personal and business incomes. In addition the receipts include borrowings from the National Bank and the nonmilitary share of the local currency generated by the United States aid program, earmarked for general budgetary items.

Most of the revenue is from customs and monopolies, pointing up the crucial role of foreign trade in the national economy. Customs receipts, which in 1957–58 generated some 70 percent of the civil budget, are based on a new tariff adopted in February 1958 to replace that adopted in 1949 for the former Federation of Indochina. These provide for increased customs rates on imported luxuries and semiluxuries and for compensatory duties on goods which compete with local products. Rates on essential imports have been reduced. In addition there are internal taxes on certain imports, special excise taxes, and a statistical tax of 2 *kip* per unit of imported goods. Direct taxes on land and on personal income are a minor source of revenue. Urban retail and wholesale businesses are taxed on their incomes although the double-language bookkeeping of the Chinese is probably too much for the inexperienced Laotian revenue officers to cope with. Many businesses in rural areas are not taxed at all, although a tax is supposed to be levied based on the size of the building frontage.

Prior to 1948 the government opium monopoly was an important source of revenue for the French administration; today the opium trade is in private hands.

The Laotian government borrows from the National Bank of Laos, but the sums involved cover only a small part of expenditures. There are no government bond flotations. Domestic savings are small and there is no local securities market. Rates of return obtainable by capital in private transactions are much higher than could be realized from the purchase of government bonds. Also there is a tendency to send profits abroad, e.g., to Hong Kong or Bangkok.

AGRICULTURE

SINCE THEIR SETTLEMENT IN THE VALLEY of the Mekong the Lao have been predominantly wet-rice farmers, living in small villages of anywhere from a few families to several hundred people where each family farms an area just large enough to supply the family needs. With the help of a buffalo — if he is rich enough to own a buffalo — and using the few simple implements he has made for himself, the farmer plants, cultivates, and harvests his crops by methods his ancestors followed centuries before.

Rice is the staple crop and the mainstay of the diet but in northern Laos, at least, the areas along the Mekong suitable for wet-rice cultivation are limited and farmers not infrequently supplement their wet-rice harvests by growing dry rice along the sides of accessible valleys. Not enough rice is grown locally to feed the urban populations and some rice is consequently imported into Laos, primarily from neighboring Thailand.

There can be no doubt that the people of Laos are at present overwhelmingly oriented toward the soil. The qualities that go to make up the rural agricultural way of life would probably rank high in the Lao scale of values. Within this way of life land is of primary importance and attachment to the land is undoubtedly one of the outstanding characteristics of the rural Laotian today.

The Lao system of land tenure rests on tradition rather than law and varies with local custom. In the days of absolute monarchy, before the arrival of the French (and even after), all land was in principle considered the property of the ruler. He had complete right to grant custody and usufruct and could expropriate at will. Such absolute domination was unenforceable over all the territory of any of the various kings and princes; it had in practice to be limited by considerations of remoteness, the strength of the tribes, and even lack of interest on the ruler's part. The principle, however, was unchallenged and unchallengeable except by war. Under this system it appears that the ruler's absolute right was seldom exercised capriciously, although individual officials or families could, and probably did, feel royal disfavor by having their lands reassigned. The commonality, on the other hand, could feel secure in their tenure of lands traditionally occupied and could at need expand their holdings by application to the local mandarin (in areas where the king's writ was in force) so long as the proper taxes and gratuities were paid. Under this system nearly every type of practical land tenure developed — individual, family, community, and tribal holdings all were practiced, according to the local tradition. There is no direct evidence of feudal holding in the technical Western sense of grants and subgrants in specific return for military service.

No concrete statement of the principles of land tenure under the present constitutional monarchy is available. The constitution contains no guarantee of the individual's right to own real property. It is therefore most probable that land tenure remains where tradition has left it: with inalienable ownership in principle vested in the state, but with *de facto* control left undisturbed in the hands of the technical usufructuaries, whether individuals, families, or communities. It is reported, on the one hand, that landholdings are nowhere actually registered, on the other, that the Lao farmers in Vientiane province consider that they own the land they work, and buy, sell, and rent it (apparently within the community). Rental, on what amounts to a sharecropping basis, is common in the vicinity of Luang Prabang and Vientiane, the landowner's share of the crop amounting to as much as 50 percent. As one leaves these urban centers, however, tenancy of this kind disappears altogether.

With respect to forest land, ownership is by tradition vested in the state, and any land unoccupied or uncultivated for three years is said to revert to the state. (In this part of the world unworked land quickly returns to forest.) There is some evidence that this principle of ownership is not universally understood; for example, the farmers in the areas not far from Vientiane are said to be unsure to whom they should apply for permission to clear new rice land.

Moneylenders in Laos do not appear to acquire the land of the debtor no matter how long the farmer may have been in debt or how deeply. Aliens are probably prohibited from owning land al-

200

though a Chinese, for example, would presumably have access to usufruct rights if married to a Lao woman.

Land is also of fundamental importance to the non-Lao upland peoples. Their systems of land tenure are not, however, in all cases similar to those of the lowland Lao. Among those groups characterized by a feudal type of social organization, for example some of the tribal Tai peoples, the land is owned by members of the noble class and worked by commoners. Among the Kha tribes, on the other hand, land is often considered the property of the village and is allotted to individual families by a council of notables acting on behalf of the village community.

Rice Cultivation

The two major farming methods in Laos, which have remained relatively unchanged for centuries, relate to the cultivation of wet rice in irrigated fields and the cultivation of dry rice in forest clearings.

So-called wet rice — almost all rainy season rice watered by the rain — is grown in paddy fields of two types, those utilizing irrigation canals and those where the system of dikes and terraces is designed merely to keep in the rain water. The fertility of the flat flood plains suitable to this type of cultivation is renewed every year by the silt deposited during the annual flooding and shallow dikes are built up both to retain the rain water and to prevent the washing away of this enriching silt deposit.

The three main varieties of rainy season rice are an early ripening variety planted in June and harvested in September, the regular paddy planted in May or June and harvested in November or December, and a late ripening rice also planted in May or June but maturing only in late December or January. In southern Laos there is in addition a dry-season crop planted after the floods have subsided but while the dikes retain the flood water, a crop which may be harvested as late as April.

The rice cycle begins, as soon as the rains have softened the ground, with the plowing of the paddy field by the farmer using a simple wooden plow pulled by an ox or water buffalo. Paddy (seed rice) from the year before, which has been soaked for four days in water, is then sown broadcast in one small area of the field and left for about six weeks. The laborious transplanting, which involves the whole family and sometimes outside help as well, follows as the seedlings are uprooted, tied together in small bunches, and transplanted at regular intervals over the entire field. After the harvest — the time of harvest depends on the type of rice — threshing is carried out by beating the plants either against boards or with sticks. To complete the cycle the rice is milled in a wooden, foot-pedaled, mortar-pestle device.

For the Lao the raising of rice is both an essential economic activity and a way of life closely interwoven with the supernatural. Each stage in its cultivation is accompanied by appropriate rituals, from the initial planting ceremonies on a day chosen as auspicious by the local astrologer to the special rites for the opening of the storage sheds after harvesting has been completed. Central to these rituals is the belief in the power for good or evil of the *phi* of the rice fields and much attention is given to their propitiation through offerings of food, alcohol, and cigarettes. Most paddy fields will contain a small altar in one corner for these offerings.

The nature of these rituals can be surmised from the transplanting ceremonies, Lein Phi Ta Hek, literally "to feed the *phi* Ta Hek," as described by Boun Than Sinavong in *Agrarian Rites in Laos* (cited by Joel Halpern in *Aspects of Village Life and Culture Change in Laos*). Glutinous rice, having been mixed with grains of paddy and shaped into ears of rice to symbolize abundance, is placed on the paddy altar together with four banana leaves rolled into horns to contain betel. The *phi* appeased, the first seven shoots of rice are reverently planted to the accompaniment of this chant:

> I plant the first shoot,
>> May you be green as the Thao.
> I plant the second shoot,
>> May you be green as the grass of the ninth month.
> I plant the third shoot,
>> May the gong of nine *kam* be mine.
> I plant the fourth shoot,
>> May ninety thousand pounds of gold be mine.
> I plant the fifth shoot,
>> May ninety thousand baskets of rice be mine.
> I plant the sixth shoot,
>> May I have a wife to sleep by my side.
> I plant the seventh shoot,
>> May a rare elephant saddled in gold and silver be mine.
> Glory!
> Prosperity!

Most of the tribal Tai and Kha of the highlands employ *rai* (swidden) agriculture, which entails slash-and-burn clearing of wooded areas. At the beginning of the dry season in January trees and underbrush are cut down to make a clearing (swidden) of adequate size for the coming year's crop. At the end of April the dried wood is set on fire. The land is cleared, except for stumps, and the wood ash supplies fertilization. The soil soon wears out, however, and the process must be repeated at another site at least after the third year. The yield may be as high as one and a half tons of rice per hectare (one hectare equals 2.471 acres) the first year but falls to about half a ton after the second harvest.

Planting methods are primitive. The plow is seldom used, partly because stumps and roots remain in the soil. Holes for two or three grains of rice are made about a foot apart with a pointed stick, the seeds are tamped in with the naked heel, and planting is finished. After the soil's fertility has been exhausted, the land is abandoned and a new plot cleared, and the cycle begins again.

Whether or not the clearings are produced by the labor of one family or of the entire community varies among the different ethnic groups, as does the decision as to whether the whole village moves to a new area. In general, there is less moving of entire villages than might be supposed; when the cultivated plots are at some distance from the village the men may move to huts near the plantings during the season of heaviest work. Except in the areas occupied by the Meo, villages are not moved unless all land within reasonable reach has been exhausted; it is also customary to return to previously used plots as soon as enough young growth has established itself to renew fertility, about twelve years.

The Meo prefer not to live at an elevation below 3,000 feet and are limited therefore in their choice of cultivable land. Their custom has been to move the entire village as the soil is exhausted. In 1912 the French became concerned about the resulting progressive deforestation in the province of Xiengkhouang and threatened the Meo with deportation if they did not replace the trees in the areas they abandoned. The Meo complied and have reportedly continued the process of reforestation.

Major Crops

In a country where the verb "to eat," *kin khao*, translates "to eat rice" it is to be expected that rice is the most important crop grown. The production of rice — predominantly a glutinous type preferred by the Lao — reached 525,000 tons in 1956-57, compared with 386,000 tons yearly average in the early 1940's. Drought and insect damage can seriously affect rice production, however, as in 1955 when northern Laos was so hard hit that rice had to be flown in by the United States and dropped by parachute to the villagers.

Second in importance is maize, grown in swidden fields wherever rice shortages are likely and used almost exclusively for food. The northern provinces account for nearly two-thirds of the maize production — the Meo often grow maize in preference to rice — but the total is only a small fraction of the rice yield and has been falling steadily since 1930. In recent years less than 10,000 tons of maize have been produced annually.

In addition to these two major subsistence crops the Laotian cultivates in his family garden or harvests from wild growth a great variety of other food crops and spices, although all only in small quantities. Pimento, cardamom, cinnamon, and a number of other spices grow wild in many parts of the country — in noticeable profusion on the Boloven plateau where spices were commercially cultivated during the French protectorate — but also are cultivated in some cases by the villagers. The gathered harvest, cultivated or wild, is generally sold locally to export merchants.

The family garden, cultivated during the dry season, is the source of a great variety of vegetables. Lao villagers in Luang Prabang province, for example, commonly raise such vegetables as cucumbers, tomatoes, salad greens, eggplant, chili, onions, cow peas, bonarista beans, and a kind of spinach. Also grown in small amounts are pineapple, cassava, mangoes, gourds, pomelo, papaya, yams, betel nut, sugar cane, and coffee.

As the towns grow larger the villagers are becoming more interested in bringing their garden products to the city markets for sale. This is particularly true at Vientiane where boats can be seen arriving each morning from nearby villages loaded down with fresh vegetables and fruits. The volume of such trade is still relatively small, however, and the towns continue to import a large proportion of their food.

Almost complete dependence on vegetable oils in Laotian cooking creates a steady demand for peanuts, castor beans, coconuts, and areca palm nuts. Both coconut and areca palms grow naturally in every village, providing a convenient source of oil. Peanuts, on the other hand, have to be cultivated and their need for a light, dry soil limits their practicality in many areas. The annual harvest of about a thousand tons is consumed locally, being either roasted or pressed for oil.

Other fruit trees regularly found in Lao villages include the banana (more than twenty-four varieties grow in Laos), fig, orange, tangerine, grapefruit, lemon, lime, pawpaw, custard apple, litchi, peach, and avocado. In addition nut trees such as walnut, chestnut, and almond are abundant and melons, strawberries, and other vine fruits are cultivated extensively.

Other Crops

Laotians have traditionally depended on textiles woven at home from fibers grown and spun locally, usually by the family itself, and cotton and mulberry for the culture of silkworms have been cultivated in almost every part of Laos. Cotton — mostly a short-staple variety of low market value — grows well along the river banks where the soil is renewed yearly by silt from the seasonal floods. Away from the rivers, and particularly in the north, cotton is planted in swiddens as a second crop immediately following the rice harvest. In addition ramie — an estimated 90 tons in 1954 — and some hemp are grown on the plateaus and in high valleys, both reportedly for local consumption only.

Before World War II rubber and coffee plantations on the Boloven plateau were worked by French interests, but neglect and abandonment during the war and subsequent Vietminh invasions resulted in widespread disease and loss of productive acreage. Experiments with rust-resistant varieties of coffee are currently underway and if successful may revive the coffee market.

The Boloven plateau is said to possess the richest soil in Laos, but several attempts to exploit it have met with indifferent success, partly because investors in the area have not had sufficient capital. A recent attempt involved a group of French war veterans who, with some financial aid from their government, established themselves on the plateau as planters. In 1953, however, only one of the group remained. The Lao government is currently encouraging small farmers to settle in this area.

The British-American Tobacco Company has experimented in raising tobacco on the Laos plateaus, particularly on the Boloven, but it abandoned the effort in 1953 because of excessive production costs due to the scarcity of labor in the vicinity and the serious transportation difficulties.

18. Livestock, Fishing, Forest Products

Opium Production

Although the sale of opium is illegal — outside the strict limits set by the government — opium continues to be bought and sold quite openly and is even used as a medium of exchange in some more remote parts of Laos. An estimated 65 tons of crude opium — a little over 20 tons after processing — are produced each year, mostly by the Meo in their high upland areas. Both the cultivation of opium poppies, which are sown at the beginning of the dry season in late fall and harvested in early spring, and their refining into smoking opium are carried out by the tribal peoples who then sell the processed drug at nominal prices to middlemen.

An undetermined amount of opium is smoked by Laotians, the rest is smuggled out of the country to Saigon or Bangkok for transshipment to Hong Kong and other ports. Though reportedly of rather poor quality, Laotian opium nevertheless is a valuable crop.

Livestock, Fishing, Forest Products

Livestock breeding has played an important part in the economy of Laos, particularly in the southern part of the country. Before World War II the livestock population was estimated at 250,000 cattle, 300,000 water buffaloes, and 250,000 pigs. Estimates in 1954 gave the same figures for cattle but showed a decrease in buffaloes to 105,000 and in pigs to 180,000. The decrease was attributed partly to lack of proper care and absence of vaccination during the days of guerrilla warfare.

Formerly, livestock was more than sufficient for the needs of Laos and was one of the few export items, but the depleted herds today produce little export income. However, livestock production is regarded by the government and its economic advisers as an item for advancing the economy of Laos. American agricultural experts have estimated that one million head of cattle could be supported on the plains of Xiengkhouang alone, and that cattle on the hoof and the by-products of slaughtering could in ten years earn $10 million in foreign exchange.

Great quantities of fish are taken from the Mekong and its tributaries each year. Most of the catch is used by the fishermen and their families, but a substantial amount reaches the larger centers of population and the village markets. The Lao are noted for their love of fishing and the average rice farmer spends a considerable portion of his time in this activity, which to him is a source of pleasure as well as an important contribution to his diet.

About two-thirds of the area of Laos is in forests, of which about one-half is estimated to be of economic interest. The forests are owned by the royal government and exploited mainly by private firms under lease. Attempts to bring the many kinds of cabinet woods to market have been costly and fuller exploitation of the forests is retarded by the high costs of transportation. Total lumber production in 1952 was 34,751 cubic meters, in 1955, 32,000 cubic meters, and in 1958, 28,000 cubic meters. During the first half of 1959, however, production rose to over 29,000 cubic meters.

In the Sayaboury region there are an estimated 173,000 acres of teak. Logs are moved over logging roads on wooden carts hauled by oxen or dragged by tractors or elephants. A few trails have also been opened recently in southern Laos. Floating the logs down the Mekong to Saigon takes about two months and occasions heavy loss and damage.

Forest products include rattan, bamboo, stick-lac, benzoin, and other resins, all of which have some export value. About 12,000 tons of charcoal were produced in 1958, compared with 3,000 in 1955.

Stick-lac is used in the manufacture of shellac and varnish and is in good demand. In recent years over 100 tons have been exported through Bangkok annually for shipment to the West. Natives of several provinces work small groves of the *pois d'angola* trees on whose twigs feed the insects that secrete the resinous substance.

Benzoin, used as a fixative for perfumes, comes from the styrax tree. The trees are planted in abandoned *rai* clearings and receive no attention other than pruning and tapping for the salable balm. About 30 tons of benzoin annually were formerly exported, mostly to France.

Role of the Government

The Lao government has taken over the agricultural experimental stations and disease-control installations once operated by the French but, owing to the lack of both trained personnel and money, has done little to develop them. Both American and French aid missions have assisted in the improvement of rural water control systems and the improvement of certain crops and livestock. Small dams and water distribution systems have been built in several of the provinces; these provide badly needed irrigation as well as water supply for the villagers. A new type of glutinous rice has been tried out which in 1958 produced yields 25 percent larger than in the previous years. Eleven other improved varieties are now being tested. Purebred Berkshire hogs from Japan have been placed in various villages and two poultry stations have been established for the upgrading of local fowl. About 1,000 of these birds have been placed with farmers for breeding purposes. The rust diseases, which have done great damage to the coffee production during and since World War II, have been identified, and a resistant variety of coffee known as Arabica is now being tested.

The Agriculture Service has one experimental station at Vientiane, one at Paksong on the Boloven plateau and two more in lower Laos. The Veterinary Service is directed from the main station at Paksong; its responsibility is to control disease, improve breeding, and inspect meat and skins. A major problem has been lack of qualified staff and sixteen Lao agricultural technicians were recently sent to Thailand and the Philippines for short-term training in an effort to fill this gap.

These and other government agricultural experimental services are charged with the development of crops in specific areas but through lack of funds and of well-defined programs have been less effective than when they were under the French. In the north some effort is being made to develop the production of sticklac, which has a ready market in France. In the south some attention is being focused on reviving and promoting the cultivation of coffee and tobacco. The experimental station near Pakse is experimenting with improvement of the culture of tea, rice, tobacco, and textile fibers.

In addition to seeking technological improvement, the present Laotian government is attempting to improve the living conditions of the farmer in a more immediate manner through a program of rural self-help. A Commissariat for Rural Affairs has been set up under the Ministry of Social Affairs and through this and regular governmental administrative offices at the provincial and district level, the United States Operations Mission has been giving assistance. Some technical and material aid is given the farmer as part of this program, but since the main purpose is to stimulate mutual aid and cooperation among villagers, material assistance is injected mainly in the form of rewards for achievement in cooperative activity. Whatever its benefits to the farmer, the rural self-help program has been a useful device for the central government to show its interest in the farmer and to combat the disaffection which had arisen in previous years through subversive propaganda and a general neglect by government of the rural population.

Laotian attitudes – of the governing elite toward agriculture and of the farmer toward government – are becoming better defined. There is increasing consciousness that government has a place in agricultural development. As for the farmer, there is some evidence that, at least close to Vientiane and probably near a few of the provincial towns of the south, he is becoming aware of the new idea that a central government could take some interest in his welfare. There are many villagers, however, who have little or no awareness of government, let alone the notion of its interest in local affairs and the welfare of the individual farmer.

INDUSTRY

THE ONLY INSTALLATIONS IN LAOS AT ALL resembling a modern industrial enterprise are a tobacco factory near Vientiane and the one small tin mine. The country's sawmills and few rice mills employ only a handful of workers each. Commercial burned-brick making, an expanding business in Vientiane, may soon reach the proportions of a small industry and foreign aid programs are currently encouraging the establishment of contracting firms and small industries for the manufacture of such items as matches, soft drinks, furniture, and cement. Garages, print shops, ice works, and the like have appeared in the vicinity of the few urban centers, mainly Vientiane, and hotels, moving picture theaters, and automatic laundries are appearing in increasing numbers, again mainly in the vicinity of Vientiane and the larger provincial capitals. But the concept of even the smallest type of factory production is still unknown to all but a very limited number of Lao elite.

The country is, however, rich in natural resources. Its forests offer a supply of both soft and cabinet woods; mineral deposits are known, and believed to abound, in various parts of the country. Although considerable prospecting was done by the French up to the time of the Vietminh hostilities, no full-scale geological survey was ever undertaken. Geological surveying and prospecting has, however, been conducted on an increasing scale during the past three years by both the American and French aid missions.

Introduction of an embryonic industry into the economy, under constant review at the national capital, becomes a formidable problem because there is almost no skilled or semiskilled labor available. The ingenuity of the peasant in handicrafting his own tools and the successful experience of the French army in training skilled workers indicate that selected recruits could in time be trained to such jobs, but most writers seem to agree that the Lao peasant could not be lured away even temporarily from the land. On the other hand, service in the army has been popular, which indicates that this conclusion may not be valid.

Along what lines industry might develop in Laos depends largely on what skills its people could master quickly and, in part at least, what products can be consumed locally. Primary industry — for instance, a furniture factory — is indicated as the most suitable for initiating production. Simple machinery is called for in the early stages of industrialization in a country where the majority of the labor potential has never known more complicated implements than the iron-tipped plow, the sickle, and the wooden hand loom.

Laos has also completely lacked other basic factors for the introduction of modern industry. Only the most limited knowledge exists about natural resources that might be utilized in manufacturing enterprises. Transportation routes which were never adequate at best for the moving of raw materials and manufactured products are still far from satisfactory. Development of these factors is necessary before any but the most simple primary industries can be introduced.

The leaders of government appear to be aware of facts and necessities; a survey of resources and improvement of waterways and land transportation routes formed part of a program advocated in 1956, and since then considerable progress has been made in the repair of roads and bridges and the installation of ferries and new airfields. The limited capacity of Laos to absorb and support industry seems to be seen realistically. A moderate program is so far being adopted, and government leaders show no tendency to stampede into an industrialization which they would not be able to maintain.

Top operating personnel and supervision for new industry would have to be brought in from outside, for there are few trained Lao administrators and managers available at present. Advisers from the United States are introducing accounting methods, about which virtually nothing has been known in Laos.

Money is available for investment in industrial development through the National Bank of Laos, although to date more consideration has been given to the promotion of imports. There appears to be a good export market for metals and wood products, but the lack of adequate transportation facilities within the country is at present a serious obstacle to competition in world markets. Foreign investment in industrial undertakings has been mildly encouraged in the past. Plans for the future, however, generally focus upon the use of funds originating in the United States and France and disbursed through their respective foreign aid programs.

Mineral Exploitation

At only one mine, located at Phontiou in the Nam Patene valley just north of Thakhek, is tin being mined commercially for export. French-owned and employing in 1957 about 700 Vietnamese workers, it has been producing annually about 500 tons of ore of 50 percent metal content. Before 1923, when the French-owned company took over the operation, the Nam Patene tin deposits were mined by native workers using primitive methods of shallow-shaft extraction. Production was very low, amounting to no more than 15 or 20 tons a year. The tin was transported over land and by river to Thailand, where it was used as ballast for fish nets. Under the French two mines were worked with a combined production prior to World War II of about 1,800 tons annually. Operation ceased from December 1953 until July 1954, during the Vietminh hostilities, then was resumed at the considerably reduced extraction rate of 10 tons a month. The recent installation of modern plant equipment will undoubtedly result in an increased labor force and increased production.

Lower Laos has few known mineral deposits other than the Nam Patene tin deposits, with which iron ores are associated. Deposits of gypsum are found on the Savannakhet plain, lead ores in the Annam Cordillera below Tchepone, and pagodite on the Boloven plateau. Oil smears have been observed in the neighborhood of Savannakhet, leading to conjecture of and reconnaissance for the presence of petroleum. Gold was once worked on the Boloven, but the ores played out by the middle of the nineteenth century.

Upper Laos, on the other hand, is highly mineralized. Four main areas of mineralization can be ascertained with only the most preliminary surveys such as have been made in the past. Around Luang Prabang ores in commercial quantities containing copper, antimony, lead, and zinc have been discovered. In the Tranninh region, near Xiengkhouang, workable antimony, lead, zinc, silver, and copper deposits have been prospected and alluvial gold is panned. In the province of Nam Tha, especially near Ban Houei Sai, alluvial gold, sapphires, and zircons are exploited from the water courses. A commercial copper deposit is known near Nam Tha in the north of the province. In Phongsaly province gypsum and antimony are found, and salt has for a long period been worked here by the Chinese methods of evaporation.

Other outlying ore deposits of commercial potentiality are the iron ores south of the Tranninh plateau, the iron pyrites deposits of Samneua, which were worked during World War II for sulphur, and the salt deposits above Vientiane worked by evaporation. Massive limestone formations appear in various areas, and their chalk seems to have been burned for lime by indigenous methods since early times.

Northern Laos is also rich in energy fuels, with sizable beds of anthracite occurring near Luang Prabang, near Phongsaly, and in the Nam Nhiep valley east of Vientiane. The Nam Nhiep deposit was worked during World War II to provide fuel for Vientiane's electric station. Lignite deposits are found in Nam Tha province and south of the Mekong in Sayaboury province. No petroleum or natural gas has been prospected or indicated in northern Laos.

Mineral prospecting has been rudimentary in Laos, and more detailed knowledge of the deposits, especially in northern Laos, awaits the detailed surveying that is now going on. It is already evident that northern Laos is potentially rich not only in metallic ores but also in nonmetallic ores and coal; southern Laos seems to have relatively little to offer besides the tin deposits, but these have large reserves and are capable of greater exploitation.

Ore working has a long handicraft tradition in Laos — gold, copper, iron, and tin have been steadily exploited. Other subsoil resources exploited indigenously for subsistence needs or trade include precious stones, salt, sulphur, anthracite coal, and limestone. But failure to solve the transportation problem of Laos in relation to the other Indochinese states and the consequent neglect of economic development in Laos inhibited commercial exploitation of any mineral deposits save the tin ores. At present, the inadequacy of Laotian or foreign capital for development as well as the still poor transportation system continue to inhibit development. Nevertheless, the mineral deposits of Laos seem significant in both their variety and richness to the future economic development of the Southeast Asia peninsula.

Power Resources

The development of power resources in Laos is at present in the earliest stages, only a few of the largest towns having even rudimentary electricity service. A new power plant with three generators of 2200 *kw.* capacity was constructed recently at Vientiane by United States engineers under contract for USOM and there are small thermoelectric plants in five other places: Luang Prabang, 110 *v.*, 110 *kw.*; Thakhek, 100 *v.*, 60 *kw.*; Savannakhet, 100 *v.*, 60 *kw.*; Pakse, 100 *v.*, 60 *kw.*; and Saravane, 100 *v.*, 60 *kw.* These stations are all strictly local, supplying current only in their immediate vicinities, and with the exception of the Vientiane plant, which uses diesel, burn locally scarce charcoal, adding considerably to the cost of their operation. The electric power produced is inadequate and erratic and could not under any conditions support industrial development. The Phontiou tin mine in addition has a wood-fueled electric generating plant.

Potential hydroelectric power in Laos, however, is probably very large. A survey of the entire Mekong river basin for development possibilities — proposed early in 1958 by Laos, Cambodia, South Vietnam, and Thailand — has begun under the auspices of the Economic Commission for Asia and the Far East. Extreme seasonal fluctuations in rainfall and the need to flood some areas now in wet-rice cultivation may make the cost of hydroelectric power from the Mekong prohibitive, but the survey, the initial phase of which is being financed by the International Cooperation Administration of the United States, should provide a realistic basis for any development of hydroelectric as well as navigational and irrigational potentialities. Further exploration will have to be made, too, of the large deposits of anthracite known to exist in northern Laos before the full power resources of the country can be ascertained.

DOMESTIC AND FOREIGN TRADE

MOST MERCANTILE TRANSACTIONS IN LAOS are carried on by foreigners, predominantly the Chinese but also French, Indians, Pakistani, Thai, and Vietnamese, most of whom are retail shopkeepers. Currency is the general exchange medium in the cities, although a considerable amount of barter still persists. Fixed prices are rare — bargaining is the general practice in cities and villages alike. Movement of goods within the country has to cope with a rudimentary transportation system that results in a wide variation in prices.

In the area of foreign trade Laos, like its neighbors, has always imported manufactured goods and exported raw materials. Of all the Indochinese states Laos was least active in international trade and remained during the period of French administration a deficit economy importing far more than it exported. Its trade deficits had to be made up by the trade surpluses of the rest of Indochina.

Since World War II United States and French foreign aid have filled the gap. Between 1946 and 1955 the foreign economic relations of Laos were regulated by joint arrangements between France and the Associated States of Indochina (Laos, Cambodia, and Vietnam). Central to these arrangements was the Indochinese customs union with headquarters in the Vietnamese port of Saigon. France and the Associated States accorded each other tariff preferences on imports and almost all trade was channeled through Saigon. Local currencies were tied directly to the Indochinese piaster, and indirectly to the French franc. France was the primary source of supply and the primary purchaser of goods entering and leaving the Associated States.

On January 1, 1955 these joint arrangements were terminated and the Indochinese customs union was dissolved. Relations between Laos, Cambodia, Vietnam and France were put on a bilateral basis and Laos was free to make whatever arrangements it chose with the rest of the world.

A branch of the International Junior Chamber of Commerce has been established in Vientiane, where there is also a Senior Chamber of Commerce and a Rotary Club. The latter two groups include representatives of foreign-owned firms. There are no other formal trade associations or cooperatives in the Western sense. The Chinese traders, middlemen, and moneylenders, as elsewhere in Southeast Asia, probably form closed, exclusive business groups that combine the functions of guilds and benevolent societies.

Transportation

Throughout the centuries the natural waterways of Laos — the Mekong and its tributaries — have been supplemented only by the most primitive trails and cart tracks, but communication by boat is well developed and Lao villages are for this reason usually located near water courses. The increasing importance of land transportation is suggested by the fact that there are at present about 1,400 trucks and 3,600 automobiles (including jeeps) in the country whereas in 1952 these classes of vehicles combined totaled less than 100. The French improved river navigation and began building a road system less to promote internal trade than to gain the military and political advantages in reducing the isolation of Laos from its neighbor states of Indochina. The war, the Vietminh troubles, and the recession of French influence contributed to deterioration of these projects and reconstruction is far from complete. Although railway construction has not yet begun, air transport facilities exist and are useful for shipping goods and doing government business.

Most rivers in Laos can be navigated all year by small native craft of shallow draft and a major part of the total distance of navigable waterways can be traversed by medium-sized vessels during high water.

The principal and most important artery of transportation in Laos is of course the Mekong. Its rapids and waterfalls and often narrow channel make navigation difficult for all but highly experienced boatmen and seriously impede river traffic, although some major navigation work has made all but two sections navigable throughout the year. The Khone falls (once bypassed by a railroad portage that was abandoned in 1945) on the Laotian-Cambodian border are impassable at all times. Motor truck transportation competes with commercial river transport from Kratie in Cambodia to Pakse at the head of the Khone falls. To ship via road is evidently less expensive and more convenient than to repair and use the old rail portage.

The Kemmarat rapids, formed by a series of ledges along an eighty-mile stretch beginning some thirty miles south of Savannakhet and including four major cascades in addition to several minor ones, can be navigated by launches and steamboats of six-foot draft during the high-water season but only by pirogues and sampans during low water. Between the Kemmarat rapids and Vientiane craft of two hundred metric tons with a draft of six feet can ply throughout the year. Between Luang Prabang and Ban Houei Sai motor-driven pirogues of five-ton capacity can travel year-long.

The French-installed channel markers on the Mekong were destroyed or fell into disrepair during the Vietminh troubles and have not been replaced, with the result that river traffic has been falling off. The Lao government has discussed with ICA possibilities of again marking the river channels. This was included in a survey of the Mekong river basin made by an American firm as part of a regional development project financed by ICA under the auspices of ECAFE.

The total navigable distance of the tributaries of the Mekong is about the same as that of the river itself. Only four of the many tributaries, however, are navigable to craft of the barge and launch class, although many long stretches can be traveled by sampan.

Pirogues and sampans are the most common type of river craft used in Laos. Although sometimes up to seventy feet long, pirogues average twenty-five to thirty-five feet in length and carry about seven passengers along with a pay cargo of half a ton. For speedier travel, especially for the transport of passengers, some large pirogues are equipped with engines of 50 to 80 horsepower. Extensive use is made of outboard motors on smaller pirogues.

In 1954 the Laos government allocated a large part of the reconstruction budget to road and bridge building. Most of the resources for this came from United States and French aid. In January 1955, with the end of all quadripartite associations, the two foreign economic aid programs were separately administered and each concentrated on particular sections of the road network. The United States program has centered on the roads running north from Vientiane to Luang Prabang and Xiengkhouang and south to the Thadeua ferry on the Mekong river. This latter stretch, though only fifteen miles long, is critical to the nation's economy since it forms a link in the main import-export artery running across the Mekong to the railhead at Nong Kai in Thailand, and thence by rail to Bangkok. In 1959 this road was still not adequate and was scheduled for complete rebuilding. French aid has centered on the improvement of the main highway leading south from Vientiane to Savannakhet. This is part of the longest and most important road in Laos, the artery between Luang Prabang and Saigon.

Laos has about 3,500 miles of roads and tracks of which only about 1,200 were surfaced in 1957, mostly in the south. The remaining mileage which was unsurfaced could not be used in the rainy season. Since then well over 500 miles have been surfaced or otherwise improved north of Vientiane. According to a report by the United States Operations Mission, some 921 bridges were still sorely needed. Of these many small ones and seven major ones were scheduled for construction in 1959.

United States aid has also been used to improve the ferries across the Mekong river. The principal one, from Thadeua in Laos to Nong Kai in Thailand, has now been modernized and four other Mekong ferries are scheduled for installation in 1960–61. Small manually operated ferries will be installed at all major river crossings where the bridges are out.

The highway system, instituted by the French but never completely developed, is based on a single south-to-north road from Saigon to Luang Prabang supplemented by a trellis of east-west roads leading to towns of the interior and in four instances across mountain passes to the coast of Vietnam. Road maintenance deteriorated seriously during World War II and the Vietminh campaigns and many bridges were destroyed, some since having been replaced by unsafe log structures. In the northern part of the country jeeps and trucks with high clearance can travel, but with some difficulty, from Thakhek to Luang Prabang. South of Thakhek the main roads are said to be better but there are still many bridges not permanently replaced.

Animal trails and foot paths have always linked the villages. Some of these trails, two meters wide and hard-packed by centuries of use can be made into motor roads without major realignment.

In the absence of an adequate system of highways great reliance has been put on air transport and the domestic as well as international air transport facilities of the country have been greatly expanded since the war. In 1957 international flights in and out of the principal airfield of Vientiane carried some 65,000 passengers and 5,000 tons of cargo, while domestic flights through the same field carried some 46,000 passengers and 9,000 tons of cargo.

Laos has three all-weather international airports located at Vientiane, Seno, and Pakse, and over thirty other ports or fields used for internal traffic only. Both United States and French aid have included plans for improvement of the facilities at Vientiane, including a new runway, drainage system, and terminal building. The United States aid program has also scheduled improvements for twelve of the smaller airports.

Both scheduled and unscheduled international flights are offered by at least four airlines. Air Laos has regularly scheduled flights to Saigon, Bangkok, Hong Kong, and Siemreap and Pnompenh in Cambodia. Air Viet-Nam operates between Vientiane and Saigon, Thai Airways between Vientiane and Bangkok, and Cathay Pacific Airways between Vientiane and Hong Kong. The Veha-Akat line offers domestic freight and passenger service by small planes to areas not accessible to the heavier Air Laos craft, particularly to the remote northern areas.

Domestic Marketing

Markets are held at regular intervals, sometimes on one designated day each week. Since most villages are too small to have a market the residents of several usually gather at a market place in a central village or one of the smaller towns. When the dry season comes and work on the land is finished villagers may load their pirogues with cloth and other handicraft products and travel to the highlands to barter with the mountain peoples. This custom assumes the proportions of an annual event, with the same individuals meeting and trading with the same people of the uplands year after year. Some of the highland products received in exchange are cereals, deer and rhinoceros horns, and ivory. Barter is the trading custom, but certain commodities are recognized as "hard currency": salt, brick tea, opium, tobacco in various forms, silver, and gold. The official currency is now finding its way into the village market place but many villagers still refuse to accept it.

Lengths of cloth woven in the traditional designs for which Laotian women are famous are taken to market; so are vegetables, fruits, cattle, buffalo, sheep, and goats. Rudely fashioned iron and copper tools and vessels are offered, and jewelry of various sorts is available for those who can afford it.

20. Domestic Marketing

There are some shops in the larger villages, usually run by Chinese or Indians. Many Chinese shopkeepers engage in money-lending as well as in trade.

While the village market is still the principal outlet for village-produced commodities, the cities are becoming increasingly important in this connection. Each morning dozens of pirogues loaded with rice, fish, fruits, and vegetables pull up at Vientiane and other centers. The products are sold in the city market places or exchanged for needed items.

The number of persons regularly engaged in trade in the larger centers is small, representing perhaps less than one half of one percent of the total population.

Most retail stores do not vary from each other in the kinds of merchandise they carry; cloth, thread, needles, buttons, an assortment of vessels and other receptacles, salt, spices, and some furniture are more or less standard. Stores are usually ranged side by side, each conspicuously narrow since taxes are levied in proportion to street frontage. Almost all merchandise is imported; the retail establishments contribute relatively little to the flow of locally produced goods.

Most retail merchants today buy direct from wholesalers who in turn depend primarily upon dealers in Hong Kong and Bangkok. In northern Laos merchants and traders have traditionally dealt with the Kha tribes, and to a lesser extent with the Meo, through an intermediary, the *lam*, himself a bilingual Lao with contacts among the various hill tribes. Although disappearing now, the institution of the *lam* is still to be found in the more remote areas. In 1957 there were no adequate warehouses in Vientiane, and when officials of the International Cooperation Administration surveyed possible storage facilities for incoming machinery and goods they found none available. At present better warehouses are planned for the major river ports, and warehousing facilities have already been provided at Thadeua.

The mercantile community is viewed with a mixture of tolerance and resentment by the Lao. The latter, wedded to the soil by tradition, at present show little tendency to engage in trade as a full-time profession. The merchants are likely to be resented as members of minority groups who do not conform to the patterns of living common to the Lao and enjoy a much higher standard of living. The organization of the Lao-Thai company, a recent innovation, may be the forerunner of a change in attitude.

Patterns of Foreign Trade

Achievement of economic self-determination was followed shortly
by several important changes in Laotian international trade. There
began almost immediately a marked shift from Saigon to the port of
Bangkok in Thailand — by 1958 almost 95 percent of Laos' exports
and imports were thus rerouted. Reflecting this trend, warehousing
facilities have been constructed with American aid at both Thadeua
and Bangkok. Part of this shift involved increasing trade with
Thailand itself, but by far the greater part consisted of overseas
shipments rerouted because of the large savings in transit time and
costs. Shipments between Vientiane and Saigon take sixteen days;
those between Vientiane and Bangkok technically take two days
although they are often held up much longer by customs difficulties.
The Laotian government has been negotiating with the Cambodian
government for use of the newly expanded facilities in the Cambodian port of Sihanoukville on the Gulf of Siam, but formal
agreement will probably come after completion of the port.

New import-export firms in Laos, conducting business on their
own rather than through the Chinese and French houses in Saigon,
have appeared. Many of these, however, are still controlled by
Chinese with Laotians only technically in charge. In some cases
new firms are financed by both Laotians and Thai, with the Laotians
holding the largest share of the investment. In addition, Japanese
importers and some of the old import-export firms in Saigon have
opened branches in Laos. One of the results of this expansion has
been to increase the importance of several provincial capitals as
trade centers and to move imported goods, formerly consumed almost entirely in the urban centers, to the more remote rural areas.

The postindependence change with the widest effect on both
the internal and external economy was the redirection and expansion of the United States aid program in Laos. Previously made
available indirectly through France and in French francs, this aid
has since January 11, 1955 been made available directly and in
dollars. The long-term goals of this program were twofold: first to
support the Laotian defense and security establishment through the
generation of local currency which augmented the Laos government
budget, and second to develop the national economy and raise the
standard of living as an adjunct to defense.

The aid program has been producing results in these general
directions, but one aspect of it, the commodity import program,
coupled with the patronage-ridden import licensing system and an

unrealistic exchange rate, stimulated a speculative trade in foreign exchange and imports which by the middle of 1958 had threatened to undermine not only the economy but also the confidence of the United States as well as the Laotian people in the government. The most obvious effect of this speculative boom was to fatten the pockets of importers and high government officials rather than to raise the standard of living of the rural people and lower income urban dwellers. At the same time the large quantities of local currency generated and kept in circulation in Laos by the aid program resulted in an inflationary rise in prices despite the large quantities of goods being imported.

The United States viewed these developments with increasing alarm and in mid-1958 temporarily suspended commodity import aid. This presented the Laotian government with a serious economic problem since it was dependent on this aid for a major portion of its local currency resources. The situation was aggravated politically by the fact that the former members of the Pathet Lao, then active in the government as well as in the rural areas, had abstained from indulging in the new luxuries of the cities and were using this restraint to gain support in both rural and urban areas.

This situation was finally resolved in July 1958 with the resignation of Premier Souvanna Phouma and the installation in the following month of a new government under Premier Phoui Sananikone. This government took immediate steps to revise its monetary and trade control policies including abandonment of import licensing and devaluation of the *kip*. The beneficial effects of these reforms were soon visible. In addressing an extraordinary session of the National Assembly on January 12, 1959 Premier Sananikone said:

> These radical measures were severely criticized in the beginning but facts show that prices on the domestic market are gradually returning to normal. . . . Modest budgets were not hard hit, and if less luxury cars are sold, it is no cause for alarm. The monetary reform completed last October . . . yielded the hoped-for results. Stopped for some time, foreign aid was resumed; the army and the police received abundant subsidies. Confidence was reborn.

Years of speculative trade in imports, geared to exchange rates rather than to the internal needs of the country, have made it difficult to sort out the specific long-term trends in Laotian trade patterns. Government statistics based on declared ultimate sources and destinations were distorted during the first three years by false declarations and by unauthorized re-exports or unloadings en route. Since the new monetary reforms of October 1958 many of these practices have been curtailed and trade statistics have become somewhat more representative of the actual situation.

In general the trends indicate that Laos is now exporting more and importing less, that it is adjusting its sources of supply on a more conservative and less speculative basis, and that it is purchasing fewer nonessential commodities.

Exports

The Laotian export trade, involving locally produced commodities, has been less affected by events since 1955 than the import trade, but it is still suffering from the effects of the war. Much of the already inadequate internal transport facilities were damaged, making it difficult to get products to the point of export. Forest and plantation products suffered from lack of continuing care and protection against disease. As a result postwar exports dropped off considerably from the prewar level. A further, though relatively minor, drop occurred in 1956 and 1957, probably due in part to the more lucrative import trade. In 1958 exports began to rise again, and by mid-1959 they had reached a total value of almost two million dollars, considerably above the 1955 level.

The principle commodities in the export trade have remained the same as they were prior to 1955 and until recently the relative importance of the various items in the export list also remained largely unchanged. Tin concentrates are still the principal export though both production and sales have dropped off noticeably since the pre-World War II days. During the 1955–58 import boom, tin mine owners complained of discrimination against purchases of mining equipment and other capital imports, stating that the government preferred instead to bring in luxury and consumer imports. Wood and wood products have increased in importance, probably as a result of the many new sawmills that have been installed since 1955. Another significant shift has been in cotton exports (mainly ginned cotton), which by late 1958 ranked in third place. Benzoin and benzoin bark continue to be major export items. Cardamom and hides have shown advances since 1955 while stick-lac and green coffee have dropped off (see Table 12).

Besides these principal commodities, Laos also exports such locally grown or collected items as opium, black pepper, chili peppers, dried mushrooms, peanuts, cotton seed, rice hulls, soya, brooms, areca nuts, deer horns, bear bones, and duck feathers. Opium, grown mainly by the hill tribes is exported illegally and the smuggling of opium probably returns a sizable income to some Laotian nationals.

Laos also has a sizable re-export trade which has been authorized, licensed, and recorded in separate government statistics. This involves such nonlocally produced items as automobiles, machinery, office equipment, motion-picture films and equipment, air conditioners, sheet metal, and various kinds of glass and metal containers salvaged from imported goods. Most of these items have been sold in Thailand, Cambodia, and South Vietnam. Much of this authorized re-export trade will undoubtedly drop off along with the unauthorized as a result of the 1958 monetary reforms and the removal of the speculative profit margin.

Imports

As a largely subsistence agricultural country, Laos has been and remains a heavy importer of manufactured goods, particularly clothing and textiles, processed foods, beverages and tobacco, transport equipment, cement, metal products, machinery and electrical equipment, gasoline and oil, and chemicals and medicines. Under the United States commodity import program, imports of these as well as other items were greatly increased between 1955 and 1958 (see Table 13).

Until late 1958 the speculative aspect of the import trade also resulted in the importation of large quantities of luxury items and items which were unessential and unsalable. Since large profits could be made simply through speculative manipulation of import licenses and foreign exchange, the ultimate disposability of the goods in Laos was in many cases irrelevant to the importer. Furthermore, many of the goods were held only temporarily in Laos and re-exported to Thailand or Cambodia where the demand was greater.

With the temporary suspension of United States commodity import aid in 1958, imports dropped off. Since the October 1958 monetary reforms and the reinstatement of this aid, imports remain high as compared to exports but have declined from the boom peak and are geared to local sale rather than exchange speculation and re-export. The officially recorded import volume now stands at an $18 million yearly level as compared with some $35 million per year before monetary reform.

224

Direction of Trade

Concurrent with these developments since independence has been the significant shift in the geographic pattern of Laos' international trade. Prior to 1955 Laos traded primarily with its partners in the Indochinese customs union. With the dissolution of the union and with cheap dollar exchange readily available through the commodity import program Laotian importers began to trade directly with a variety of other countries.

At the end of 1955 the principal suppliers of Laotian imports were, in order of importance in value, France (including Algeria), Thailand, South Vietnam, Japan, the United States, Hong Kong, Indonesia, the United Kingdom, and West Germany. By 1957 this pattern had changed. Japan moved to the lead followed in order by the United States, France, Hong Kong, West Germany, the United Kingdom, Indonesia, and South Vietnam. Statistics for the first half of 1959 indicate that the pattern was again changing, with the United Kingdom the principal supplier of imports followed closely by Japan. France and Indonesia were in third position, followed by the United States, Thailand, and Hong Kong.

Japan is the major supplier of clothing and textiles. The United States is a major supplier of gasoline and oil as well as transport equipment and parts, pharmaceutical products, and dry cell batteries. Indonesia supplies mainly mineral products. France and the United Kingdom supply a variety of manufactured items. Hong Kong provides large quantities of food items, both raw and dried.

In addition to these major sources, Laos also imports from many other countries in Western Europe, from British Commonwealth countries, from French Community countries, from its neighbors Cambodia and Burma, from the Philippines, South Korea, and Formosa, and from the Communist countries of the People's Republic of China, North Vietnam, and Czechoslovakia.

Since the port of Bangkok has become the primary transit point for goods entering and leaving Laos, it is difficult to assess Thailand's role as a supplier of locally produced goods to the Laotian market and as a consumer of goods produced in Laos. Although traders are required to show ultimate sources and destinations on their bills of lading, false declarations were an integral part of the recent import and exchange manipulations and have probably distorted statistics in some measure since. This situation tends to inflate the statistics for trade between Thailand and Laos. On the import side, Thailand is known to supply Laos with such locally produced items as rice, fruits and vegetables, cigarettes, rubber products, kapok, furniture, and household utensils but the total value of these imports probably places Thailand lower on the list of principal suppliers to the Laotian market than government statistics would indicate.

On the export side, ordinary overseas exports in 1959 showed the following major destinations: Thailand, South Vietnam, Hong Kong, Singapore, and France. Exports were also shipped to Cambodia, England, the United States, and West Germany, but in limited quantity. The United States and France have been the primary buyers of tin concentrates and benzoin, but tin sales to the United States have dropped or been stopped since 1956. Most of the green coffee has in the past gone to Hong Kong. Most of the sticklac, cotton, and wood goes to Thailand but large quantities of these items are probably re-exported overseas.

Balance of Trade

Laos has always had an unfavorable balance of trade, with the total value of imports considerably in excess of exports (see Table 14). The prewar trade deficit was widened by wartime setbacks to the export trade and by the speculative import boom after 1955. With the marked rise in exports during 1958 and a dropping off of imports as the boom subsided, the gap appears to be narrowing again although the data against which such trends might be measured are not very reliable. The differential is still large, however, and will probably remain so as long as the Laotian economy is heavily dependent on other countries for its manufactured goods or until the export trade can be strengthened through improvement of the internal transport system and the rehabilitation of major productive and extractive processes.

Foreign Aid

Laotian foreign trade deficits, recorded as the balance of international payments and receipts of the Laotian national economy, are in effect covered today entirely by foreign aid funds. The largest foreign aid totals are those contributed by the United States. France likewise contributes a substantial amount of aid, with smaller amounts, principally in the form of technical assistance, coming from the Colombo Plan nations, specialized agencies of the United Nations, and the Philippines, Japan, and Thailand.

Although Laos trades with Communist China and North Vietnam, it has, unlike its neighbor Cambodia, so far refused eco-

226

nomic aid from any Communist country. During 1956, however, under Premier Souvanna Phouma, Laos came close to accepting aid from Communist China. A general accord was signed between the two countries in mid-1956 and later in the year China offered Laos $70 million in aid. The Pathet Lao favored acceptance of this offer and in December 1956 made it an additional condition for a reunification agreement after an earlier agreement had been reached. Premier Souvanna refused to accept this condition, and his refusal resulted in a temporary breakdown in negotiations with the Pathet Lao.

United States Aid

The United States aid program for Laos, under the Mutual Security Program, is administered by the local operations mission of the International Cooperation Administration — the United States Operations Mission or USOM. The over-all program has two separate but related parts. The first is a combination of cash grants and the commodity import program both of which are designed primarily to generate local currency for the use of the Laotian government in supporting its defense and security establishments. Under the commodity import program, dollar credits allocated to the Laotian government are made available through a Procurement Authorization system to local importers in exchange for local currency. The cash grants supply dollars sold by the National Bank to importers. These dollars thus do double duty. On the one hand they permit a high level of commodity imports and on the other they return to the government large amounts of local currency which the government can use in its defense budget, as well as to pay the salaries of civil servants, police, teachers, public health doctors, and others. Although the system of cash grants has been questioned as basically inflationary, it has been defended on the ground that it is appropriate in a country such as Laos where exchange controls do not now exist and direct government control of dollars is impossible and unwarranted in view of the operation of the price and market mechanisms.

The second part of the program consists of the USOM's own operations variously referred to as Project Assistance, Technical Cooperation, or Economic Assistance. These include a variety of activities in agriculture, industry, mining, public works, public education and health, public administration and safety, and rural self-help. The USOM has its own dollar funds, primarily for external expenses, and in addition draws on some of the local currency generated by the cash grants and commodity import program and allocated to the government's Defense Support Fund. Thus the Laotian government and the USOM both have dollar and local currency resources available to them to spend on their respective activities (see Tables 15 and 16).

From 1954 through fiscal 1959, United States aid totaled over $225 million dollars, averaging slightly over $40 million a year from mid-1955 through 1958. For the fiscal year 1959, United States aid amounted to $25 million which represents a considerable drop from previous years, partly due to use of accumulated balances (see Table 17). For fiscal 1960 the figure is approximately $40 million.

By far the largest share of this dollar aid — about two-thirds — has ultimately gone to the defense support program. Some critics have pointed out that this is an absurd amount to maintain an armed force of 25,000 which is apparently undermanned, but defense support includes many supplementary expenses which are not strictly military in nature. The remaining one-third has gone to support the activities of the USOM, and about one-quarter of this amount, to development of the transport system.

Although there have been criticisms suggesting that the American aid program has not been well planned or coordinated, it has nevertheless enabled Laos to maintain its defense and internal security establishment, to import goods, and to provide higher salaries to government employees and the military to pay for these goods. Through the USOM it has also produced some visible and continuing results of a developmental nature and in a variety of economic and social areas. The opening and improvement of roads, ferries, and airports, the installation of a powerhouse in Vientiane, the improvement of water control, crops, and livestock, and the expansion and training of the civil service corps, particularly in teaching, health, and public administration have all been aided by the USOM program. Through participation in regional projects involving Laos' neighbors as well, the USOM has made contributions to the eradication of communicable diseases, the development of the Mekong river for power and water control, and the installation of a regional telecommunications system.

French Aid

The French Mission for Economic Aid and Technical Assistance to Laos was established in 1955 as part of a five-year program of aid and technical assistance to the three former members of the Federation of Indochina. To date France has allocated some $8 million in

228

francs to Laos, a major share of which has been used for rebuilding roads linking Laos to South Vietnam and for airfields. The remainder has been spent on training programs, technical studies, telecommunications, rural irrigation works, hospitals and schools. Included in these expenditures have been the salaries of French military instructors and of teachers in the primary and secondary schools, scholarships enabling some 170 Laotian students to study in France, and surgical and radiological equipment for the hospitals in Vientiane and Luang Prabang.

Japanese Aid

In late 1958 an economic and technical cooperation agreement was signed between Japan and Laos. Amounting to about $2.75 million in yen over a two-year period, this aid will be partly in Japanese products and partly in advisory services and will be used on various projects agreed on by both governments, including a projected waterworks for the city of Vientiane.

Commercial Agreements

Laos has only a few commercial agreements with other countries. With Cambodia and South Vietnam, Laos has concluded payments agreements providing for a settling every six months of the balances arising out of transactions with each of these countries. Other accords with these countries authorize a continuation of a form of the mutual tariff preferentials on imports similar to those in effect under the old Indochinese customs union. So far these accords have not been implemented. With Thailand, Laos has a transit agreement which permits continued use of the rail facilities between Bangkok and the Laos-Thailand border.

To foster the development of this route, Laos has negotiated a customs arrangement with Thailand under which goods entering Bangkok from overseas markets and consigned to Laos are exempt from customs levies. Shipments re-exported by Thailand to Laos — not including the above-mentioned transit shipments — entitle the Thai importer to a rebate of seven-eighths of the duty he paid when the goods entered Thailand. The agreement also provides that in customs administration neither party will discriminate against imports from the other. Both parties also agreed to take steps to control smuggling between the two countries.

A commercial convention with France provides for the general application of most-favored-nation principle to French-Lao trade plus a continuation of limited preferential arrangements. So far Laos has not acceded to the General Agreement on Tariffs and Trade (GATT) — the multilateral trade liberalization agreement in which the United States and most of the free world participate.

NATIONAL ATTITUDES

THE STATUS OF LAOS AS A POLITICAL entity within the Indochina federation was an artifical creation of the French. This fact has posed a special set of problems for Laos' leaders as they seek to find the human and material resources necessary to the functioning of a politically responsive industrialized society, capable of intelligent representation within the modern community of nations.

The Lao are not, however, without a traditional heritage — common traditions of origin, recorded events, and cultural symbols — capable of lending itself to the development of national attitudes. This national symbolism is inherited in a direct line of descent from the fourteenth-century kingdom of Lan Xang, the 350-year ascendancy of which is the Golden Age of the Lao. The full and traditional name of the country, Muong Lan Xang Hom Khao (Land of the Million Elephants and White Parasol), is emphasized in the flag and emblem of the state. The elephants (white) — represented by three joined elephant heads and forelegs — stand under a nine-tiered white parasol of state. The "Palladium of the Kingdom" — a designation of the statue of Buddha commonly called the Pra Bang, located at the royal and religious capital — also commemorates the Golden Age, for the old annals record that this Buddha was presented to the first king of Lan Xang by his Khmer mentor and father-in-law.

All Laotians, even the illiterate, know the legends of Lan Xang and the most famous kings of its royal line. For this reason changing the country's name from Laos, a French invention, back to Lan Xang has been considered. It has been said that many in remote parts of the country find neither meaning nor significance in the word "Laos."

Until very recently any real awareness of Laos as a national entity was shared only among the Western-educated members of the old royal and mandarin families. Today this small elite is expanding as foreign aid programs begin offering new educational and economic opportunities to a broader segment of the population and as younger members of an emergent middle class begin moving into positions of influence and power. It is probably safe to say that to the traditional elite of the monarchy — once absolute, now constitutional — is the symbol of unity. To them, the unity visualized is a unity of all the Lao under the central government with the king at its head and with the mass of the population continuing to accept their traditional leadership.

For the vast majority of the people of Laos, however, their world view does not extend much beyond the confines of the village and the seasonal routines of an agricultural way of life. They may know that somewhere there is a king and a government and most have, by now, voted, but probably with no clear idea that this act is designed to procure for them a responsible representative at the distant capital. A recent survey carried out by an American research organization (*Information and Attitudes in Laos,* Bureau of Social Science Research, Inc.) under the auspices of the Lao Ministry of Information indicates that most Lao, if they know anything at all about the government, tend to view it in a passive sense, as something which may be affecting their lives but in which they themselves are not personally involved. Indicative of the level of political awareness was the fact that some three-quarters of the villagers interviewed failed to respond at all to a question asking them to give the names of the two men whom they would consider the most important leaders in Laos today. The number of "don't know's" to this question was somewhat lower in the provincial capitals, but still came to slightly over 50 percent. The results of this survey indicate that awareness of foreign aid, in particular American economic aid, may be more widespread in rural Laos than knowledge of most other aspects of the national scene. For example, 45 percent of the villagers questioned reported a knowledge of American aid while in the provincial capitals and in Vientiane the number rose to between 65 and 70 percent.

The Laotian government is attempting to further a concept of nationalism through such devices as Constitution Day, which falls annually on May 11, and Independence Day, celebrated as a national holiday annually on July 19. These artificially created holidays must, however, compete with the traditional secular and religious festivals and it is doubtful whether their observance extends much beyond the larger towns and provincial capitals.

Thus far the Lao, the dominant ethnic group in Laos, have proceeded cautiously or not at all with respect to the problem of integrating the various ethnic groups within the country into a larger national culture. Laotianization of these other groups has occurred to a slight extent, as with those Kha tribes living in close proximity to the larger centers of Lao influence. Relatively little is known, however, about the extent and rapidity of such changes or about the attitudes of the various groups involved. The Tai tribes, although closely related to the lowland Lao, reportedly consider themselves superior to the latter which presumably makes them poor candidates for Laotianization. The Meo, although among the groups most distant from centers of Lao influence, are the only ethnic minority in Laos to have a representative within the national government.

It is doubtful whether for these diverse ethnic groups the possession of citizenship has much significance, at least in terms of personal identification. Under the constitution citizens are defined as all permanent residents of the country not already citizens of another nation. Membership in an ethnic group is likely to be a more important factor in self-identification. The ideal man is the superior family head and devout Buddhist, rather than a personification of civic virtue in any political sense. Only those holding political office would assume a party label, and some officials prefer to be known as of no party.

Among the elite there are many who see a unified nation as something to be highly desired, but the circumstances under which Laos as an independent country came into being and has existed ever since have denied it the conditions requisite to developing any real unity. Dependence on protection from outside and a consequent insecurity foster frustrations which are reflected in factionalism. Lacking a firmly based government, the elite are thrown back on loyalties they know are operable — those of the family. Motivations can most successfully be sought in analysis of whether action taken or desired benefits a family, its prestige, or its clients; country very often takes second place. By the same token, what by Western standards appears clearly traitorous conduct is apt to be judged entirely in the family context; if a family (or its head) chooses to condone aberrant action, as was apparently the case in the return of Prince Souphanouvong, it is a matter for that family, and not the nation. It is possible, too, that the Buddhist principle of refraining from the moral judgment of others applies here as strongly as in everyday relationships.

But national unity is only one aspect of the problem. The aspirations of leaders and key groups for the future of the country are also colored by a realization of the weakness and insecurity of Laos. Action to meet recognized necessities — such as development of the considerable natural resources and the provision of basic public services—has been deferred repeatedly. A vicious circle has come into operation: unity and true independence are seen as stemming from economic viability but a start toward economic improvement cannot precede the achievement of the security inherent in unity.

In their search for unity the Lao have relied heavily on compromise, accommodation, and the art of gentle persuasion. On the other hand, as shown in their negotiations with the French during the difficult months following V-J Day, the Lao possess a hard core of reality and an ability to sort out the various elements in a complex problem and to deal with them one by one. Patience and tact have stood the new nation in good stead thus far and it is reasonable to suppose that these same qualities will be in evidence as Laos continues to face the difficult problem of creating a homogeneous society and a national culture — a problem which, interestingly enough, faced the rulers of the Kingdom of Lan Xang some five hundred years ago.

External relations during the next decade will likewise pose serious problems for the Laotian government. Both sides in the current world ideological struggle regard Laos as a strategic area. Lacking either military or economic leverage, the Lao leadership will probably rely on its traditional realism, compromise, and restraint in an attempt to maintain some semblance of national sovereignty in the midst of the political maneuvering of the major powers. Whether this approach can be successful remains to be seen, but it may be significant in this context that the history of Lan Xang is not without parallels to the present situation, and that historically the Lao have shown a considerable aptitude for political maneuver and political survival in the face of apparently overwhelming odds.

Table 1. LIST OF LAOTIAN RULERS

I. The Kingdom of Lan Xang (1353-1707)

1353-1373	Fa Ngoun
1373-1416	Sam Sene Thai
1416-1428	Lan Kham Deng
1428-1438	Nang Keo Phimpha
1438-1479	Sai Tiakaphat
1479-1486	Thene Kham
1486-1496	La Sene Thai
1496-1501	Som Phou
1501-1520	Visoun
1520-1547	Photisarath
1548-1571	Setthathirath
1571-1575	Sene Soulintha
1575-1579	Maha Oupahat
1580-1582	Sene Soulintha
1582-1583	Nakhone Noi
1583-1591	Interregnum period
1591-1596	Nokeo Koumane
1596-1622	Thammikarath
1622-1623	Oupagnouvarath
1623-1627	Photisarath II
1627-1637	Mone Keo, Tone Kham, Visai
1637-1694	Souligna Vongsa
1694-1700	Tian Thala
1700	Nan Tharat
1700-1707	Sai Ong Hue

II. Laotian Principalities (1707-1836)

A. Vientiane

1707-1735	Sai Ong Hue
1735-1760	Ong Long
1760-1778	Ong Boun
1778-1782	Interregnum period
1782-1792	Chao Nan
1792-1805	Chao In
1805-1828	Chao Anou

B. Luang Prabang

1707-1726	King Kitsarath
1726-1727	Khamone Noi
1727-1776	Intha Som
1776-1781	Sotika Koumane
1781-1787	Tiao Vong
1787-1791	Interregnum period
1791-1817	Anourout
1817-1836	Mantha Thourath

III. Period of Siamese Expansion (1836-93)

1836-1850	Souka Seum (King of Luang Prabang)
1851-1869	Tiantha Koumane
1872-1894	Oun Kham

IV. Modern Period (1894-)

1894-1904	Zakarine
1904-1959	Sisavang Vong
1959-	Savang Vatthana

Source: Adapted from Gerald C. Hickey, *Area Handbook on Laos*, pp. 54-55.

Table 2. **POPULATION ESTIMATES BY PROVINCE AND BY PRINCIPAL TOWNS, 1958**

Province	Minimum	Maximum	Principal Towns(a)
Luang Prabang	210,000	280,000	Luang Prabang, capital, from 7,000 to 15,000. Of six other places classifiable as towns, the largest is Muong Sai with population estimated from 1,000 to 3,000.
Vientiane	180,000	250,000	Vientiane, capital, from 45,000 to 80,000. A more recent census of Vientiane (April-August 1959) gives 68,206. The maximum estimated population (1958) of the five other towns listed for Vientiane province is 3,000.
Savannakhet	270,000	350,000	Savannakhet, capital, from 7,000 to 10,000.
Khammouane	120,000	160,000	Thakhek, capital, from 4,000 to 7,000.
Champassak	170,000	220,000	Pakse, capital, from 6,000 to 10,000.
Attopeu	60,000	90,000	Attopeu, capital, from 2,500 to 3,000.
Saravane	160,000	200,000	Saravane, capital, from 2,000 to 2,500.
Sayaboury	140,000	180,000	Sayaboury, capital, from 2,000 to 3,000.
Nam Tha	65,000	100,000	Nam Tha, capital, from 1,500 to 3,000.
Xiengkhouang	130,000	170,000	Xiengkhouang, capital, from 3,000 to 4,000.
Phongsaly	70,000	100,000	Phongsaly, capital, from 2,000 to 3,000.
Samneua	80,000	110,000	Samneua, capital, from 2,500 to 3,500.
Total	1,655,000	2,210,000	

(a) The range between minimum and maximum figures reflects the varying definitions of town boundaries in Laos.

Source: Kingdom of Laos, Ministère des Finances de l'Economie Nationale et du Plan, *Bulletin Statistique du Laos,* 1958.

Tables

Table 3. **ETHNIC COMPOSITION OF POPULATION BY PROVINCE, 1921**

(percentages of total)

Province	Lao and Lu	Tai	Kha	Meo and Man	Ho, Kho, Others	Totals
Houa Khong (Nam Tha)	23	6	47	6	6	29,000
Phong Saly	25	4	50	3	12	26,000
Houa Phans (Samneua)	....	75	18	6	....	44,000
Luang Prabang[a]	50	2	42	4	n[b]	225,000
Tran Ninh (Xiengkhouang)	57	18	....	20	n	51,000
Vientiane	70	22	1	2	n	68,000
Khammouane	80	20	....	....	n	70,000
Savannakhet	48	31	19	....	....	80,000
Saravane	38	27	33	....	n	69,000
Bassac (Champassak)	89	....	8	....	n	105,000
Attopeu	18	....	81	....	n	52,000
LAOS	52	15	27	3	0.8	819,000

(a) Includes Sayaboury province.
(b) n = negligible.

Source: Adapted from Kingdom of Laos, Ministère des Finances de l'Economie Nationale et du Plan, *Annuaire Statistique du Laos, 1951-1952,* pp. 38-39.

Table 4. **ETHNIC COMPOSITION OF POPULATION BY PROVINCE, 1953**[a]

Province[b]	Population	Percentage of Thai Peoples[c]	Percentage of Kha Peoples	Percentage of Meo and Yao Peoples
Nam Tha	46,809	36.54	57.25	6.21
Luang Prabang	136,821	48.74	46.35	4.91
Sayaboury	98,516	87.69	8.29	4.02
Xiengkhouang	93,609	47.10	30.01	39.89
Vientiane	186,269	98.77	.17	1.06
Khammouane	108,603	91.88	8.12	....
Savannakhet	214,974	79.89	20.22	....
Saravane	125,957	52.00	48.00	....
Champassak	122,078	96.47	3.53	....
Attopeu	43,350	29.70	70.30	....

(a) This table does not include European, Vietnamese, Chinese, or Siamese, who reside primarily in the towns.
(b) There are no figures given for Phongsaly and Samneua provinces which at the time were under the control of the Pathet Lao.
(c) Includes both Lao and tribal Tai.

Source: Compiled by Joel Halpern from various Laotian government sources.

Table 5. **NUMBER OF STUDENTS IN ELEMENTARY SCHOOLS, 1959**

Province	Schools(a) Male	Female	Pagoda schools Male	Female	Total
Vientiane	12,349	7,168	990	656	21,163
Khammouane	6,354	2,332	235	119	9,040
Savannakhet	9,548	2,438	832	219	13,037
Champassak	6,488	2,832	1,576	917	11,813
Saravane	3,220	1,005	1,152	211	5,588
Attopeu	2,173	778	17	12	2,980
Luang Prabang	6,625	4,114	38	14	9,791
Xiengkhouang	4,430	1,027	25	2	5,484
Sayaboury	3,806	1,531	187	73	5,597
Samneua	3,055	527	2,119	207	5,908
Nam Tha	2,104	621	....	....	2,725
Phongsaly	538	349	....	....	887
Total	60,690	23,722	7,171	2,430	94,013

(a) Including rural education centers.

Source: Compiled by Joel Halpern from various Laotian government sources.

Table 6. **NUMBER OF STUDENTS IN SECONDARY SCHOOLS, 1959**

	Secondary schools						Professional				Technical				Total
	Lycee		Collèges		Normal		Law		Medicine		Arts		Trade		
Province	M(a)	F	M	F	M	F	M	F	M	F	M	F	M	F	
Vientiane	738	224	......	......	190	66	83	4	9	9	23	21	58	......	1,425
Khammouane	......	......	132	19	......	......	......	......	......	......	......	......	......	......	151
Savannakhet	......	......	237	26	......	......	......	......	......	......	......	......	34	......	297
Champassak	......	......	188	51	......	......	......	......	......	......	......	......	......	......	239
Saravane	......	......	......	......	......	......	......	......	......	......	......	......	......	......	......
Attopeu	......	......	......	......	......	......	......	......	......	......	......	......	......	......	......
Luang Prabang	......	......	116	58	......	......	......	......	......	......	......	......	......	......	174
Xiengkhouang	......	......	92	18	......	......	......	......	......	......	......	......	......	......	110
Sayaboury	......	......	......	......	......	......	......	......	......	......	......	......	......	......	......
Nam Tha	......	......	......	......	......	......	......	......	......	......	......	......	......	......	......
Samneua	......	......	......	......	......	......	......	......	......	......	......	......	......	......	......
Phongsaly	......	......	......	......	......	......	......	......	......	......	......	......	......	......	......
Total	738	224	765	172	190	66	83	4	9	9	23	21	92	......	2,396

(a) M = male; F = female.

Source: Compiled by Joel Halpern from various Laotian government sources.

Table 7. **NEWSPAPERS RECENTLY PUBLISHED IN LAOS** [a]

Name	Language	Published	Circulation	Publisher or political party affiliation
Ana Chak Lao	Lao		Unknown	CDIN
Anaked	Lao		5,000	RLP
Kham Mouan	Lao	Bimonthly	2,500	RLP
Lao Hak Sat	Lao	Weekly	10,000	Neo Lao Hak Sat
Lao Haksa Sat	Lao	Weekly	15,000	CDIN
	French	Bimonthly	10,000	
Lao Huam Lao	Lao	Bimonthly	5,000	RLP
Lao Huam Samphan	Lao	Weekly	5,000	National Union
Lao Lan Yang	Lao	Bimonthly	Unknown	RLP
Lao Mai	Lao		Unknown	Bong Souvannavong
Lae Presse	Lao	Daily	2,000	Government organ
	French	Daily	1,600	
L'Avenir du Laos	French	Bimonthly	1,500	
La Voix du Peuple	French	Bimonthly	2,000	RLP
(Sieng Rajsadorn)	Lao		Unknown	
Le Maha Sohn	Lao		Unknown	Phoui Sananikone
L'Independant	French	Weekly	Unknown	Phoui Sananikone
Midthaharn	Lao	Weekly	3,000	Army
Prachathipatay	Lao		1,500	Democratic
Santiphab	Lao		Unknown	Neutrality
Sieng Lao	Lao	Biweekly	Unknown	Democratic
Tamruaj Samphan	Lao	Weekly	10,000	Police department

(a) Exclusive of newspapers published by foreign nationals.

Source: United States Information Service, *Briefing Notes on the Royal Kingdom of Laos*, 1959.

Table 8. WAGES PAID IN THE CONSTRUCTION INDUSTRY IN VIENTIANE AND VICINITY, 1956

(in kip per month)(a)

Classification	Ministry of public works	Private contractors	
		Laotian	Vietnamese
Blacksmith	2,000 to 2,500		
Blacksmith, chief	3,500		
Carpenter	3,000 to 3,500	150 to 190(b)	220 to 330(b)
Clerk, stock	2,500		
Driver, light vehicles		2,000 to 3,000	
Driver, truck	2,800 to 3,200		
Driver, heavy trucks		3,500 to 4,800	
Driver's assistant		2,300 to 3,000	
Fitter (mechanic)	3,000		
Laborer	35 to 40(b)		
Laborer, chief	2,500 to 3,000		
Laborer, female		35 to 45(b)	
Laborer, male	40 to 45(b)	40 to 55(b)	
Laborer, skilled		50 to 65(b)	
Mason		140 to 180(b)	200 to 300(b)
Mason, experienced	4,500	6,500 to 7,000	7,500 to 8,200
Motor rewinder	4,000		
Operator, diesel			
Operator, engine	3,500 to 4,000		
Operator, engine, asst.	2,200 to 2,500		
Operator, lathe	4,000		
Operator, milling mach.	5,000		
Operator, road roller	3,000		
Plumber	2,500 to 3,000		
Plumber, sanitary		160 to 220(b)	200 to 320(b)
Wheelwright	2,000 to 2,200		
Woodworker	3,000 to 3,500	150 to 200(b)	220 to 330(b)
Woodworker, experienced		7,500 to 8,300	7,000 to 7,800

(a) 35 kip: $1.
(b) Wages per day.

Source: Adapted from various United States government sources.

Table 9. MONTHLY SALARIES OF GOVERNMENT PERSONNEL AT LUANG PRABANG, 1959
(in *kip*)(a)

Category	Number of Persons in Each Category	Percent	Amount Paid(b)
Less than 2,000	9	1.35	16,950
2,001 - 2,500	10	1.73	21,660
2,500 - 3,000	7	1.47	18,549
3,001 - 3,500	54	14.67	184,612
3,501 - 4,000	55	16.56	208,274
4,001 - 4,500	26	8.83	111,505
4,501 - 5,000	18	6.71	84,506
5,001 - 5,500	17	7.04	88,651
5,501 - 6,000	12	5.50	69,110
6,001 - 6,500	8	4.00	50,382
6,501 - 7,000	12	6.38	80,194
7,001 - 7,500	10	5.74	72,304
7,501 - 8,000	5	3.10	39,105
8,001 - 8,500	3	1.96	24,624
8,501 - 9,000	4	2.76	34,679
9,001 - 9,500	5	3.65	45,691
9,501 - 10,000	3	2.32	29,278
10,001 - 10,500	2	1.63	20,562
10,501 - 11,000	......	......	....
11,001 - 11,500	2	1.80	22,657
11,501 - 12,000	3	2.80	35,227
Total	265	100	1,258,520

(a) 80 *kip*: $1.

(b) These amounts do not include family allotments, which range from 800-950 *kip* per month for a wife and 400-500 for each child.

Source: Compiled by Joel Halpern from various Laotian government sources.

246

Table 10. MEDICAL FACILITIES IN LAOS, 1957

Province	Hospitals	Infirmaries	Dispensaries
Phongsaly		1	3
Nam Tha		1	5
Luang Prabang	1	1	12
Sayaboury		1	5
Samneua		1	8
Xiengkhouang	1		6
Vientiane	1		17
Khammouane	1		9
Savannakhet	1		13
Champassak	1		9
Saravane		1	11
Attopeu		1	2
Total	6	7	100

Source: United States Operations Mission, A. H. Holloway, *Basic Data for Planning a Public Health Program in the Kingdom of Laos,* October 1957.

Table 11. MEDICAL PERSONNEL IN LAOS, 1958

Lao *médicins indochinois*	31
Lao physician trained in France	1
Lao physician trained in Thailand	1
Thai physician	1
Japanese physicians	2
French physicians (3 in private practice; 13 in military)	16
Filipino physicians with Operation Brotherhood (1959)	19
Iranian physician (on USOM staff)	1
World Health Organization physicians	2
American physicians	3
Lao nurses (male and female)	450
French army nurses	12
Filipino nurses with Operation Brotherhood	30
French dentists	2
Filipino dentist with Operation Brotherhood	1
Total	572

Source: United States Operations Mission to Laos, *American Cooperation with Laos,* 1959.

Table 12. **LAO EXPORTS BY COMMODITIES, 1956-58**

(in thousand *kip*)(a)

Commodity	1956	1957	First nine months of 1958
Tin concentrates	16,285	18,050	11,700
Benzoin and benzoin bark	8,720	4,984	4,315
Coffee, green	7,435	3,338	2,018
Stick-lac	279	2,159	274
Cardamom	2,854	1,583	4,433
Wood and wood products	2,654	1,613	6,319
Hides and skins	3,302	1,173	1,352
Cotton, unginned	763	1,009	1,699
Cotton, ginned	....	....	3,223
Other commodities	1,980	3,835	5,782

(a) 35 *kip*: $1.

Source: Adapted from United States Department of Commerce, *Basic Data on the Economy of Laos,* 1958; and Kingdom of Laos, Ministère des Finances de l'Economie Nationale et du Plan, *Bulletin Statistique du Laos,* No. 1-3, 1958.

248

Table 13.   LAO IMPORTS BY COMMODITIES, 1956-58
(in thousand *kip*)(a)

Commodity	1956	1957	First nine months of 1958
Yarns, textiles, and clothing	276,436	311,468	122,151
Transport equipment and parts	144,477	219,785	101,615
Metal and metal products	99,987	157,477	101,346
Processed foods, beverages, tobacco	104,033	151,803	98,216
Chemicals and products	67,016	100,960	41,240
Mineral products	52,194	96,566	105,973
Fruits, vegetables and products	141,572	93,717	42,217
Machinery and parts	52,507	60,075	80,034
Paper and paper products	47,888	39,689	39,493
Animals and animal products	24,194	38,132	10,464
Shoes, umbrellas and hats	24,482	28,280	8,035
Stoneware, ceramics, glass, and products	16,552	27,714	14,658
Plastic and rubber products	20,498	25,730	13,005
Wood and wood products	36,092	20,293	7,824
Animal and vegetable fats, and oils	1,863	13,261	4,299
Scientific instruments, clocks, etc.	22,338	7,305	4,953
Leather, skins, and leather products	5,399	6,312	1,693
Arms and ammunition	1,743	6,276	1,269
Precious stones, metals and jewelry	2,718	768	272
Other (electrical equipment, toys, art objects, etc.)	17,357	55,290	14,350

(a) 35 *kip*: $1.

Source: Adapted from United States Department of Commerce, *Basic Data on the Economy of Laos*, 1958; and Kingdom of Laos, Ministère des Finances de l'Economie Nationale et du Plan, *Bulletin Statistique du Laos*, No. 1-3, 1958.

Tables

Table 14. TRADE BALANCES, 1955-58
(in thousand *kip*)(a)

Year	Exports	Imports	Balance
1955	48,025	662,969	− 614,944
1956	44,272	1,236,043	− 1,191,771
1957	37,744	1,460,873	− 1,423,129
1958	54,000(b)	1,200,000(b)	− 1,146,000(b)

(a) 35 *kip:* $1.
(b) Estimated.

Source: United States Department of Commerce, *Basic Data on the Economy of Laos,* 1958; and Kingdom of Laos, Ministère des Finances de l'Economie Nationale et du Plan, *Bulletin Statistique du Laos,* No. 1-3, 1958.

Table 15. TOTALS OF UNITED STATES PROJECT AID TO LAOS FOR FISCAL YEARS 1958 AND 1959
(in thousands of dollars)

	1958	1959
Agriculture	142	301
Industry and mining	114	215
Transportation	1,062	2,325
Health and sanitation	40(a)	61(a)
Education	333	434
Civil police administration	188	149
Public administration	97	57
Community development	659	600
General and miscellaneous	6	100
Total	2,641	4,242

(a) Does not include Asian Economic Development Fund regional appropriation for malaria eradication in Laos totaling $237,000 in 1958 and $120,000 in 1959.

Source: United States Operations Mission to Laos, *American Cooperation with Laos,* 1959.

Table 16.   **UNITED STATES PROJECT AID TO LAOS FOR FISCAL YEAR 1959 BY PROJECT**

(in thousands of dollars)

Project	Dollars	Kip[(a)]
Agriculture and natural resources		
Agriculture extension	50	21
Irrigation development	53	302
Livestock and poultry	100	57
Crop development	70	29
Forest resources	28	25
Subtotal	301	434
Industry and mining		
Mining and mineral survey	215	......
Vientiane power	......	27
Subtotal	215	27
Transportation		
National road system	1,265	875
Rivers, harbors, and ferries	295	
Vientiane airport	765	
Subtotal	2,325	875
Public health		
Yaws eradication		9
Training of health workers	61[(b)]	9
Malaria eradication		157
Subtotal	61	175
Education		
Teacher training	384	269
Rural education	50	88
Subtotal	434	357
Public administration, police, and other		
Police	149	940
Government purchasing office	42	31
Public administration	......	......
Banking	12	......
Customs	3	88
American aid commission	......	16
Statistics and census	......	19
Subtotal	206	1,094

Table 16. (continued)

Project	Dollars	Kip(a)
Community development		
Xiengkhouang Demonstration Project	70	15
Civic action	70	579
Rural self-help	210	313
Operation Brotherhood	250	......
Subtotal	600	907
Miscellaneous		
Lao Photo Press	100	114
Subtotal	100	114
Total for Laos	4,242	3,983

(a) Figures converted into United States dollars at 80 *kip:* $1.

(b) Does not include Asian Economic Development Fund regional appropriation for malaria eradication in Laos totaling $237,000 in 1958 and $120,000 in 1959.

Source: United States Operations Mission to Laos, *American Cooperation with Laos,* 1959.

Table 17. **TOTAL FUNDS OBLIGATED IN UNITED STATES AID TO LAOS FOR FISCAL YEARS 1958 AND 1959**
(in millions of dollars)

	1958	1959
Military budget support	19.8	11.2
Other nonproject assistance	7.5	7.2
Project assistance	2.6	4.2(a)
Technical support of USOM program	1.5	2.8(b)
Total	31.4	25.4

(a) Does not include Asian Economic Development Fund regional appropriation for malaria eradication in Laos totaling $237,000 in 1958 and $120,000 in 1959.

(b) Including special appropriation for USOM housing construction.

Source: United States Operations Mission to Laos, *American Cooperation with Laos,* 1959.

A SELECTED BIBLIOGRAPHY

A SELECTED BIBLIOGRAPHY

This bibliography is intended to provide an introduction to the literature on Laos. For more complete lists the reader is referred to the bibliographic sources listed below. Those items marked with an asterisk were found to be especially helpful in the preparation of the present volume.

ABADIE, M. *Les races du Haut-Tonkin.* Paris: Challamel, 1924.

Annuaire des Etats-Associés: Cambodge-Laos-Vietnam. Paris: Diloutremer et Havas, 1953 to present.

ARCHAIMBAULT, CHARLES. "Les techniques rituelles de la pêche du Palom au Laos," *Bulletin de l'École française d'Extrême-Orient,* XLIX, No. 1 (1958), 297-335.

—————. "Les rites agraires dans le moyen-Laos," *France-Asie,* XVI, Nos. 160-63 (1959), 1185-94; 1274-83.

AYMONIER, ETIENNE. *Voyage dans le Laos.* 2 vols. Paris: Leroux, 1895.

BARNEY, GEORGE L. "Christianity: Innovation in Meo Culture: A Case Study in Missionization." Unpublished Master's thesis, University of Minnesota, 1957. 100 pp.

—————. "The Meo and Incipient Church," *Practical Anthropology,* IV, No. 2 (1957).

BENEDICT, PAUL K. "Languages and Literatures of Indochina," *Far Eastern Quarterly,* VI (1947), 379-89.

—————. "Thai, Kadai, and Indonesian: A New Alignment in Southeastern Asia," *American Anthropologist,* n.s., XLIV (1942), 576-601.

BENEDICT, RUTH. *Thai Culture and Behavior.* (Data Paper No. 4, Southeast Asia Studies.) Ithaca: Cornell University, 1952. Mimeographed. (Written in 1943; contains information on the Lao of northeast Thailand.)

* BERNARD, N. "Les Khas, peuple inculte du Laos française," *Bulletin de Géographie Historique et Descriptive,* XI (1904), 283-388.

256

Boun Oum, Prince. "Allocution à l'occasion de la signature des Conventions franco-laotiennes," *France-Asie*, No. 46-47 (January-February 1950), 629-31.

Briggs, L. P. *The Ancient Khmer Empire*. Philadelphia: American Philosophical Society, 1951.

Broderick, A. H. *Little Vehicle: Cambodia and Laos*. London: Hutchinson, 1949.

Bulletin Economique de l'Indochine (monthly). Saigon, 1898 to present.

* *Bulletin de l'École française d'Extrême-Orient* (quarterly). Hanoi, 1901 to present.

* *Bulletin de la Société des Etudes Indochinoises* (quarterly). Saigon, 1883 to present.

Bulletin des Amis du Laos (quarterly). Hanoi, 1937-40.

Bulletin des Amis du Vieux Hué (quarterly). Hanoi, 1914-44.

Burchett, W. T. *Mekong Upstream*. Hanoi: Red River Publishing House, 1957.

Bureau of Social Science Research, Inc. *Information and Attitudes in Laos* (Raymond Fink, Study Director). Washington, 1959. (Mimeographed.)

Cady, J. F. *The Roots of French Imperialism in Eastern Asia*. Ithaca: Cornell University Press, 1954.

* Canada. Department of Mines and Technical Surveys. *Indo-China: A Geographical Appreciation*. (Foreign Geography Information Series, No. 6.) Ottawa, 1953.

* Coedes, G. *Les Etats hindouisés d'Indochine et d'Indonésie*. Paris: E. de Boccard, 1948.

Cordier, G. *Bibliotheca Indosinica: Dictionnaire bibliographique des ouvrages relatifs à la Péninsule indochinoise*. 4 vols. Paris: Imprimerie Nationale, 1912-14.

Cupet, Pierre P. *Voyages au Laos et chez les sauvages de Sud-Est de l'Indochine*. Introduction by A. Pavie. (*Mission Pavie: Indochine, 1879-1895, Géographie et voyages*, Vol. III.) Paris: Leroux, 1900.

d'Erceuil, C. "Le Laos dans le Drame du Sud-Est Asiatique," *L'Afrique et l'Asie*, No. 23 (3rd Quarter, 1953), 50-66.

d'Orleans, Henri. *Around Tonkin and Siam*. London: Chapman and Hall, 1894.

de Malglaive, Marie C. L. J. and Armand J. Riviere. *Voyages au centre de l'Annam et du Laos et dans les régions sauvages de l'est de l'Indochine*. Introduction by A. Pavie. (*Mission Pavie: Indochine, 1879-1895, Géographie et voyages*, Vol. IV.) Paris: Leroux, 1902.

* DE REINACH, LUCIEN. *Le Laos*. 2 vols. Paris: A. Charles, 1901. (Posthumous edition compiled by P. Chemin-Dupontes. Paris, 1911.)
* DEYDIER, HENRI. *Introduction à la Connaissance du Laos*. Saigon: Imprimerie Française d'Outre-Mer, 1952.
————. "Le Râmâyana au Laos," *France-Asie*, IX, No. 78 (1952), 871-73.
————. *Lokapâla: Génies, Totems et Sorciers du Nord Laos*. Paris: Librairie Plon, 1954.
* DEYOUNG, JOHN. *Village Life in Modern Thailand*. Berkeley: University of California Press, 1955.
DIGUET, E. *Les Montagnards du Tonkin*. Paris: Challamel, 1908.
DOBBY, E. H. G. *Southeast Asia*. New York: Wiley, 1950.
DOOLEY, THOMAS A. "Foreign Aid: The Human Touch," *New York Times Magazine*, April 20, 1958.
————. *The Edge of Tomorrow*. New York: Farrar, Strauss, and Cudahy, 1958.

EMBREE, JOHN and LILLIAN OTA DOTSON. *Bibliography of the Peoples and Cultures of Mainland Southeast Asia*. New Haven: Yale University, Southeast Asia Studies, 1950.
* EMBREE, JOHN and WILLIAM L. THOMAS JR. *Ethnic Groups of Northern Southeast Asia*. New Haven: Yale University, Southeast Asia Studies, 1950. (Mimeographed.)

* FALL, BERNARD B. "The International Relations of Laos," *Pacific Affairs*, XXX, No. 1 (March 1957), 22-34.
Far Eastern Economic Review (quarterly). Hong Kong, 1946 to present.
Far Eastern Survey (fortnightly). New York, 1932 to present.
FINOT, LOUIS. "Recherches sur la littérature laotienne," *Bulletin de l'École française d'Extrême-Orient*, XVII, No. 5 (1917), 1-218.
France. Ambassade de France. *Laos Benefits from French Economic Aid and Technical Assistance*. New York: French Press and Information Service, January 1960.
* *France-Asie* (monthly). Saigon, 1946 to present.

Geneva Conference, 1954. *Conférence de Genève sur l'Indochine, 8 mai-21 juillet 1954; procès-verbaux des séances, propositions, documents finaux*. Paris: Imprimerie Nationale, 1955.
GILKEY, ROBERT. "Laos: Politics, Elections, and Foreign Aid," *Far Eastern Survey*, June 1958, 89-94.
GIRONCOURT, G. DE. "Recherches de géographie musicale en Indochine," *Bulletin de la Société des Etudes Indochinoises*, n.s., XVII (1942), 1-174.

258

GOUROU, PIERRE. *Land Utilization in French Indochina.* 3 vols. Washington: Institute of Pacific Relations, 1945.
————. "Land Utilization in Upland Areas of Indochina." Pages 24-42 in Institute of Pacific Relations, *Development of Upland Areas of the Far East,* Vol. II. New York: Institute of Pacific Relations, 1951.
————. "The Quality of Land Use of Tropical Cultivators." In William L. Thomas Jr. (ed.), *Man's Role in Changing the Face of the Earth.* Chicago: University of Chicago Press, 1956.

* HALL, D. G. E. *A History of South-East Asia.* London: Macmillan, 1955.
* HALPERN, JOEL MARTIN. *Aspects of Village Life and Culture Change in Laos.* (Special report prepared for the Council on Economic and Cultural Affairs, prepublication copy.) New York: Council on Economic and Cultural Affairs, August 1958.
————. "Trade Patterns in Northern Laos," *Eastern Anthropologist,* XII, No. 2 (1958), 119-24.
————. "Economic Development and American Aid in Laos," *Practical Anthropology,* VI, No. 4 (July-August 1959), 151-71.
HAMMER, ELLEN J. *The Struggle for Indochina.* Stanford: Stanford University Press, 1954.
* HICKEY, GERALD C. (ed.). *Area Handbook on Laos.* HRAF Subcontractor's Monograph No. 23. University of Chicago, 1955. (Mimeographed.)
HOLLOWAY, A. H. *Basic Data for Planning a Public Health Program in the Kingdom of Laos.* Vientiane: United States Operations Mission to Laos, October 1957. (Mimeographed.)

Indochina. *Codes laotiens: Code civil, code pénal, code de procédure.* Hanoi: Imprimerie d'Extrême-Orient, 1908.
Indochina. Direction des affaires économiques, Service de la statistique générale. *Annuaire statistique de l'Indochine.* Hanoi and Saigon, 1927-49.
Indochine, Sud-Est Asiatique (monthly). Paris, 1951 to present.
* Institut d'Emission des Etats du Cambodge, du Laos, et du Viêtnam: Service des études économiques et financières. *Etudes et documents* (quarterly). Saigon, 1952 to present.
International Commission for Supervision and Control of Laos. *First Interim Report, August 11, 1954–December 31, 1954.* London: H. M. Stationary Office, 1955.
* IZIKOWITZ, KARL GUSTAV. *Lamet: Hill Peasants in French Indochina.* (Etnologiska Studier, No. 17.) Göteborg: Etnografiska Museet, 1951.

A Selected Bibliography

JANSE, O. R. T. *The Peoples of French Indochina.* (Smithsonian Institution War Background Studies, No. 14.) Washington: Smithsonian Institution, 1943.

JOHNSON, RAS OLIVER. *A Study of Education in Laos.* Vientiane: United States Operations Mission to Laos, November 23, 1956. (Mimeographed.)

Journal of Asian Studies (quarterly). Ann Arbor, 1956 to present. (Successor to *Far Eastern Quarterly.*)

KAUFMAN, HOWARD K. *Village Life in Vientiane Province.* Vientiane: United States Operations Mission to Laos, October 1956. (Mimeographed.)

————. *Lao Village Life.* Vientiane: United States Operations Mission to Laos, 1957. (Mimeographed lecture.)

Keesing's Contemporary Archives (weekly). London: Keesing's Publications, 1931 to present.

KENE, THAO. *Bibliographie du Laos.* Vientiane: Ministère de l'Éducation Nationale, Editions Comité littéraire lao, 1958.

* *Kingdom of Laos: The Land of the Million Elephants and of the White Parasol.* René de Berval (ed.). Saigon: *France-Asie,* 1959. (Contains an extensive bibliography. First published in French in 1956 as *Présence du Royaume Lao* in Nos. 118-120 of *France-Asie.*)

KLAUSNER, WILLIAM J. *Report* (on village of Nong Khon near Ubon, Thailand). Bangkok: United States Operations Mission to Thailand, November 6, 1956. (Mimeographed.)

LAFONT, PIERRE-BERNARD. *Slash-and-Burn Culture Methods among the Mountain Peoples of Central Vietnam.* Bangkok: Ninth Pacific Science Congress, 1957. (Mimeographed.)

Laos. Royal Embassy of Laos, Press and Information Service. *About Laos.* Washington, 1957.

————. Royal Embassy of Laos, Press and Information Service. *Laos Information Bulletin* (quarterly). Washington, 1958 to present.

————. Royal Embassy of Laos, Press and Information Service. *The Facts behind the Pathet Lao Affair; Conference Given by Sisouk Na Champassak, Secretary of State for Information and Youth, 23 June 1959.* Washington, 1959.

————. Commissariat du Plan. *Plan de développement économique et social du Laos; periode de 5 ans du 30 juin 1959 au 1ER juillet 1964.* Vientiane, 1959.

————. Ministère des Affaires Etrangères, de l'Éducation Nationale et de l'Information. *Constitution du royaume du Laos, 11 mai 1947. Texte revisé et adopté par le Congrès National en sa Séance du 29 septembre 1956.* Vientiane, 1957 (?).

260

————. Ministère d'Information. *Bulletin Quotidien d'Information.* (Roneotyped daily information sheet.) Vientiane, 1952-55.

————. Ministère des Finances, de l'Economie et du Plan: Direction de la Statistique. *Annuaire Statistique du Laos.* Vientiane, 1950 to present.

————. Ministère des Finances, de l'Economie et du Plan: Direction de la Statistique. *Bulletin du commerce exterieur: importations-exportations* (irregular publication). Vientiane, 1950 to present.

————. Ministère des Finances, de l'Economie et du Plan: Direction de la Statistique. *Bulletin statistique du Laos* (quarterly). Vientiane, 1950 to present.

* LE BOULANGER, PAUL. *Histoire du Laos Français; Essai d'une Etude Chronologique des Principautés Laotiennes.* Paris: Librairie Plon, 1931.

Le Laos. Introduction by Jean-Paul Marchand. Paris: J. Peyronnet, 1948.

LE CLERE, ADHEMARD. *Histoire du Cambodge depuis 1ᴱᴿ siècle de notre ère, d'apres les inscriptions lapidaires, les Annales chinoises et annamites et les documents européens des six derniers siècles.* Paris: P. Geuthner, 1914.

LEFEVRE-PONTALIS, PIERRE. "Voyages dans le Haut Laos et sur les frontières de Chine et de Birmanie." Introduction by A. Pavie. (*Mission Pavie: Indochine, 1879-1895, Géographie et voyages,* Vol. V.) Paris: Leroux, 1902.

LEERBURGER, FRANKLIN J. "Laos: Case Study of U. S. Foreign Aid," *Foreign Policy Bulletin,* XXXVIII, No. 5 (January 1, 1959), 61-63.

LEROI-GOURHAN, ANDRE (ed.). *Ethnologie de l'union française. Pays d'outre-mer: colonies, empires, pays autonomes: peuples et civilisations d'outre-mer,* 6th series. (Vol. II.) Paris: Presses Universitaires de France, 1953.

LEVY, PAUL. "Les traces de l'Introduction du Bouddhisme à Luang-Prabang," *Bulletin de l'École Française d'Extrême-Orient,* XL (1940), 411-24.

————. "Les tatouages laotiens," *Bulletin et Travaux de l'Institut Indochinois pour l'Étude de l'Homme,* IV, (1941), 113-18.

LEWIS, NORMAN. *A Dragon Apparent: Travels in Indochina.* New York: Charles Schribner's Sons, 1951.

MADGE, THOMAS CHARLES. *Survey before Development in Thai Villages.* (Series on Community Organization and Development.) New York: United Nations, 1957. (Mimeographed.)

MASPERO, GEORGES. *Un empire colonial français: l'Indochine.* 2 vols. Paris: Van Oest, 1929.

MEEKER, ODEN. *The Little World of Laos.* New York: Charles Scribner's Sons, 1959.

A Selected Bibliography

MILLER, HAYNES. "A Bulwark Built on Sand," *Reporter,* XIX, No. 8 (November 1958), 11-16.

MOUHOT, HENRI. *Voyages dans les royaumes de Siam, de Cambodge, de Laos et autres parties centrales de l'Indochine. Relation extraite du journal et de la correspondance de l'auteur par Ferdinand de Lanoye.* Paris: Hachette, 1868.

NHOUY ABHAY, THAO. "Le Royaume de Champaçak," *France-Asie,* III, No. 25 (April 1948), 460-68.

————. *Aspects du pays lao.* Vientiane: Ministère de l'Éducation Nationale, Editions Comité littéraire lao, 1956.

OGANESOFF, IGOR. "Living It Up in Laos," *Wall Street Journal,* April 9, 1958.

Pacific Affairs (quarterly). New York, 1926 to present.

PARMENTIER, H. "Le Wat laotien et ses annexes," *Bulletin des Amis du Laos,* No. 2 (June 1938), 9-64.

————. "Eléments du Wat laotien," *Bulletin des Amis du Laos,* No. 3 (August 1939), 7-49.

————. *L'Art du Laos.* 2 vols. Hanoi, Ecole Française d'Extrême-Orient, 1954.

* PATHAMMAVONG, SOMLITH. "Compulsory Education in Laos." In *Compulsory Education in Cambodia, Laos, and Viet-Nam.* Paris: UNESCO, 1955.

PAVIE, AUGUSTE. *A la conquête des coeurs: Le Pays des Millions d'Éléphants et du Parasol Blanc.* Paris: Bossard, 1921.

PELZER, KARL J. *Climate, Vegetation and Rational Land Utilization in the Humid Tropics.* Bangkok: Ninth Pacific Science Congress, 1957. (Mimeographed.)

PHOUVONG, PHIMMASONE. "The That Luang of Vientiane: An Historical and Bibliographical Study," *Asia,* III, No. 9 (June 1953), 91-101.

PIETRANTONI, ERIC. "La population du Laos de 1915 à 1945," *Bulletin de la Société des Etudes Indochinoises,* n.s., XXVIII, No. 1 (1953), 25-38.

————. "La population du Laos en 1943 dans son milieu géographique," *Bulletin de la Société des Études Indochinoises,* n.s., XXXII, No. 3 (1957), 223-43.

POINDEXTER, HILDRUS. "Epidemiological Data on Laos," *Reports to ICA from USOM.* Vientiane, April 4, 1955.

————. "Some Observations on Major Health Problems in Laos," *Reports to ICA from USOM.* Vientiane, April 4, 1955.

262

Présence du Bouddhisme. R. de Berval (ed.) *France-Asie,* XVI, Nos. 153-157 (February-June 1959).

RAQUEZ, A. *Pages laotiennes: le Haut-Laos, le Moyen-Laos, le Bas-Laos.* Hanoi: Schneider, 1902.

ROBEQUAIN, CHARLES. "Deux villes du Mékong: Luang-Prabang et Vieng-Chane," *Cahiers de la Société de Géographie de Hanoi,* XI (1925), 1-24.

————. *The Economic Development of French Indochina.* London: Oxford University Press, 1944.

ROCHET, C. *Le Laos dans le Tourmente.* Paris: Vigneau, 1946.

ROFFE, G. EDWARD and THELMA W. ROFFE. *Spoken Lao: Books I and II.* Washington: American Council of Learned Societies, 1956-58.

ROUX, HENRI. "Quelques Minorités ethniques du Nord-Indochine," *France-Asie,* Nos. 92-93 (January-February 1954), 143-413.

SASORITH, KATAY D. *Le Laos, Son évolution politique: Sa place dans l'Union française.* Paris: Editions Berger-Levrault, 1953.

SEIDENFADEN, ERIK. *The Thai Peoples.* Bangkok: The Siam Society, 1958.

SIMMONS, J. S., *et al.* "Global Epidemiology." In *India and the Far East,* Vol. I, pt. 1. Philadelphia: J. B. Lippincott, 1944.

SINAVONG, BOUN THAN. *Agrarian Rites in Laos.* Bangkok: Ninth Pacific Science Congress, 1957. (Mimeographed.)

"Sisavang Vong, King of Laos," *Current Biography,* April 1954.

SMALLEY, WILLIAM A. *Outline of Khmu Structure.* Unpublished Ph.D. dissertation, Columbia University, 1956.

————. "The Gospel and Cultures of Laos," *Practical Anthropology,* III, No. 3 (1956).

STANTON, EDWIN F. "A 'Presence' in Laos," *Current History,* XXXVIII, No. 226 (1960), 337-41.

THOMPSON, VIRGINIA. *French Indo-China.* New York: Macmillan, 1937.

THOMPSON, VIRGINIA and RICHARD ADLOFF. "Laos: Background of Invasion," *Far Eastern Survey,* XXII, No. 6 (May 1953), 62-66.

————. *Minority Problems in Southeast Asia.* Stanford: Stanford University Press, 1955.

United Nations. Ad Hoc Committee on Forced Labor. *Replies from Governments to the Questionnaire on Forced Labor.* Geneva, June 18, 1952.

A Selected Bibliography

————. Department of Economic Affairs. *Development of Mineral Resources in Asia and the Far East.* New York, 1953.

————. Economic Commission for Asia and the Far East. *Economic Bulletin for Asia and the Far East* (quarterly). Bangkok: 1950 to present. (See special supplements: *Economic Development and Planning in Asia and the Far East: Social Aspects,* X, No. 3, December 1959; and *Economic Survey of Asia and the Far East, 1959,* X, No. 4, March 1960.)

————. United Nations Educational, Scientific, and Cultural Organization. *World Survey of Education, II.* Paris, 1958.

————. Food and Agriculture Organization. *Statement Prepared by the Government of Laos for the Special Technical Meeting on the Economic Aspects of the Rice Industry.* (CCP/RI-54/5.) Rangoon, November 11, 1954.

————. Food and Agricultural Organization. *A Survey of the Investigations Required for Planning Development of Agriculture, Forest, and Fisheries in the Lower Mekong Basin.* Rome, February 1959.

United States. 83rd Congress, Second Session. Senate Committee on Foreign Relations. *Report on Indochina.* (Report of Senator Mike Mansfield on a study mission to Vietnam, Cambodia, and Laos, Oct. 15, 1954.) Washington: Government Printing Office, 1954.

————. 85th Congress, Second Session. House Committee on Foreign Affairs. *Mutual Security Program in Laos.* (Hearings before the Subcommittee on the Far East and the Pacific, May 7 and 8, 1958.) Washington: Government Printing Office, 1958.

————. 86th Congress, First Session. House Committee on Government Operations. *United States Aid Operations in Laos.* (Hearings before the Foreign Operations and Monetary Affairs Subcommittee, March 11-June 1 1959.) Washington: Government Printing Office, 1959.

————. 86th Congress, First Session. House Committee on Government Operations. *United States Aid Operations in Laos.* (7th Report by the Committee, June 15, 1959.) Washington: Government Printing Office, 1959.

————. Department of Agriculture: Office of Foreign Agricultural Relations. *The Agriculture of French Indochina.* Washington, 1950.

* ————. Department of Commerce: Bureau of Foreign Commerce. *Basic Data on the Economy of Laos.* (World Trade Information Service, Economic Reports, I, Nos. 58-69.) Washington, 1958.

————. Department of Labor: Bureau of Labor Statistics. *Labor Conditions in Indochina.* Washington, November 15, 1950.

————. Department of State. *Comments by the Department of State and ICA on the Report of the House Committee on Government Operations (United States Aid Operations in Laos, June 15, 1959).* Washington: Government Printing Office, 1959.

264

————. International Cooperation Administration: United States Operations Mission to Laos. *Cooperation for Peace and Prosperity, Laos-America.* Vientiane, May 28, 1957. (Mimeographed.)

* ————. International Cooperation Administration: United States Operations Mission to Laos. Report of the Director. *American Cooperation with Laos: A Vital Link in the Chain of Mutual Security.* Vientiane, July, 1959.

————. International Cooperation Administration: United States Operations Mission to Laos. *Quarterly Statistical Bulletin No. 6, July-September, 1959.* Vientiane, January, 1960.

————. Library of Congress. *Indochina: A Bibliography of the Land and People.* Washington, 1950.

* ————. Library of Congress: Orientalia Division. *Southern Asia Accessions List* (quarterly). Washington, 1952 to present.

————. U.S. Information Agency. *Briefing Notes on the Royal Kingdom of Laos.* Vientiane, 1959.

VIRAVONG, MAHA SILA. *History of Laos.* New York: U.S. Joint Publications Research Service, 1958.

WIENS, HAROLD J. *China's March toward the Tropics.* Hamden, Connecticut: The Shoestring Press, 1954.

INDEX

282

149, 180, 198, 205, 212; in early history, 7, 10, 14; power potentials of, 31, 213, 227; transport on, 3, 17, 25, 26, 206, 215 ff.

Mekong River Project, 161

Meo, tribal groups, 7, 15, 17, 33, 36, 38, 41, 81, 83, 105, 128, 132, 167, 177, 188, 202, 203, 219; language, 36, 41 f.; political awareness, 131, 232; religion, 44, 59, 60; social organization, 72, 73

Merchants, 2, 33, 219. *See also* Chinese; Indians; Shopkeepers; Thai; Traders

Merit, in Buddhism, 44, 51, 53, 57, 65, 70, 96, 101, 102, 175

Metempsychosis, belief in, 45, 59

Miao. *See* Meo

Middle class, development of, 4, 76, 231

Middlemen, 215, 219

Midthaharn, army newspaper, 138, 243

Midwives, 186, 187

Migrations, historic, 7 f., 33

Migratory labor, 164

Military alliances, 147, 152

Millet, cultivation of, 40

Mineral resources, 25, 209, 211 f. *See also* Tin deposits

Mines, 168. *See also* Tin mine

Mining, 226. *See also* Tin mine

Ministries, 122 ff.; Commerce and Industry, 193; Cults, 81; Finance, Agriculture, National Economy, 82, 124, 193; Foreign Affairs, 132; Information, Tourism, Propaganda, Public Welfare, 136 ff., 139, 231; Interior, 125, 128, 130, 133, 196; Justice, Culture, Sports and Youth, 132; National Defense and Veterans Affairs, 132; National Education, Fine Arts, 81 f., 84, 124, 173, 196; Public Health, 124, 173, 184, 196; Public Works, Planning, Transports and Telecommunications, 81, 124, 166, 196, 244; Religious Affairs, 50, 85; Social Affairs, 173, 207

Minorities, ethnic. *See* Ethnic groups

Missionaries, 13, 60, 187

Missions, Christian, 60, 173

Mobile schools. *See* Schools

Molotov, Vyacheslav M., 146

Mon, tribal groups, 7

Monarchy, 11, 108, 121; constitutional, 6, 20, 115 f., 119, 199; succession to, 120, 121; traditional, 103, 115, 119, 198 f., 231. *See also* King, role of; Royalty

Monasteries, 79, 102. *See also* Pagodas; Sangha

Monastic community. *See* Sangha

Monastic schools. *See* Schools

Mone Keo, King, 237

Monetary system, 147, 189 ff., 193; reforms in, 154, 160, 189 f., 221 f., 223. *See also* Currency; Foreign exchange

Moneylenders, 33, 43, 194 f., 200, 215, 219. *See also* Chinese; Indians

Mongols, 7

Mon-Khmer languages, 35, 36, 39, 42. *See also* Cambodian

Monks. *See* Bonzes

Monopolies, state, 197

Monsoon cycle, 2, 25, 28, 30, 94 f.

Monsoon forest, 30

Moral code, Buddhist, 44, 47 f., 52, 79, 97, 98

Mortality rate, 32, 182

Moslems, 15

Mother, role in family, 67

Motion pictures. *See* Films

Motor transport, 164, 215 f., 217. *See also* Roads

Mountains, region of, 25, 26 f., 28, 62, 170, 172, 174; agriculture in, 2, 40, 41, 200, 202. *See also* Hill peoples; Tribal groups

Moving picture theaters. *See* Cinemas

Mulberry, cultivation of, 204

muong. See Districts

Muong Lan Xang Hom Chao. *See* Land of the Million Elephants and White Parasol

Muong Sai, town, 238

Muong Swa. *See* Luang Prabang

Muong Theng, town, 8

Museums, Buddhist, 86

28 DAYS